Architectures of Sound

Michael Fowler

Architectures of Sound

Acoustic Concepts and Parameters for Architectural Design

Birkhäuser
Basel

Introduction

This is a book about ideas. It is about architecture too, though most of all, it is a book about sound and listening and how these concepts might change our notions of the experience of the built environment. The lens through which these elements are examined and interrogated is the meta-theory of *critical listening*. As a framework, critical listening might best be described as an approach to reading sound. But it is also a theory about the simulation of acoustic space, not through direct digital computational means, but rather through the development of an informed and constructive auditory imagination. It is a means thus in which to read the relationship between architectural environments and the ways in which they curate and compose particular acoustic signatures. Consequently, it is a book that is just as much about modes of listening as it is about ways of reading sound-space.

As a way in which to engage in this type of auditory imagining, and from the pedagogical standpoint of starting from zero, *Architectures of Sound* is bookended by two related short stories. Both are musically inspired, and thus are what I have called a *Prelude* and a *Postlude*. But rather than seeking merely to place the book into a non-standard or superficially novel state, these two paired chapters of science fiction are used in what the composer and theorist R. Murray Schafer may have called an "ear cleansing" process. These short chapters, "Sounding City" and "Wang's Dream," track how a protagonist, Wang, encounters and understands an acoustic environment of a future megacity.

But instead of attempting to describe a wholly unknown acoustic world of the future as a character that in itself might draw us away from the situation of our own "contemporary" acoustic environment, the idea of the *Prelude* and *Postlude* is to begin and end the argument of the book proper: that is, that architecture and the built environment greatly impact the way in which we experience sounds.

Hearing then is at the core of the initial jump into the unknown of what *Architectures of Sound* engages in. But instead of simply describing or formally defining hearing or its related and sometimes confusing partner, listening, both the *Prelude* and *Postlude* seek to center and highlight what might be understood as "critical" when we speak of hearing or listening. The first ear cleansing then of "Sounding City" is an attempt to not simply describe sound and the auditory experience in absolute terms, but moreover, to question the what, why and how of auditory phenomena. I see these bookends then as extremely important because they are a means by which to engage and open the imagination to new types of auditory consequences. In short, to be a critical listener is perhaps simply that: not simply to observe the auditory environment as a passive attendant, but to go further and actively discover what influences, structures and states perpetuate such qualities of our sounding environment.

The role of architecture within this type of method is of course extremely relevant and important. Most of us today live in a built environment, an environment that has design elements, landscapes, planning regulations, aesthetic and developmental concerns, not to mention ecological and sustainable strategies written directly into law. Sounds live there too, but moreover, they are fundamentally affected by these approaches to the design and maintenance of the built environment. The first proposition of *Architectures of Sound* is to thus imagine (critically) what a building would be if it could be described as an ear, as a device for listening? "An Architecture of the Ear," the first chapter proper, is one that posits that the methods, function, geometry and site of the human ear can be consequently imagined as a type of architecture. But this architecture is also a series of characteristics that can be consequently assigned and understood within the context of the built environment, and of design. If the facade of the building is the interface between the outside and the inside, it is also a potential listening device that through its form, porosity and temporality enables modes of listening to occur both exterior and interior to its program.

Following on from this initial investigation comes the notion of how we can account for scale in terms of listening experience. While for Le Corbusier or Étienne-Louis Boullée the objective relation between the architectonic and the human physical dimension becomes a defining metric, auditory experience and the sense of what is large and small is a more complex and indeed subjective matter to contend with. The chapter "On Auditory Scale" therefore establishes a continuum between two extreme rooms, the anechoic chamber (complete absorption) and the reverberation chamber (complete reflection). Scale acts as a pivot between the acoustic qualities, geometry and dimension of a space as gauged against its auditory qualities and characteristics. This approach is supported in part through John Cage's most famous encounter at the anechoic chamber at Harvard in the 1950s, which consequently led to his silent piece 4'33". But rather than drawing wholly on Cage's iconoclastic aesthetics of musical upheaval, it provides a suitable foil for reading how philosopher Michel Serres hears the world as a superfluous series of interconnected boxes originating at the ear.

But if the question of what auditory scale is can be induced from a more critical lens or mode of listening, the pragmatics of how such scales can be defined in architectural terms remains unknown. The chapter "Dumb Holes and the Acoustic Horizon" thus sets out to explore the main argument of the meta-theory of critical listening. By examining numerous projects by various architects from Bernhard Leitner, NOX, Hodgetts + Fung Design, OMA, etc., a series of theoretical concepts is explored that, when considered as an assemblage, assists in describing the very dimensions by which the auditory experience is defined through the architectonic articulation of space. By examining, (re)defining and theorizing on the auditory implications of the facets of texture, form, materiality, structure and program, a new series of fundamentals is understood in relation to the physical properties of architecture and the built environment. Though some of these facets are already known and defined within architectural praxis, they are used here in particular orbits and definitions as a means to tease out the auditory within architecture.

In addition to these explorations of what the assemblage of facets means for defining the dimensions of auditory scale, the chapter seeks also from its outset to call into account the notion of what an acoustic horizon and acoustic arena are. As two concepts that become ephemerally generated through the facets of texture, form, materiality, structure and program, the difference between the acoustic horizon and the acoustic arena can be readily abstracted into the emphasis on either the position of the sound source or the listener. Naturally both points of view have significance for the built environment, but what is emphasized within "Dumb Holes and the Acoustic Horizon" is the utility of reading anthropologist Tim Ingold's concept of the interconnectedness of "knots on a mesh." That is to say, the notion in which activities and sounds arise and are curated through the articulation of architecture and its influence on the acoustic horizon and acoustic arena.

A most basic inquiry of whether sounds can be distinctly located *in* space or whether they themselves *produce* space is the thesis of the fourth chapter, "The Taxonomy of a Meta-theory." I nominate critical listening as representing a meta-theory because it is aligned and seeks to theorize on two extant acoustic theories: that of aural architecture by Barry Blesser and Linda-Ruth Salter, and soundscape by R. Murray Schafer and Barry Truax et al. It is thus a theory of theories in that it positions itself as a root from which the work of Blesser, Salter, Truax and Schafer unfolds. Taking on this meta-theory status also allows for an objective and critical examination of the brief history and perceived weaknesses of both soundscape and aural architecture.

The intent of critical listening though is generally utilitarian. It seeks to be an analysis tool as well as a theoretical lens and potential design framework. At its heart is the notion that the representation of architecture and of built form, like a musical score, is a suggestion of a world to be constructed, lived, experienced, critiqued and, most poignantly, heard. In testing this thesis, the two paired chapters of "Re-hearing Icons of Architecture I. & II." seek a return to some of the most obvious and perhaps misunderstood architectural projects of the mid- to late 20th century. In suggesting that those icons from such practices as Archigram, Archizoom, Superstudio and Hans Hollein may have been previously somehow marginalized is to suggest that the lens of critical listening presents here a new and critical commentary on these diverse works from the perspective of the potential auditory experience. To test the limits or indeed the inclusiveness of critical listening is thus to run its methods, concepts and priorities on known and measured exemplars in an effort to forge some new knowledge trajectory or quality. It is clear that this approach warrants a new type of sensory awareness, given that such projects inherently play out across multiple layers of experience. But it is these deeper hidden qualities that have been overlooked because of the current hegemony of visual information and ocular communication within architectural discourse.

The propensity for visual modes of communication in architecture is of course an inherent, vital and completely necessary element, though the question of what lies in store for the future of the built environment, given the rapid increase in population densities and settlement patterns, remains. These issues are already being addressed through traditional applications in urban planning and building regulation strategies and this trend is expected to grow as more and more information becomes relevant, disseminated and utilized through the growth of digital networks. Added to the infrastructure strain of new settlement patterns occurring between rural and urban spaces is the flow-on issue of increased noise and the related health concerns from such population inversions. In the chapter "Acoustic Futures" the current approaches taken by acousticians and noise engineers (and not designers) to regulate through top-down models at the urban scale indicates how the relationship between architecture and the sounding environment that it enables and curates is becoming separated through fragmentation. By drawing on the concepts of theoretical physicist and philosopher David Bohm regarding the notion of an implicate and explicate order, this chapter seeks to argue that ultimately the fragmentation of architecture from sound and acoustics has created a limitation to the traditional guardianship of architecture as a humanistic art in which multisensory spatial experiences are enabled through built form.

This move towards "wholeness" and the need to avoid fragmentation is what is suggested in philosopher Alphonso Lingis's account of experiencing a traffic jam in Tehran. In the final chapter, "'Like Quail Clucking …,'" I examine what Lingis (via a hitchhiker's observation) suggests as the quality of wholeness of the sounding environment. For Lingis there is an inherent and underlying symbiosis occurring in the mutual creation of a sound environment such as what is experienced in a city. Here, in a similar manner to "quail clucking when feeding on a ripe wheat field," the individual sound-actions of people, objects, architecture and nature, etc., become merged hyper-events which contribute to the dynamics and qualities that become the whole. But this characterization also enables us to come full circle and return again to the architecture of the ear. We might subtly concede that this symbiosis that Lingis describes is again much like what Bohm suggests as to the relationship between the enfolding (that is, as I argue, found in the form of architecture) and the unfolding (that is, the form of sound events) within any environment. This means that sounds and architecture are not separate entities but interrelated states. Just as the architecture of the ear both enables and dictates particular modes of listening, while at the same time being located as a part within our bodies and within an environment, it seems that the notion of Serres's iteration of boxes extends as both an outwards-unfolding order and an inwards-enfolded order.

There is perhaps an unwritten notion that the composition of this book is somewhat circuitous in its argument. While there may be truth in this suggestion, what I can allude to is that the book seeks to function as a series of essays, some of extended length, others not. It was originally conceived as an arc of writing in which, like a *sonata* or *symphony*, movements build on each other such that, at the larger scale, each individual chapter or movement partakes in much more than forming an impetus and drive that satisfies its own conclusions. Thus the greater arc that runs through the entire work consumes any small pauses. In this sense there is an unending quality to the unfolding of the book such that to take only a single chapter is to not completely see its vital and dynamic place within the entire phrase that is the complete work proper. Thus the concept and main argument of *Architectures of Sound* is developed through a series of seemingly open questions. Each of the chapters begins with one of these basic questions, such as "how do we experience sounds?" or "what then of the future sound of cities?" as a means to both set up the chapter and its flow of text while concurrently moving deeper into the development of the meta-theory of critical listening.

I should mention one final point: that the language and approach of *Architectures of Sound* is one of interdisciplinarity and inclusivity, but at the same time, an approach that is obvious in its acknowledgment of the vast and important discourse that is architectural theory. One of the arguments for the instigation of critical listening as a meta-theory is that there is a division between applied acoustics, soundscape theory and aural architecture in regard to the theoretical discourses of architecture and of design. Though critical listening does not see itself as a theory of architecture, architecture is at its heart, as is the notion about the experience of listening itself, and the way in which sounds communicate a rich variety of information to us. Perhaps like soundscape theory and aural architecture, critical listening partakes too in the idea of awareness, an auditory awareness as an essential starting point to engage in the multisensory nature of reality. But once we begin to look into, or at, the built environment, or even the natural environment—whose form and materiality play equally important roles in producing certain types of sound behaviors—there must be a point at which the question of what architecture is and how it functions arises. Thus architecture's influence in producing acoustic signatures and sound profiles is where critical listening seeks to provide a starting point as well as bridging method and interpreting language. With these tools and tactics, we might accordingly speak of how architecture functions in terms of its delicate balancing of visual and acoustic space.

Prelude

Wang slowly walked from his terminal, taking a beeline to stairwell C4 so as to avoid Janovich's desk and be safely delivered directly to the rear exit of the building, then into the subdued environs of Hertz Boulevard. "Friday at last," he said aloud to the mute streetscape without the slightest forethought as to what the weekend might bring. All that mattered now was to get to the soundrag in time and without incident. This would be his fifth attendance at a soundrag event after receiving a wholly cryptic and anonymous invitation last quarter: "Hearing is believing, soundrag Helmholtz Avenue, link below." It was an internal e-memo, and as far as Wang could ascertain, it came from somebody in the G-Kredit department on the 10th floor. Wang suspected it was from the now missing Tilsky, though he couldn't be sure, and nor did he want to investigate any further—all that mattered was that he was being kept in the loop.

As a subtle form of protest against the highly homogeneous nature of city sound regulations and enforcement—especially all those silent zoning ordinances—soundrags had developed out of what Wang saw as the prevalent "modding" subculture of the younger Generation-y kids. Much like the celebration of radical car and engine modification in his grandfather's age (with those monotonous-sounding, fossil-fueled dinosaur engines), acoustic modding had turned into an artform with the electric car, and, moreover, into a viable form of protest, especially when one encountered those hordes of modders gathered to crawl through the streets and re-tune the city with a soundrag. In fact, auditory modification of a car was all one could do these days to bring any personalized qualities to a vehicle, considering the highly restrictive laws of acoustic car classifications and zero-modification tolerance of any other kind of alteration. Added to this were the constant presence of surveillance drones and the threat of heavy G-Kredit deductions or even travel blackouts for offenders whose auto specs deviated even in the slightest way from the dominant standard.

He felt the still and heavy air outside the colorless office building fall on his face like a wet towel. It was thick and humid. "Perfect," murmured Wang; it was the type of night that made sounds travel faster. But a night like tonight also meant that the soundbeams were operating at an equal peak rollover. "Mustn't forget my sound map," he reminded himself, delving quickly into a pocket to fish out what seemed to his colleagues like an arcane piece of hardware: a small leather-bound notebook replete with gold embossing, real paper pages and the musty smell of a bygone age. "Wow, that looks like it could even be pre-iPhone," Janovich had remarked facetiously upon seeing the curious artifact, adding sarcastically, "Has it got voice control?" Wang looked forlornly at the cover, remembering his own reaction when he first held the notebook: its small, beautifully patterned creases, its rough texture under the fingers and its perfect size—practically speaking it was a time machine, and the ultimate device for privacy, he thought, not connected and not in the cloud.

The route from the monolithic office building of OptaKM-Solutions to the soundrag on Helmholtz Avenue was one that Wang had taken before. He crossed the street assuredly and saw what must be the new "Hypersonic Listening Parlor" that Gregor had

mentioned. Behind the lightly tinted glass storefront windows Wang clearly saw what looked like cocooned figures lying motionless in sparkling white pods, each curvaceous sarcophagus decorated in a sublime manner with small loudspeakers. "The HSE junkies," he thought to himself while fondling the soft cover of the leather notebook hidden deep within his worn rain jacket pocket. From what Gregor had told him, such places gave clients a 90-minute treatment of HSE, or the "hypersonic effect": "Yeah, get this, so you go in, lie down and listen to silence for 90 minutes," reported an incredulous Gregor. "What gives?" inquired Wang. "Well, you're not actually listening to silence," stressed Gregor, adding a pregnant pause to denote his perceived command of the subject. "You are played-back frequencies over 20 kHz — you know, like what you used to get in a rainforest, but people can't hear it! Funny thing is you get all drunk and trance-like, better than any drugs — at least that's what my cousin says and he's addicted to it." It had been a curious discovery and one that was often mentioned as the most significant neurological finding of the late 21st century: the ability to "hear," or at least feel, the euphoric effects of sound frequencies that lay outside the range of human hearing. There had been numerous attempts at explanations in which the skull acts as a type of resonator, but what needed no explanation was its impact on the production of all manner of audio playback and electroacoustic communication devices and the subsequent addiction and abuse sought by so many of the new breed of HSE junkies. In a few short years, with the increased availability of HSE loudspeakers and HSE devices able to deliver any type of auditory content one wanted, what seemed like an epidemic of rapidly increasing proportions had begun to unfold onto a hitherto seemingly deaf public. Wang could not imagine what the future held, given the vociferous appetite of so many for the sensation of HSE.

Approaching the listening parlor, he could clearly see the faces of the Mummies now, just as Gregor implied, beatific smiles staggering out into the hot and muggy night from the nondescript storefront, apparently drunk on HSE. "Well," Wang thought to himself, "better that than being stuck in a soundbeam for 90 minutes." Somewhat concerned that his brief pause at the parlor might attract unwanted attention, he hurried head down along the busy street, weaving through the numerous obstacles of people, vending machines and surveillance drones. From what he had been told, the soundscape of the contemporary city had changed irretrievably since the introduction of the electric car, soundbeams and nano-facades. His grandparents had told him of a past in which those living within cities had routine health problems from elevated noise levels — psychosocial, cardiovascular and sleep disturbance issues to name a few! His grandfather recalled that the rapid mechanization and reliance on fossil fuels had produced deafening cities filled with dreary sounds like that of the internal combustion engine, air-conditioner fans and other bland-sounding signals all so hopelessly uninteresting to the contemporary ear that they might cause nausea or insanity to anybody experiencing them today.

Up ahead, Wang saw the final obstacle in achieving the goal of the evening's sojourn, Sabine Lane. It was a shortcut to Helmholtz Avenue and the soundrag, but it required a delicate maneuver to successfully navigate the narrow sloping path so as to avoid the soundbeams. Wang stood at the threshold atop the hill surveying the near-silent spectacle. Scores of people pushed in and out of the space, apparently oblivious to the soundbeams and their all-consuming product placements. Yet Wang could see on their bellicose faces the toll of living in an environment in which the idea of private acoustic space had long since been released to the Globalized Corporates. In the distant past, the notion of acoustic space had been connected to the notion of privacy and consideration—an arcane concept these days, particularly in regard to the public arena. Of course, public space now was public in every sense; ownership of a space within the city included ownership of the air bounded by a free volume. It had become a ruthless scheme with some Airspace agents resorting to selling ridiculous 1m³ sections along the sidewalk to the Globalized Corporates so that they could use such thoroughfares for invisible advertising programs—"unrestricted yet public" was the slogan Wang heard continuously regarding these acquisitions.

He gently fingered the small leather notebook in his pocket, carefully fishing it out in such a way as not to draw undue attention to it, in case an inquisitive surveillance drone might find fancy with his arcane treasure. He quickly glanced over the hand-drawn sketches that described the route. The notebook felt reassuring in his hand now; briefly admiring his own drawing skills, he studied the arrows, notes and cross-hatchings of his map. Though a curious artifact from a distant past, it was a talisman still. Looking up, he saw the monolithic concrete buildings of the lane were adorned on each floor with numerous balconies, each of them rudely jutting out and punctuating the indifferent sky, and many of them in possession of a small dish pointed downwards at the lane—the source of the soundbeams. Apparently you could earn excellent G-Kredit by renting your balcony to the Globalized Corporates, but at the cost of hurling mind-numbing advertising 24/7 directly down into the heads of unsuspecting victims while perpetuating the insane economy of Airspace agents with their sell-offs, rentals and futures market. The furtive nature of the soundbeam, a shallow beam of modulated ultrasound only audible within the narrow "spotlight" of the beam, meant that advanced detection of the hidden auditory net was impossible for the passerby—until, of course, it was too late. The beauty, if one could call it that, was that Airspace was a rental market in which no one could tell who was renting what volume of Airspace. Any movement through the city was also a potential encounter with an Airspace renter, who was inevitably one of the Globalized Corporates seeking to sell all manner of wares, gadgets or the latest knowledge management system. If the city of his grandfather was saturated with mechanical sounds of engines and cooling systems, today's city was awash with invisible beams of sound that penetrated all nooks, crannies and corners, boulevards, streets and thoroughfares with devastating precision and undivided apathy.

Wang casually eased into the lane. According to his handwritten map, the route to avoid the soundbeams was 50 paces down the left edge, turn 90° at the G-Kredit vending machine, cross the lane and walk 60 paces as close to the far wall as possible while bending over with head down (try to avoid suspicion, and above all, those loitering Gen-y teenagers outside EcoFauxSushi@#$!), step back into the lane and backtrack for 10 steps, turn right 45° and then walk diagonally to the corner junction where the lane meets Helmholtz Avenue. Wang cut a curious figure amongst the other hurried and chaotic pedestrians. His passage was assured and confident while others (probably Eco-tourists he thought) visibly cowered, covered their ears and swore in Chinese and Hindi.

Finally reaching Helmholtz Avenue, he quickly looked at his watch. Already 20:15, though not too late. The soundrag should be starting very shortly he thought, pleased

with his efforts so far. Soon other people he recognized started arriving, a couple of Geisha girls he saw here last quarter, and the occasional bewildered Ecotourist who must have heard about the event through an e-memo somewhere and was seeking desperately to join an "authentic subcultured social mob" in the hope of impressing those back home who were not as fortunate with their right-of-travel applications. Of course, too, Wang immediately noticed other Technokrats of his ilk, like him, completely disenchanted with the Globalized Corporates and their vision of the new hyper-economic block, yet unlike those attention-seeking nihilist Gen-y kids, content with generating more passive or subversive means for protest. In a moment of contemplation, he vaguely and halfheartedly scanned the crowd for the missing Tilsky, while at the same time wondering if he himself was being tracked.

Some of the first cars appeared. Of course, they looked no different from the other traffic on Helmholtz Avenue, but you could clearly hear their acoustic modifications. The usual subdued pings and aesthetically pure, though saccharine, melodious and highly regulated electroacoustic tones of the traditional electric car were magnificently transformed into all manner of fantastic swooshing, hissing, thunderous, pulsating and deeply bulbous noises that seemed to emanate from every panel of the cars at high volume, while engulfing all eager listeners nearby into a frenzy of cacophonous proportions. But something didn't seem completely right to Wang. As the first cars of the soundrag slowly marched by, their unique sounds dissipated as quickly as they had appeared. Someone had yet to hack the nano-facades, thought Wang! The ability to instantly change the acoustic properties of a building's facade through the manipulation of its material structure at the nanoscale had changed so many things about the soundscape of the city. As Wang's grandparents had so often told him, in their day, the city was a very noisy place, filled with the reverberation of sound waves bouncing off everything, and in turn becoming amplified through the numerous hard and nonporous surfaces. Today, the opposite was true; the city street was but a mere whisper, a dead place with no possibility of shared acoustic delights. To walk the street was like living in an anechoic chamber or receiving, as Gregor had sagely proclaimed, "a pair of deaf 20th-century ears"—at least this was the case outside the soundbeam zones.

But the severity of the acoustic situation was offset by the ability one had to change the absorption characteristics of all surfaces and building facades, whose normal state was in total absorption mode or active noise-cancellation mode. Hacking into the source code of nearby building facades was not difficult, given the openness and ease of access to local digital infrastructure networks across the city and the fact that those networks were inevitably hard-coded to particular buildings (as Gregor had pointed out, one could even occasionally find the odd ancient physical port in walls within back alleys for direct access). This kept the Gen-y kids busy: each of them seeking out how much further one could push the functionality of a facade through clandestine control. Not only could one change the acoustic behavior of a building's facade, one could also make it sing or hum (if you had prima coding skills of course). Wang had even overheard the Geisha girls saying that you could theoretically destroy a building (or at least the facade) through coding an excitation algorithm that resonates a fundamental wavelength throughout the structure—find the right frequency and one could theoretically destroy the building.

In that moment, the melodious cacophony of the soundrag suddenly exploded with a tenfold force upon those gathered, the sounds of the cars appearing to shoot upwards into the dark encroaching night, then swirling through the air and back down to the gathered swooning crowd, penetrating what seemed like every cell of one's body. The Geisha girls squealed in a rapid hocket of high-pitched delight. Just in time! With the code of the facades now fully hacked, all the local surfaces including the street and buildings had switched function to become monumentally reflective and emphatically resonant: in essence, a giant and superlative echoic chamber, prima amplifier and jacked-up musical effects box all in one. As the acoustic modders drove by, their eclectic gaggle of fanciful sounds madly bounced through the air, appearing to submerge and engulf not only Wang and the other listeners, but also the entire avenue. Suddenly it was as if the architecture of the city had become a musical instrument, a living composition that both curated and encouraged the flight of acoustic delights, while delivering and feeding the aural imaginations of those who were witness to this divine soniferous garden. Wang marveled at the sounds, textures, rhythms and inventiveness of the sound designs: hearing is believing he thought.

1
An Architecture of the Ear

Organs of hearing
Membranes
Vibrations

An Architecture of the Ear

Organs of hearing

How do we experience sound? To our protagonist Wang of "Sounding City" this could not be more simply answered: sound is something we feel as an omnipresent force. It is something that can be seemingly touched, something that cannot be ignored in our daily lives nor easily rationalized as always completely necessary or considerate. But to begin in even more simplistic terms, as I envisage this book as both an exploration and analysis of the role of sound in architecture, we can turn to the organ of hearing itself. The ear is both a fantastic device and an innovative architecture that enables us to make sense of what, in purely physical terms, are simply vibrations within the medium of the air we breathe. Yet from these vibrations come distinct feelings, distinct notions about space, about time, and our connection to the immediate environment. Indeed, as Walter J. Ong argues, "The centering action of sound (the field of sound is not spread out before me but is all around me) affects man's sense of the cosmos." (Ong 1982, p. 72) Whereas we cannot see behind ourselves, nor that much to our peripheries, we can indeed hear behind, above and below our bodies: we can even hear inside our bodies.

Hearing penetrates our immediate environs in ways that seeing cannot. Sitting within any urban environment and listening for even a brief moment reveals to us that what can be heard is often well beyond that which we can see — what you see is not always what you hear. Anthropologist Edmund Carpenter understood this too, particularly in his detailing of the acoustic concepts born from his time studying Inuit tribes in the polar regions:

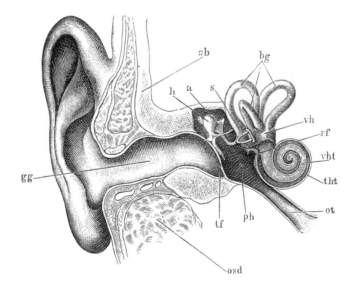

Figure 1. "Ear in a vertical position, **gg:** The ear canal; **tf:** Tympanic Membrane; **ph:** Tympanic Cavity; **h:** Malleus; **a:** Incus; **s:** Stapes; **bg:** Semi-circular Canals; **vh:** Organ of Corti; **tht:** Vestibules; **vht:** Cochlea; **ot:** Eustachian Tube; **osd:** Temporal bone; **sb:** Mastoid bone; **rf:** Round Window."

Auditory space has no favored focus. It's a sphere without fixed boundaries, space made by the thing itself, not space containing the thing. It is not pictorial space, boxed-in, but dynamic, always in flux, creating its own dimensions moment by moment. It has no fixed boundaries; it is indifferent to background. The eye focusses, pinpoints, abstracts, locating each object in physical space, against a background; the ear, however, favors sound from any direction. (Carpenter 1959, p. 37)

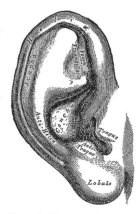

Figure 2. "The auricula. Lateral surface."

While the common usage of a window of a building is as an opening or opportunity to pinpoint the immediate visual space beyond, it is also a filtering device that enables an auditory view to the world at large. But this view, afforded to us by the organ of hearing, is as Carpenter suggests, vast, dynamic and temporal. The sound of a distant train, bells ringing at a church or temple, the impetuous sounds of car horns and traffic can be experienced outside their immediate visual vicinities, outside their points of enactment. Just as Ong argued, sound is a trigger for the imagination, a vehicle for connecting and contemplating the intangible. Hence sound is an important and indeed inseparable aspect of architecture and the built environment, yet its vitality and vitalness remains as one of the greatest unknown dimensions to the practice of architecture, in spite of its ubiquity. Thus, the human ear and the auditory system are important delivery devices for the communication of information about the state of architecture, about its atmosphere, its materiality, its program and those increasingly important affordances that may bring a sense of intimacy or place to our experiences of the built environment. It should then be considered as a fundamental tenet to any notion or conceptualization regarding the design of habitable space.

Indeed a few architects, perhaps visionaries, have sought to agitate the canon regarding sound and its fundamental grounding to built space. Perhaps the most famous is Juhani Pallasmaa, who has argued that the power of sound as an illumination of architecture demands a reconsideration of the nature of the auditory and its importance within design: "The sense of sight implies exteriority, but sound creates an experience of interiority. I regard an object, but sound approaches me; the eye reaches, but the ear receives. Buildings do not react to our gaze, but they do return sounds back to our ears." (Pallasmaa 2005, p. 49)

This returning of sounds back to us is achieved through a most efficient yet practical means: by way of the outer ear or *pinna* (Figure 1). As an interface between architecture and its inherent curation of sounds, the pinna, or auricle, is at first glance a seemingly expertly designed object whose form of sensuous folds, ridges and undulating surfaces might immediately call to mind the rise of computational strategies of the blobitecture movement in architecture (Waters 2003) rather than the product of thousands of years of human evolution. The pinna is not only adept at collecting sound waves and channeling them through to the middle ear via the auditory canal, but also enables incoming sounds to be both amplified and filtered through its highly complex geometry.

Take for example the *tragus*, the small bulbous lump that is located in front of and below the *concha* (Figure 2). Its backwards-projecting stance over the meatus or ear

Figure 3. *Hochschule für Musik, Theater und Medien* Hanover, designed by Rolf Ramcke and completed in 1973

canal is highly specialized in that it allows us to hear sounds that emanate from be-hind our bodies. In fact, the nature of the form of the *tragus* and its partnered forma-tion, the *anti-tragus*, assist in sensing the difference between sounds that come from in front of us and those that are from the rear. This is because those sounds coming from behind are ever so slightly delayed due to the morphology of the tragus. It is then an enabling form, a type of structure that, as a product of evolutionary forces, follows a particularly discreet function that has been tested and refined over time. But the fil-tering of incoming sounds into the pinna is also a privileging process in that the pinna allows those frequencies within the range of human speech (that is, those roughly be-tween 75 and 300 Hz) to be more present. In addition to this function, the reflection of higher-frequency sounds off the complex geometry of the pinna around the *helix, anti-helix* and *scapha* also plays an important factor in generating directional information that allows us to have (unlike the act of seeing) a particularly wide omnidirectional auditory field. This field allows us a good sense of the location of sound sources occur-ring not only in front of us, but above, behind, below or to either side: as Hildegard Westerkamp notes, "we are encapsulated and embedded within our sounds of the en-vironment." (Westerkamp 2006, pp. 84–89)

It may make sense then to read the literal translation of the form of the pinna into the design for the Hochschule für Musik, Theater und Medien in Hanover (Figure 3) by Rolf Ramcke as simply a novelty or postmodern frivolity, as an example of what Robert Venturi came to label as "ducks," given a condition "where the architectural systems of space, structure, and program are submerged and distorted by an overall symbolic form." (Venturi, Brown & Izenour 1977, p. 87) But embracing such a stance, even in favor of the notion of the "decorated shed," may prematurely jettison an important con-ceptualization about how a building might function if it were indeed an ear. As Peter Eisenman elaborates:

> For Venturi, a duck was a building that looked like its function; for example, a hot dog stand that looked like a giant hot dog. A decorated shed was more of a stage set, like the scenographic images of main street in a Hollywood western—all front and no rear. Ducks were volumetric, decorated sheds were facade screens. While

at the time Venturi's classification was useful, as buildings became more complex these distinctions began to blur. (Eisenman 2006, p. 139)

In light of Eisenman's reading of Venturi, and indeed to serve the purpose of an interrogation into architecture as an auditory system, a useful catalyst is found in the notion of transmediation by Marjorie Siegel. According to Siegel, transmediation is a process in which a sign system in one media is reappropriated into another. (Siegel 1995, pp. 455–475) Here, Siegel suggests that the power in understanding a sign system arises in the usurpation of the fundamental or identifiable structures of the system such that they become appropriated and retooled for use in other media. What is mapped perhaps approaches a structuralist semiotics in the vein of Claude Lévi-Strauss, whose theory of *différence*, though primarily demonstrated through language, mythmaking and kinship relations, inevitably sought to expose culture and cultural behaviors as of the domain of exchange and of communication. (Teyssot 2008, p. 45)

We find then the architectonic manifestation of a pinna at the Hochschule in Hanover as enfolded not only through the materiality and geometry of its surfaces, but similarly in its orientation. Sitting close to the city center and straddled between a main transport infrastructure and a park, the building and its footprint seek perhaps to provide an interface between the city, with its plethora of chaotic sound sources, and those more rarefied experiences of a classical concert hall, not to mention the natural sound world of a small, wooded arena that feeds an opening between its *tragus* and *anti-tragus*. Is the *modus operandi* then of the building—particularly in light of a forthright reading of it as one of Venturi's "ducks"—one in which it actively seeks to transfer and corral these sounds? To collect them, and within its interiority, to transform them so that mechanized noise becomes music, the everyday becomes the rarefied and the public becomes the private? To venture such a program is to also imply Aldo van Eyck's reading of those structuralist influences of Lévi-Strauss within architecture, for which Georges Teyssot observes that,

> for van Eyck, a building should present a structural analogue to the human being, and include anthropomorphic pairings, such as breathing in and out, front and back, spirit and body … space is made in the image of man, and, accordingly, architecture begins to function in a system of imitation, with each level of the similarity, or analogy, "imitating" the next: from the scale of theological to the anthropological. (Teyssot 2008, p. 37)

To read Ramcke's *Hochschule* in van Eyck's terms as a "system of imitation" brings to bear its nature as a listening device. As an ear to the city then, it is all hearing and indiscriminate as to those sound sources that approach it—of course not tentatively but boldly. Windows littered across its facade then act out other roles, ones that serve as indeterminate filtering devices that cast the exterior conditions as an otherness from the more acoustically controlled interior. Each random or considered opening presents an opportunity for the building to breathe in, to consume, to regulate and to acoustically mediate. A condition that was already seemingly understood in the advice given to architects in the late 1950s from the *Bundesministerium für Wohnungsbau* (Ministry for Housing) in West Germany regarding an acoustic sensitivity required for

BAUT RUHIGE WOHNUNGEN

Figure 4. 1950s brochure
(cover) from the Ministry
for Housing, West Germany,
pertaining to advice on
building quieter houses

new housing projects of the *Wirtschaftswunder*, given the rapid rise in population densities of the postwar period.

But it is just this type of seemingly analog account of the facade as pinna that for Joel Sanders and Karen Van Lengen provided an opportunity to embrace the technical means with which to situate architecture as an interactive digital interface to the acoustic environment. A congruent stance to what Laurent Stalder has similarly argued: that architecture is itself a technological system of objective parameters such as construction, materials or indeed functional operations that together form commodities in which "technological developments not only lead to the change of the built environment but also to a change of their experience and their use." (Stalder 2009, p. 69) Thus for Sanders and Van Lengen, the notion of using architecture as a device for dynamic acoustic mediation through the collection of sounds via electronic means gives their *Mix House* of 2006 a special place in the reconceptualization of architecture. By approaching Stalder's notion of architecture as technology, the *Mix House* becomes an auditory enabler by re-imaging architecture as a replete and functioning auditory system. The result of this focus is that the project provokes to expand the modernist notion of the transparent. It seeks to see into, yet hear beyond, those glass box paradigms of Philip Johnson or Mies van der Rohe by incorporating two sound-gathering volumes (fitted with microphones) within a suburban house that are equipped with three audiovisual windows to essentially approach sound design within the domestic realm as a DJ might at a dance party.

The curved profile of each of these sonic windows is composed of two elements: a louvered glass window wall that regulates the sound of the airborne ambient environment, and a parabolic dish that electronically targets domestic sounds and transmits them to an interior audio system controlled from the kitchen island. From this sound command center of the house, occupants are free to design original domestic soundscapes by mixing media-sponsored sounds [music, speech, etc.] with the ambient noises of the neighborhood. (Sanders & Van Lengen 2006)

Membranes

But this notion of actively controlling the immediate acoustic environment through envisaging the facade as a pinna had also arisen within the performance experiments of the New York School that emerged in the 1950s, through its embrace of Happenings, chance operations and the influence of the Fluxus and Dada movements. In fact, using the perforations of a facade as opportunities for enabling "chance hearings" from an exterior environment to enter into a musical work was integral to iconoclastic American composer John Cage's *Variations IV* of 1963. The work is generated according to the free juxtaposition of transparent sheets of points and lines over a plan of the performance space (Figure 5). The resulting score documents those points where sounds are to occur with the possibility that (numerous) sounds might be located outside the building. Furthermore, the structure, duration and type of sounds are freely chosen by the performer(s): as Cage notes, the thematic materials consist of "any sounds or combination of sounds produced by any means with or without other activities." (Cage

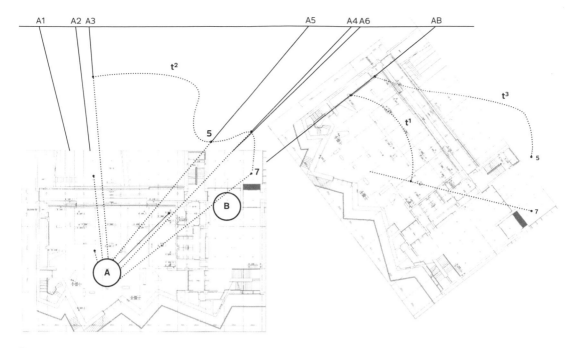

Figure 5. John Cage, *Variations IV* (1963) realization method (detail) at Nono Hall, Akiyoshidai International Art Village, Yamaguchi, Japan. Lines that connect points to circles A and B are also extended beyond the building envelope to locate possible positions of sound sources.

1963) In addition to these freedoms is Cage's erudite deconstruction of the notion of a necessary divide between exterior and interior sound worlds. In fact, those sound events that occur outside the building may simply be understood as opportunities for the listeners to experience those chaotic non-intentional sounds of the exterior environment—a particularly dynamic one when a performance is presented within a dense urban environment.

Thus, unlike the technologically fortified media space of the *Mix House*, Cage's *Variations IV* draws us into a circuitous route back to a technologically unmediated architectural space—back to the notion that a building might be an ear to its site. Architecture remains as a technology, as a technological system, though in *Variations IV*, architectural form functions not as an encapsulation of space, but instead as an acoustic mediator that connects two diverse auditory centers. Cage's notion of spatiality then is one in which music is not constrained by the traditional questions of exactly which thematic materials may best serve the purpose of communicating musical meaning nor by what sites best acoustically isolate the exterior world from the idealized constructs of music-space. In this sense, *Variations IV* seeks to take the building back to the landscape, by conceptualizing the acoustic space of music as one that is comfortable as both an interior and an exterior experience. Hence the facade as a pinna is one through which sound might be channeled, essentially unadjusted and uncensored, but above all, as an aid towards intensive listening.

This type of channeling, or acoustic transparency, was what Carpenter also glimpsed within the materiality and technics of the architecture of the Inuit peoples of the Arctic regions. Both the igloo and the sealskin tent are acoustically transparent, yet

Figure 6. Sketch of sealskin tent by Frederick Varley

completely immersive environments. This is not simply due to their materialities, which may be considered situational or indeed endemic to a cold climate, but a function of an embodiment of particular cultural values, and indeed of particular acoustic expectations:

> Visually and acoustically the igloo is "open," a labyrinth alive with the movements of people. No flat static walls arrest the ear or eye, but voices and laughter come from several directions and the eye can glance through here, past there, catching glimpses of the activities of nearly everyone. The same is true of the sealskin tent. Every sound outside can be heard within, and the women inside always seem to be turning and stretching so they can peer out through the hole in the tent. (Carpenter 1959, p. 26)

It seems that Cage too was comparably convinced of an actively negated role of architecture to deliver isolated acoustic spaces (even for the presentation of art music) through his disregard for the acoustic occlusion of a building. Indeed, the Inuit notion of not referencing a singular sphere of acoustic activities as a predilection for control, but recognizing an interpenetrating of acoustic realms as a necessity of societal and cultural coherence, would not have been foreign to Cage's own goals or philosophy regarding the function of music in society at large.

In fact, in a manner analogous to Manuel De Landa's descriptions of positivist or empiricist philosophies (De Landa 2012), the design of the traditional concert hall reduces an observed cause and effect into a constant conjunction—that is, the elimination of nonmusical sounds of the outside through codified procedures of architectural

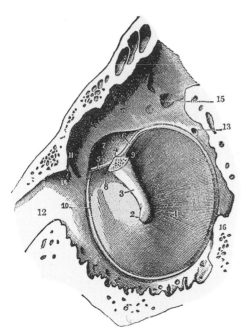

Figure 7. "The tympanic membrane viewed from within. (Testut.) The malleus has been resected immediately beyond its lateral process, in order to show the tympanomalleolar folds and the membrana flaccida. **1.** Tympanic membrane. **2.** Umbo. **3.** Handle of the malleus. **4.** Lateral process. **5.** Anterior tympanomalleolar fold. **6.** Posterior tympanomalleolar fold. **7.** Pars flaccida. **8.** Anterior pouch of Tröltsch. **9.** Posterior pouch of Tröltsch. **10.** Fibrocartilaginous ring. **11.** Petrotympanic fissure. **12.** Auditory tube. **13.** Iterchordæ posterius. **14.** Iterchordæan-terius. **15.** Fossa incudis for short crus of the incus. **16.** Prominentia styloidea."

form applied through particular materials. To say that architecture then becomes political would not be an overestimation, especially in light of Cage's vowed anarchic tendencies. (Cage 2010) In this redefinition of the function of the building's facade, that which is occurring outside, and the acoustic properties of this outside sound world, is not exclusive or foreign to the interior properties of the building. *Variations IV*, like the habitable spaces of the Inuit peoples, allows us to cast the architectural structure as an ear, in that it is centered on the reconciliation of the aural qualities and events of the surrounding context (the arena of the unintentional) with that of the architectural interior (the arena of the intentional).

But to focus in a little further, and to examine in more detail this potential transition of sounds from the exterior to the interior, from the city in through the facade as a pinna, we can see that the detail of Ramcke's building does not stop at the likeness presented by the building as an analog to the outer ear. Within the interior courtyard can be found a representation of the eardrum or *tympanic membrane*. Ramcke uses a bright yellow cone approximately two meters in diameter at its circular base and some three meters in depth at its apex. Suspended through cables, and as if floating within the courtyard, its form recalls the notion that at the inner canal of the middle ear is a threshold, a point at which a second interior (the inner ear) lies beyond the wall of the *tympanic membrane*.

This in-between space as the nexus of the middle and inner ear is where sound vibrations from the exterior excite sympathetic vibrations in the tympanic membrane. It is where a confluence and a synthesis between the exterior and interior collide such that the actuation of the transmediation of vibrations in the medium of air is mechanized via the membrane. The architecture of the ear is such that its materiality allows for sympathetic resonances to be further perpetuated on a smaller scale, at the scale of the ear canal. Sounds emanating from distant sources, at the scale of architecture, at the urban scale, become ostensively miniaturized, contained and interpreted by the mechanism of the membrane. Often, the causes of hearing loss, particularly that of high-frequency content, are tied to the decreased sensitivity of the tympanic membrane, to the deterioration of the muscles and ligaments surrounding it.

Connected to the membrane are the smallest bones of the body, the *malleus, stapes* and *incus*. They work in concert as a natural lever, the *ossicular chain*, such that the vibrations occurring across the membrane become amplified through a mechanical advantage that further enables the transformation of these vibrations to disturb the liquid located within the *cochlea*—vibrations in air become vibrations in a liquid, a classic case of Siegel's transmediation. The threshold of the tympanic membrane then is an operable state in which a transmediation via mechanization and scalar diminution produces a sense of place, a sense of activation, or perhaps as Aldo van Eyck might reason, an "image of occasion." (van Eyck 1968, p. 101) It is indubitably also the kernel of an auditory awareness. As van Eyck would assert, the role of archi-

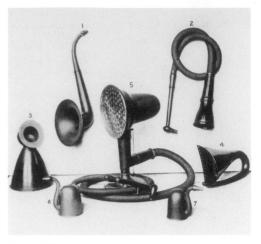

Figure 8. "Mechanical aids to hearing"

tecture and of urban design must be to identify space as the meeting place of humanity, itself a composite of dualities such that the dialectic of these oppositions must be reconciled through architecture: "inside and outside, here and there, small and large, part and whole." (Teyssot 2008, p. 38) Thus the notion of space and time correlates to the architectonics of place and event. At the tympanic membrane too we find a meeting, a creation of place given it is the point of articulation of our sense of the auditory qualities, the auditory dimensions of architecture. These are always unfolding in time such that the in-between that is represented by the membrane, its moment of excitation and our sensation of sound and space become reconciled as the inside/outside dichotomy is brought to bear as an auditory awareness of our surroundings.

But this structural condition of the membrane, between those vibrations in air and those vibrations occurring across the membrane, represents a paradigm. It is a necessary binary state of the type that Pierre von Meiss asserts is adept at embracing the totality of its spatial continuum:

> Each relationship between two places or between an interior and an exterior proceeds from two aspects of dependence. It provides both separation and connection, or, in other words, differentiation and transition, interruption and continuity, boundary and crossing. Thresholds and spaces of transition become places in their turn: places in which the world reverses itself. (von Meiss 2013, p. 148)

Sitting then at its own threshold, both exterior to the building yet cradled within the outer-facing facade as a pinna, we find the bright yellow cone of Ramcke's courtyard sculpture, also a keen reminder of the historical mechanization of hearing, of the technological beginnings of what Raymond Kurzweil predicts as our inevitable slide towards the transhuman. (Kurzweil 2005) In fact, by an account of Keith Ansell Pearson, there is valuable currency in highlighting Heidegger's error, given his aversion to technics and technology. (Heidegger 1977) Pearson contends that, because of Heidegger's massive underestimation of "the extent of technology's invention of the human animal and the nature and extent of its investment in mankind" (Pearson 2012, p. 153),

Figure 9. "Fig. 3. The Audiphone properly adjusted to the upper teeth; ready for use. (Side view.)"

there is accordingly an erroneous notion perpetuated that technology is a cause for dehumanization.

Ramcke's conical sculpture then must certainly evoke the ghost of Beethoven's own hearing instruments, of the attempt of a technological intervention to thwart a cruel and ironic deficiency in the composer's ability to hear his own music. Indeed, by the onset of Beethoven's complete deafness sometime in 1814 (Davies 2001), ear trumpets had already been popular for at least twenty years, as their effectiveness had increased greatly through improved design, though sadly for the master, no such amplifying device could assist in the treatment of his acute disability. The capability of such contemporary devices was limited to pure amplification, essentially through mimicking the physiology of the outer and middle ear. In the special case of sufferers of *otosclerosis* (of which it is conjectured that Beethoven was a potential candidate), a much later means to circumvent the deprecated *ossicular chain*, in which vibrations fail to reach the cochlea, is approached through bone conduction. As R. A. Tange describes, these later devices operated through a placement of the instrument in the mouth:

> The first hearing aids for otosclerosis were bone-conducting teeth stimulators developed by R. S. Rhodes (1879) and T. W. Graydon (1880). Otosclerosis being a bone-conducting disease, these fans were an acceptable help in hearing rehabilitation. The Audiphone of Rhodes and the Dentaphone of Graydon conveyed sound to the inner ear through the teeth. (Tange 2014, p. 38)

To hear through the teeth and indeed via the temporal bone allows for a bypassing of the organs of the middle ear as a means to directly access the cochlea and the *vestibular system*. Both of these organs are recessed within a special cavity in the skull, the *osseous labyrinth*. The *vestibular system* comprises a series of canals (the *posterior, anterior* and *horizontal*) that sense rotational movement in addition to the very small *otolithic organs* that detect linear accelerations. Though this system is embedded within the mechanism of the ear, it is directly connected to the neural structures that control eye movement and the muscles that allow one to stand without falling over: just as Pallasmaa had already poignantly observed, "the ears often help the eyes." (Pallasmaa 2005, p. 48) But perhaps the most important part of the inner ear is the *cochlea*: a very small shell-like structure filled with fluid, which is responsible for converting those sound waves that enter the ear into electrical signals. The cochlea is thus the organ that is responsible for sending electrical impulses on to the brain to be interpreted and heard. The inner ear then is an interior space, both in the sense that it is located within the body, as well as being a system that interiorizes external stimuli into the sensation of hearing.

Ramcke's Hochschule is also conceivably a site for the conversion of sounds. At the inner courtyard, protected from the transport infrastructure on its western side and leading on its eastern side to a heavily tree-covered park, sounds of the city and sounds of nature converge, merging and entering into the building through open-

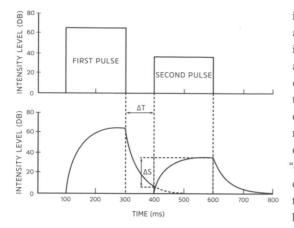

Figure 10. Diagram of the stimulus level (upper) and the sensation level (lower) in regard to time of two pulses. First proposed by Plomp (1964).

ings, through chance meetings and via auditory windows. But within the building, beyond the sculpture of the ear cone as a tympanic membrane, sounds are indeed transformed through the production of music. In interior corridors, antechambers and vestibules, the notion of music, or that which early electroacoustic composer Edgar Varése understood as "organized sound," becomes a living and cultural phenomenon. Musical space is therefore conceived as open rather than bounded, thus producing an encapsulating atmosphere of creative conversion.

What might architecture gain from such acts of *critical listening*? Listening itself is born of sensation, whether it proceeds from the observance of the qualities and acoustic behaviors of the architectonic or the production and realization of musical thematics, it is active, and an activation of an attention to aurality. As Plomp forwarded in 1964, the decay of auditory sensation is a gradual one such that given two pulses separated by silence, the decay of the sensation of the first pulse is not immediate and lingers within the silence between pulses. (Plomp 1964) This is consequential given that our experience then of the built environment is a perpetual unfolding, it represents an interminability offered to us in which we are in effect constantly processing acoustic information about our surroundings—whether we are succinctly aware of this or not. Sounds appear in almost every facet and every moment of our lives, from the functional or unwanted to the musical or aesthetic. Architecture too though has an important role given that it is often both an aid and a deterrent to achieving a sense of balance of acoustic appropriateness. Certainly, the notion of critical listening begins with this sensorial paradigm. Moving through and understanding the dimensions of auditory space presented to us by the architectonic is in effect an ongoing processing in which to be critical is to be immersed in the fact that auditory sensation is not easily or readily set aside, at least at the neurological level.

A dissonant theme then for the protagonist Wang of "Sounding City" is the comprehension of a listening experience that seemingly negates the sensation of listening to a form that ostensively bypasses the point of conversion occurring at the cochlea. What remains mystifying is that though the sensation of listening is reduced, muted or abrogated, the effects of listening remain intact, perhaps even amplified—the HSE junkies can attest to this fact. The range of human hearing operates through a relatively fixed frequency band of between 20 Hz and 20 kHz. The inner ear mechanism works at its most efficient between 512 Hz and 8 kHz (nominally the range of human speech). At an HSE parlor, and through hypersonic content (that is, frequencies outside the range of human hearing), audibility is no longer about the activation of the tympanic membrane or the malleus, incus and stapes as energy transfer systems for the delivery of sensory information directly to the brain's cortex via the cochlea. Instead, this transfer of energy occurs through some other means such that even a wider gamut of sounds can be "experienced."

It might seem that the usurpation of such a fantastic notion as HSE is purely a means to coercively subjugate the status quo of architecture and its somewhat timid relation to sound and to listening. Surely could such a plot device not have been more fanciful as a utility for auditory awareness had it not already entered the scientific discourse as a potential paradigm-shifting discovery. Though the disputations of the validity of hypersonic listening are still well formed, in the year 2000, Tsutomu Oohashi, Emi Nishina and their collaborators published an account of the hypersonic effect (HSE) in the *Journal of Neurophysiology*. (Oohashi et al. 2000) Their study of subjects who listened to recorded music containing excerpts that had significant high-frequency components (that is, content above 20 kHz, abbreviated HFC) and excerpts that contained no HFC found increased brain activity in the HFC-augmented music samples, as well as tangible physiological and psychological effects as measured by alpha-EEG scans and questionnaires. Researchers discovered "an intensification of the pleasure with which the sound is perceived, and envisage the participation of the neuronal pathways in connection with reward-generating systems." (Oohashi et al. 2000, p. 3557) Evidently, the effects of hypersonic listening are present even though the physiological means of activation are still unknown. Oohashi and colleagues speculate that the human brain's deeper neurological structure might somehow be activated or that the bone-conducting auditory pathway might become a resonator at hypersonic frequencies—a curious parallel to those late 19th-century teeth-actuated devices, the Audiphone of Rhodes and the Dentaphone of Graydon. But the most intriguing outcome of this initial study of HSE is the subsequent research suggesting how such a phenomenon might impact the sound design of the built environment and the role of the architectural in curating listening experiences.

Six years after their initial studies, Oohashi's colleagues Nishina and Nori Kawai presented a proposal for an "urban sound design system" at the World Forum for Acoustic Ecology conference in 2006. Building on research into HSE, their investigation sought to provide richer urban acoustic experiences by projecting recordings of rain forests within public spaces in Japan through a specialized six-channel loudspeaker delivery system. (Nishina et al. 2006) Samples of pristine Malaysian rain forest sites revealed naturally occurring HFC of up to 130 kHz—a dramatic contrast to the typical Japanese urban area in which upper-frequency ranges drop off at around 10 kHz. Nishina and colleagues' auditory design concept found an ad hoc testing ground in Hikone, Shiga Prefecture, Japan. A publicly accessible site in a high-density area with a large amount of pedestrian traffic provided an auditory zone for the diffusion of the source sounds through specially adapted loudspeakers. The researchers' intentions for

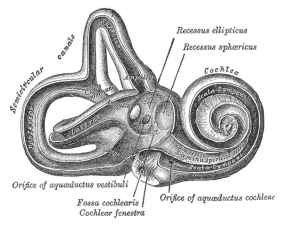

Figure 11. "Interior of right osseous labyrinth"

Figure 12. *Signal* public loudspeaker array, Melbourne, Australia

urban sound-space design stem from an underlying desire to return to a putative original acoustic environment that modern human beings have never heard. The project's impetus is the original-adaptation model of environmental informatics that postulates that the cradle of human gene evolution occurred over millions of years within rain forests in central western Africa. (Brunet et al. 2002) As such, their goals are to "establish, nourish and put into practice a systematic strategy by which to bring about a revival in an urban space of the original sound environment imprinted on human genes in the rainforest." (Nishina et al. 2006, p. 373)

That such approaches to the amelioration of the acoustic environment within cities have found some footing within urban planning models is further evidenced in a similar system located in Melbourne, Australia. Though not established as a means by which to bring us back, at least acoustically, to what Albert Borgman (1984) identifies as the necessary correction to a dehumanized technologically saturated contemporary condition via a reversion to "a good life" with an emphasis on "focal things and practices," the *Signal* site along the Yarra River in Melbourne includes multimedia facilities for the presentation of public art. Like Nishina's original design in Hikone, the *Signal* urban loudspeaker array is located in a thoroughfare witnessing high pedestrian traffic. In addition to the eighteen paired loudspeakers situated along a pathway parallel to the Yarra River (Harvey 2013), facilities for the production and reproduction of creative auditory content are housed in an adjacent building, itself once a signaling tower for the nearby suburban railway system.

Both of these systems are pitched as urban renewal projects and thus pay homage to the greater urban sound design interventions nominally envisaged by Kevin

Lynch, in particular his vision for an environmentally controlled yet sustainable city sound-space that would be aided by, among other things, the inclusive fomentation of "acoustic perfume":

> Provisions for the control of noise, or of the micro-climate, including the use of planting of shielding devices, the control of noise at the source, the orientation and spacing of buildings, the design of ground surfaces in regard to the way they reflect or absorb radiation, the introduction of desirable sounds or "acoustic perfume." (Lynch 1995, p. 310)

But such a tactic then seemingly reverses the aesthetic of the *Mix House* of Van Lengen and Sanders—the building not as a listening device, but instead as sounding instrument. The concept that architecture and buildings might emit sound beyond the purely obvious case of the electroacoustic refitting, modernizing, or what Adorno termed the *Technifizierung* (Adorno 1999, p. 199) of a structure or series of standardized methodologies would seem at odds with the conceptualizations I have brought to bear here on the notion of the facade as a pinna, or architecture as a potential auditory system. Any building can make any sounds given the addition of loudspeakers, perhaps as Venturi's "decorated shed," where as functional spaces, "decorative symbols are [simply] applied." (Harries 1998, p. 73) Such a situation then duly places the responsibility on listeners to make meaningful experiences of the site, to read and comprehend the symbols, or at least for them to attempt to reconcile the auditory image with that of the architectural image. This is particularly acute in light of the rise of Musak in the 1930s and its purpose to be a "psychologically active, sonic accompaniment, carefully designed to remain below the threshold of common attention." (Radano 1989, p. 450) But rather than seeking to speculate on the conception of sounds that simply accompany architecture, a more pertinent idealization is to address those sounds that are of architecture, those sounds that cast themselves as a function of the architectonic.

Vibrations

To return once again to the ear, it may not be surprising to know that, as a consequence of its particular physiological traits and materiality, the ear is frequently engaged in producing sounds. First predicted by Thomas Gold (1948) and then verified through experiments by David Kemp (1978), the cochlea is considered the point of origin of two types of *otoacoustic emission* (OAE): sounds that are spontaneous and those that can be evoked through clinical stimulation. OAEs are thought to arise in the cochlea and are considered a byproduct of the amplification system of the cochlea in which the outer hair cells act to increase the amplitude and frequency selectivity of sound vibrations through electromechanical feedback. Though most people are unaware of their OAEs (and those who are aware describe them in similar terms to tinnitus), the sounds themselves are relatively stable and occur at between 500 Hz and 4500 Hz (within the range of human speech), and are considered so unique to each individual that they might be utilized for biometric identification. The clinical evocation of an OAE is actuated through audio: sending signals (in the presence of a microphone) into the ear canal and then measuring the difference between the stimulus waveform and the recorded waveform, which is essentially the sum of the stimulus and the OAE.

Such approaches are commonly used for hearing tests for newborn babies as it has been concluded that after damage to the cochlea (or similarly, in the case of defects), OAEs no longer appear. Hence the utilization of such tests is considered noninvasive, and requires no patient input or verification.

What then for architecture? Indeed, a fundamental physical consequence true of all matter is its state of being in constant vibration. At the atomic and even subatomic levels, motion, waves and excitations are inseparable characteristics of the physical constraints and state qualities that bind the fundamental elements of materials together. We can, without a great deal of conceptual effort, further concede that architecture not only curates particular types of acoustic behaviors, or particular acoustic typologies, but furthermore, architecture, in its very nature, builds sounds and constructs sound worlds. This concept has a particular richness that is only slightly tempered by these sounds being, for the most part, hidden from us though certainly not inaccessible. Indeed, for John Grzinich and his *New Maps of Time* series of sound workshops, this hidden auditory world of architecture proved the catalyst for seeking out methods in which to "map spaces (mental, architectural and natural) using sound as a means of expressing actions within a space." (Grzinich 2016) The approach by Grzinich is not so much to pinpoint the qualities of the sound design proper of architectural spaces, but instead to reveal the hidden acoustic qualities of a space, and indeed the sound of what lies beyond the visual articulation of a building's form. Thus unlike the frame of the "scientific" applied to traditional acoustic analysis, Grzinich's work is born of architecture, in the architectural, and thus seeks not to describe a building or structure by its acoustic qualities in mathematical terms, but simply to redress our common notions about the sound of architecture by disclosing it in raw and direct terms through the lens of what I would contend is critical listening.

This is variously achieved through myriad placements of inexpensive contact microphones along structures such as suspension bridges, within walls of a building, in floors and on other surfaces and transport infrastructures. The audio recordings of such results are truly extraordinary, given the wealth of sounds and textures that emerge, their rhythmic vitality and the oft-surpassed point of incredulity that the structure and its bellows of ecstatic protest and delight might be labeled as anything other than animated form, that the building is speaking to us in no uncertain terms. If, as by van Eyck's desire, architecture becomes an expression that approaches a "system of imitation," then through the mappings of Grzinich, we are indubitably convinced of a forthright challenge to the notion of a stasis inherent in the built form, of a fundament of pedestrian immobility within architecture.

But if Grzinich's acoustic mappings are born simply of a desire to identify and hear architecture as a vibrating object, the work of David Byrne and his *Playing the Building* installation seek to take the notion further, and to manipulate and perform through the building's structure. First installed at Färgfabriken, an exhibition space located in a Kunsthalle at a former factory in Stockholm in 2005, Byrne's installation incorporates an old pump organ that is used as a controller and centrally located in the space. The organ's keyboard triggers the actuation of motors that variously bring into audibility numerous structures, surfaces, beams and pipes of the building through direct contact. There is no traditional tuning or mapping of the pitches of resulting sounds to the geography of the keyboard; instead, it is public and interactive, and only through

Figure 13. David Byrne, *Playing the Building*, Battery Maritime Building, New York, 2008

"play" and experimentation are the capabilities for sound combinations, rhythms and textures discovered. The activations also include blowing air through plumbing as well as striking objects such that a rich tapestry of sound colors and a vast depth regarding the frequency and pitch content are literally teased out of the building. None of the motors or actuators make any sound themselves, so that the focus is on the generation of sound purely from the infrastructure of the building itself. Byrne considers architectural space and the work of *Playing the Building* in relative volumetric terms vis-à-vis the notion of architecture as a container that can be filled with sounds:

> As far as space goes, I sense that different architectural spaces "want" to have specific kinds of sounds inside them. The space creates a hole for sounds to fill, psychologically and physically—but only specific sorts of sounds seem to "fit" in each kind of space. The inherent acoustics of a room have far-reaching effects: they make you walk different and talk different. They make you feel different. (Byrne 2016)

Byrne's conceptualization of the relationship between sound and architecture is particularly telling. What is revealing is his adjudging of architecture as a vessel, as a volume pregnant with a potential sound world that has not yet been born yet demands a highly considered sensitivity with reference to its formal characteristics. This conceptualization of architecture speaks directly to the difficult notion surrounding sound and site

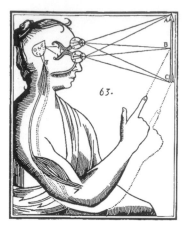

Figure 14. Explanation of the pineal gland

specificity, particularly regarding introduced sounds. In a site such as the one found at *Signal*, where the capability of auditory content and playback is limitless, the rather problematic issue of exactly what is an appropriate sound design for the site ensues. What may adequately serve a musical or sound art program may not best serve an architectural program. There must certainly be then a qualitative difference between the erudite integration of sound into a site and a simplistic juxtaposition of sounds (towards which the concept of Muzak heavily leans).

Byrne then seems to recognize such differences and, by acknowledging that his work seeks to act out and emphasize the "act of careful listening," tacitly fortifies the argument that to hear architecture is to be cognizant of the undertaking of a process of sense-making, or what Grzinich identifies as the nature of acute listening, indeed of critical listening, as an apparatus to "explore the subjectivity of personal and collective experience." (Grzinich 2016) The resultant of this materialist process is in De Landa's terms a function of a causality that "is considered to be an objective relation of [the] production between events, that is, a relation in which one event produces another event." (De Landa 2012, p. 7) The events here are the act of acute listening and the resulting auditory awareness of the architectural properties of a space, which themselves are a direct addressee to both the necessity of participatory affirmation by the listener and a recognition of those deep running connections that bind architecture to site.

But *Playing the Building* also brings to light the notion between architecture as an already-sounding object, that is, as a vibrating manifold nominally unheard, and those volumes in which it enables sounds to propagate, to live, move and infiltrate the immediate surroundings. This perhaps creates yet another duality, a potential threshold between the micro and the macro. Indeed, this notion that the lived space of architecture and our experience within it in some manner bears the nexus of two acoustic conditions, two potential sound worlds, was similarly petitioned by German composer Karlheinz Stockhausen and his 1968 text work *Aufwärts* (upwards) from *Aus den sieben Tagen* (From the seven days) (Stockhausen 1968). Here too, in a simple directive to the performers, who are to improvise intuitively on the directive, Stockhausen asks for an apprehension of the seemingly conflicting and conflated sound worlds of the very small and the very large:

> Play a vibration in the rhythm of your smallest particles
> Play a vibration in the rhythm of the universe
> Play all the rhythms that you can
> distinguish today between
> the rhythm of your smallest particles
> and the rhythm of the universe
> one after the other
> and each one for so long
> until the air carries it on …

But these directions too might also ask us to consider what such an ostensive or irreconcilable scale means for architecture as a sounding body. Whereas Descartes had postulated that the substance of the mind and body are distinct such that there is no easy manner in which they could casually interact (the body has no real feelings, these are produced in the mind), the duality of the acoustic spaces of architecture is tied to the ostensively unheard micro-vibrations of its underlying structure and those voids that enable discrete acoustic behaviors and the sensations of introduced sounds to propagate within it. If the walls and supporting framework of architecture, its skeletal structure, is its cochlea, by which tiny unheard emissions, OAEs, dissipate and diffuse outwards into its voids, then we are left with considering what those other sounds are, and how they will function within the materiality, geometry and volumes of the voids of the architectonic, across its pinna and middle ear. What is intriguing then about the work of Byrne and Grzinich is that it collapses this duality back onto itself. It takes Stockhausen's directive of seeking to acoustically map out a scalar continuum by diffusing those micro-sounds of the vibrating body and distributing them into the voids of the body itself at an adjusted and exploited scale through amplification—either with microphones or via mechanical actuations.

If we look at the building as its own universe, as a body, one can essentially build a recursive relationship or axiom between the very small and the very large. The micro-vibrations of the structure are heard at the largest scale that the body of architecture can offer; at the same time we hear the acoustic properties of the volumes of the body, the behaviors of the sounds in terms of their reflections, presence and energy within the space. Thus to conceive architecture as an auditory system, as an ear to a site, obliges us to acutely access all its auditory facets and qualities, to identify and reconcile its acoustic dualities, to initiate a critical listening towards its predilections of the micro and macro, its exterior and interior, the heard and unheard, the void and the structural. It is peradventure, as Stockhausen asked, to listen to sounds and their journey through space and through time and to seek out an expediency in which to comprehend the seemingly tangible and physical constraints of built form to the ephemeral and intangible qualities of auditory sensations.

2
On Auditory Scale

Boxes
Dimensions
Continuum

On Auditory Scale

Boxes

What is scale in terms of listening experience? Without the assistance of the ocular, of visual sensation, this question may be more poignantly reduced to a querying of what are the limits, in terms of both the infinitesimally small and the extraordinarily large, of our notion of the dimensions of space when they are defined purely by sound? Sounds that approach us find their way through the pinna into the middle ear and finally into the cochlea and are a result of an interaction with the materiality of the surrounding environment. Sound waves possess energy, which is only dissipated and spent through the interaction of the waves with various mediums—air, architectural surfaces, liquids, the earth. There are of course direct sounds that approach us too, coming from a source without any diversion, without an excursion: a direct face-to-face conversation, a whispered thought in another's ear, headphone listening. These occurrences exist without any agency of diffusion that had caused them to firstly map out a corner, a border or a terminating surface that had subsequently triggered them to reflect back towards us, into us.

But the fundamental means of how we sense the auditory dimensions of architectural space is through the auditory channel as a neurological computation, firstly as a sum of vibrations that each approach the ear at slightly varied time distributions and, according to William T. Preyer's 1886 study, from twenty-six discernible directions. These variations or delays are the result of sound waves essentially mapping out the physical boundaries, the tangible architectonics of the reflective surfaces that surround us. They are, as Heidegger described, encounters within thematic space as a function between *Dasein* and myriad localized objects. (Heidegger 2008) But these types of objects, and those boundaries between ourselves and the numerous worlds we encounter exterior to us, are also what Michel Serres considers "boxes," perhaps not only in philosophical terms:

> Every possible kind of audible finds sites of hearing and regulation. It is as though the body were constructed like a box, a series of boxes, through which these cycles pass. As though the collective forms itself into a box or boxes through which these flows circulate. And as though knowledge, a world crying out for more attentive hearing, constructs the largest white box of all. (Serres 2008, p. 111)

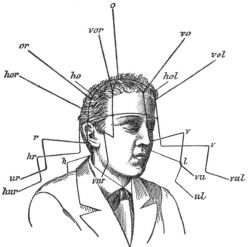

Figure 15. Diagram of Preyer's twenty-six perceivable sound directions

Le Corbusier too seemed fixated on the notion of the box, not necessarily in architectonic terms, but certainly as a container for the idea of proportion, scale, and the relationship

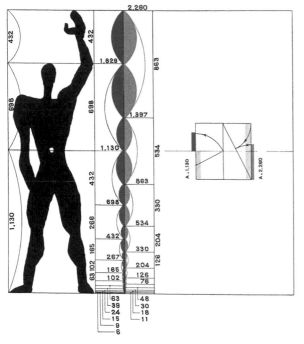

Figure 16. Graphic representation of the *Modulor*

between the human body and lived spaces. Built architecture has necessarily acquired an immutable connection to the human body, its range of motion, physiological characteristics and the ways in which we psychologically perceive and engage with a spatial program. Given Teyssot's assertion that "since the Greek canon and Vitruvius, an intrinsic aspect of the Western tradition has been to embed human proportions into a building," (Teyssot 2008, p. 37) it is not surprising that Le Corbusier found an absoluteness in his vision for a proportional metrics in architecture, as found in his *Modulor 1 & 2* (1948/1955). Here, the architect's argument for a system for aesthetic and practical management of proportions regarding the design of built space through the utilization of two reference scales (one red, one blue) is conditioned and even idealized through its use of a ladder of golden means found in the Fibonacci series (Gans 2006)—thus representing an inherent naturalness to the proportions as a synthesis of man (and vicariously architecture) to the natural world. As a foil then to those past models such as from Vitruvius, the *Modulor* greatly emphasizes the human body as a utility for the extradition of scalar proportions that may be used to guide architectural design—an inner box to inform the outer container of architecture? Indeed, as Le Corbusier argued, "the human being is at the same time the source and purpose of architecture. Therefore, the human body with its proportions should be the centre of all order." (Kanach 2008, p. 12)

There are then of course implications for the box as an architectonic concept and its relation to human proportions in terms of listening, in terms of the metrics of auditory sensation. If the human body is a box latent with sensation, what becomes of the containment of architecture? What becomes of the box outside the box? The auditory qualities that can be sensed within enclosed spaces are a function of the reflection of sound waves off surfaces. Not only are those qualities such as depth, envelopment, loudness or clarity communicable, but equally, the notion of the physical dimensions of a space (indeed whether it is located exterior or interior to a building). We are extremely adept at sensing and locating sounds sources relative to our bodies due to evolutionary forces of survival. Within enclosed spaces, this sense awareness of the physical dimensions inherent within the containment of architecture is communicated via a sense of the prolongation of sounds sources, namely of a room's reverberation.

Assessing then the graphic representation of the *Modulor*, one notices that the proportions extend from the navel of the figure of a man both incrementally upwards and downwards (presumably continuing ad infinitum in both directions). What is the

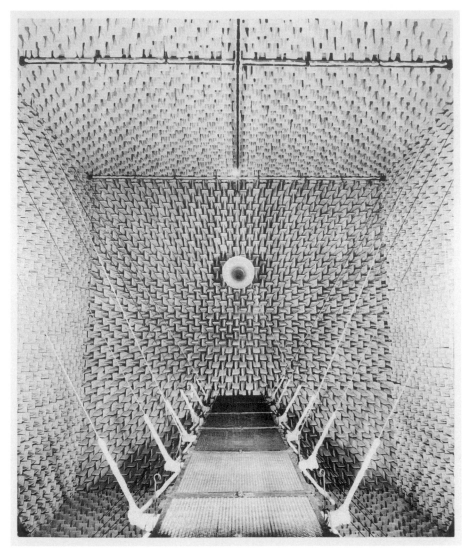

Figure 17. The former anechoic chamber at the Cruft Laboratory at Harvard that Cage visited in 1951

notion of an ever incrementally increasing and decreasing scale of auditory sensation, or a scale of reverberation? Such a continuum is perhaps best revealed through two acoustic typological extremes of the box (in terms of both architectonics and sensation): the anechoic chamber and the reverberation chamber—one, a space that allows only for the experience of direct sounds, the other, an overtly efficient distributer of reflected sounds.

Experiencing the anechoic chamber is perhaps John Cage's most retold anecdote given its significance in regard to the composer's most infamous and polarizing work, 4'33", the silent piece of 1954. Upon visiting Harvard in 1951 and being invited to experience a silent room, Cage, after sitting still for a while within the chamber, noticed (perhaps to his delight) that in spite of the ostensive engineering feat of managing to completely isolate all sound and negate the potential for sound reflections within the chamber, two distinct sounds were indeed audible. Querying the engineer on the significance and source of the sounds, given that Cage had expected to hear nothing, (Foy 2010, p. 64) it was explained to Cage: "the high one was your nervous system in operation. The low one was your blood circulation." (Cage 1968, p. 134) Naturally, Cage concluded that in all certainty there is then no real silence *per se*, as evidenced from his experience situated within a room with no reverberation and completely isolated from any extraneous sounds. Though quietude certainly exists as a metaphysical concept, perhaps as a quieting of the mind, actual total silence can never be fully realized. It was left to the body, in this situation, to take over as noise generator, to fill in, or provide a

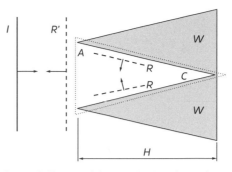

Figure 18. Diagram of the minimization of sound wave reflections by the walls of an anechoic chamber. Wedges, *W* of height *H* cause an incident wave *I* to be caught within the airspace (*A*) between them as a series of internally reflected waves, *R*. The acoustic energy of *R* is dissipated by *A* as well as the vertex *C*. Due to the highly absorptive materials of *W*, any reflected waves *R'* are significantly reduced in energy.

proxy for reading off the dimensions of this anti-room, a box bearing a strong, even considered visual aesthetic, yet in possession of no identifiable acoustic signature. The rest, as it were, changed musical history when, in 1954, pianist David Tudor sat in silence (with notated score: a prop perhaps, pregnant with sounds) at the *Woodstock Music Festival* for a total of 4 minutes and 33 seconds. This chance-determined time bracket provided only a structural guide, an empty plan, for which the thematic materials of the work at hand consisted solely of the extraneous sounds occurring within the concert hall at the time of the performance. These incidental sounds were no doubt exacerbated through a nervous collective anticipation on the part of the audience that something was about to happen given Tudor had a stopwatch to observe exactly the length of the three movements of the work from his unfailing score-as-prop.

What is perhaps most overlooked though in Cage's seminal silent work is its patent decentralization of auditory space. Though the piece aptly and blatantly seeks to question the very nature of thematic materials, asking of us exactly what sounds are appropriate to constitute a musical work and thus communicate meaning, this emphasis overshadows how 4'33" exposes a new reading of what Barry Blesser and Linda-Ruth Salter have nominated as the acoustic arena. Here, auditory space is defined through the extent and volume by which any sounds can be heard. The acoustic arena is an auditory zone,

> where listeners are part of a community that share the ability to hear a sonic event. An acoustic arena is centered at the sound source; listeners are inside or outside of the arena of the sonic event. (Blesser 2007, pp. 22–23)

In Cage's refiguring of musical space, a strident consequence is the refocus not on the point of musical performance as a centering of sounds within a site, as a definitive point from which the acoustic listening space is defined, but instead, the larger arena of the concert hall as a homogeneous set of possibilities and indeed probabilities given various contexts, audiences and of course history. There can perhaps not ever be another authentic performance of the work, given its global reputation and the inevitable knowledge of contemporary audiences of what the work is about and what it seeks to redefine.

Perchance as a forbearing apparition to his later *Variations IV*, the arena defined by 4'33" is the entire architectural body. Sound from, and within, the architecture of the site becomes the composition. It is notable too that numerous concerts at Woodstock took place in an old wooden barn. Hence the sound of architecture is placed on equal terms to traditional musical materials. Furthermore, those numerous points within the audience seating, not to mention those sounds that might also be leaking inwards from the exterior, similarly came to define a multitude of acoustic arenas, each interpenetrating one another to form a sound world as a function of the building. The acoustic arena then of 4'33" ceases to be a hierarchical premeditated point of stasis in which all sounds will spread out from this point, on the stage, from an instrument, vocalist or speaker. There is then an inherent spatiality to this decentralization in that though the actual size of an arena may not change between a performance of 4'33" and, say, Beethoven's *Sonata Op. 31a* in the same performance space, the sense of where the listener is placed in regard to the arena, and indeed how many arenas are being created, may change radically.

The implications for music are architectural in nature in the sense that space for the delivery of music, in Cage's new reading of sound-space, need not be tuned, or designed for homogeneous, rarefied listening experiences. Cage, it would seem, attempts to construct an architectonic music in which sound forms and their spatial location bring and demand new modes of critical listening. Modern concert halls are constructed on the premise of finding a way in which every seat in the hall passes a certain minimal acoustic quality test, what Herbert A. Simon called satisficing, that is, the extended search of all available alternatives in order to fulfill an acceptability threshold. (Simon 1959) The consequences are that there will always be exceptional listening points, and others that are less exceptional though satisfactory according to standardized acoustic parameters as metrics. Reading the new definition of the acoustic arena in 4'33" means that every seat in the house is equally scaled to satisfy an exceptional auditory value because it can potentially be a point of origin for an unfolding acoustic arena.

But Cage's precedent auditory experience to 4'33" within the anechoic chamber at Harvard can also be read in terms of an extreme diminution of the acoustic arena through the removal of reverberation. The notion of reverberation, of the scale of the room at hand, is nominally connected to the physical dimensions of architecture. We expect reverberation times, that is, the prolongation of sounds, to increase in some fashion, given a regularity or stability in materiality, as a space increases in size. This expectation innately connects the apparent size of the acoustic arena to the length of the prolongation of sounds heard within a space. Reverberation then is a result of the inherent qualities of all materials to absorb and reflect sound waves at different capacities and at different frequencies bands. The more porous a material is, the greater ability it displays in the absorption of sounds (according to frequency band), while the harder it is the more reflective it becomes (often at higher frequencies). The auditory dimensions then of the anechoic chamber, a room completely lacking in any sense of a room, could be heard as sitting somewhere on the extremes of Le Corbusier's

Modulor: either infinitely large, like the sonic experience of a vast open meadow (the energy of the waves dissipates in the air before they can interact with anything solid), or infinitely small, such as the experience of the sounds from our bodies, the box within us. Reverberation and its interrelated acoustic arena thus track the acoustic typologies of architecture and provide a resultant feeling of depth, of volume, and of the spaciousness of architecture—even when the eyes are closed. It is the sound of walls and objects, and as such, of the activation within our minds of the dimensions of the space in which we are situated.

Room Type	T60 (seconds)
Classrooms	0.6–0.7
Movie Theaters	0.9–1.2
Concert Halls	1.7–2.2
Band Rooms	0.9–1.1
Recording Studios	0.4–0.8
Church	1.2–1.8
Theaters	1.2–1.4

Table 1. Typical reverberation times for various rooms. The metric *T60* is a measure of the amount of time required for the level of a steady sound to decay by 60 dB after the sound has stopped.

Consequently, the notion of reverberation as tool for imagining the infinitely large provided the cathedral builders of the medieval period with a tool for the communication of the almighty, of eternity, otherness, and the incomprehensibility of a space in which sounds seemed to float upwards, perhaps directly to God, given the wealth of hard reflective surfaces and large open volumes. Such spaces played heavily off their acoustic qualities and particularly long reverberation times as both providing an ideal environment for the production of vocal music, particularly, in the first instance of monophony (such as Gregorian chant), but also as an absolute extreme to the typical domestic (and in fact urban) acoustic typology of the period. What could be more contrastive than hearing the sound reflections from wood (often described in terms of warmth, clarity and the subdued) from floors or roughly rendered walls of a small dwelling, to the diffuse sweetness, lightness and unending spaciousness of the cathedral? It is as if the domestic dwelling represented, in an auditory sense, the containment of the finite, a directness of the human-made, and for evermore relegated to the human scale, while the cathedral embodied the intangibility of the infinite, that which cannot be truly understood by the human mind, the complete stratification of otherness. Thus what emerged, and what we have inherited today, is the first strong sense of an auditory continuum between two acoustic extremes.

The acoustic typology of the anechoic chamber then problematizes a generally linear sense of the relationship between physical dimensions of the box and its acoustic dimensions, and moreover, what the appropriate size of its acoustic arenas ought to be. It conceivably deforms and bends the scalar proportions developed in the *Modulor* back around onto itself such that its end becomes its beginning. An anechoic chamber, such as the one Cage visited, might be of relatively large dimensions, yet its feeling of acoustic intimacy, of the auditory scale of the box, is completely unexpected—it essentially reduces the acoustic arena to an occupation of our bodies, rather than a field that unfolds within the chamber. But the notion of Serres's (silent) box within the anechoic chamber is also, as Chris Smith alludes, a place of forceful architecture:

I would argue that the most forceful architecture is not that which generates perceptions but rather that which flees them. In this respect, this architecture is not a "softening." That is, it is not the production of music from sound or the softening

Figure 19. Étienne-Louis Boullée's *Deuxième projet pour la Bibliothèque du Roi* of 1785

of an already tender flesh that these architectures activate. Rather these architectures are a hardening. A hardening of the world. Making it harder against the body. Not in the sense that they break bodies, but in the sense that they cut and bang and silence them in the world. Or, at the very least, cut and bang and silence sensibilities, often in order to activate sensations. (Smith 2015, p. 34)

What occurs in terms of listening experience and of sensation within the anechoic chamber is not only a hardening of architecture, but equally the presentation of a threshold. The anechoic chamber sits between what may be conceptualized as a box of infinitesimally small dimensions and one of extraordinarily large proportions: a similarly difficult area for modern science and its search to reconcile the peculiarities of nonlinear equations of quantum mechanics (the imperceptibly small) and the linear nature of gravity, stars and the workings of galaxies (the monstrously large). (Weinberg 2011) Indeed, the acoustic qualities of an anechoic chamber are most often described as representing a vacuum-like "free-field" condition in which, given the expected sense of a room, of the containing box, an amorphous proxy seemingly negates the qualities of any sense of a room through the complete removal of the reverberation time. The resultant "room" is as close as one might come to floating in a windless sky, as what in 1783, Étienne-Louis Boullée similarly described as the loss of self when regarding scales of the vast which in turn produce in us both an ecstasy and a resignation towards inconceivable space:

> It is the same on a balloon floating in the heavens, having lost sight of everything on earth and seeing nothing of nature but the sky. Wandering thus in immensity, in this abysmal expanse, man is overwhelmed by the extraordinary spectacle of inconceivable space. (Boullée 1976, p. 91)

Boullée's notion, a resolute product of an ocular centering, appears here entirely applicable to describing the loss of an auditory tangibility, of the experience within an anechoic chamber. In fact, much of Boullée's theory of scale, that which he nominated as embracing either the "gigantic" or a "bigness," has an implicit auditory quality. Indeed, Boullée's argument for the failure of St. Paul's in London and St. Peter's in Rome is due to the perceived lack of "an impression of space" within the two sites, given the propensity of their designers to focus on equally grand objects that are found within them such as columns and arched doorways. (de Vallée 1976, p. 91) In contrast, Boullée seeks to embody "bigness" through a focus on the space itself, as is effortlessly captured in his *Deuxième projet pour la Bibliothèque du Roi* of 1785. But here there must also be acknowledged the potential of the design to generate an echo within the space, perhaps the auditory signature of that which is "big."

Echoes, unlike reverberation, are a distinct replaying of a sound source some time after the original source has dissipated. The ear, if presented with a reflection of a sound source after a delay of thirty milliseconds, will perceive the source as a prolongation of the sound, as reverberation. But if a sound source reflection comes to the ear after this short time bracket, it is heard as a second source, a repetition of the original sound. This small time difference makes a distinct and lasting difference to the auditory impression. Thus Boullée's notion of the need for the reduction of a swarming of large, intruding objects within a vast space to achieve "bigness" has implications for the acoustic qualities. There is, not least, the negation of the chance for any absorption at higher frequencies as well as the encouraging of sounds to seek out further distant walls for reflection—thus extending the potential time lags between original source and reflection given the speed of sound is nominally 340.29 meters per second. In a space such as the one described in *Deuxième projet pour la Bibliothèque du Roi*, the chance for echo effects is greatly increased through its geometry, unobstructed depth, materiality and volume. But perhaps the presence of a potential echo in such a space is but a confirmation of Boullée's theory on the need to manifest "an impression of space." For Brandon LaBelle, the power of the echo is in its performative function and the manner in which it brings to life a spatial impression of architecture:

> The echo exaggerates the passing of sound, staging it as a performance. The echo literally continues the vector of sound, staggers it, and supplements it with a further set of sound events that ultimately fill a given space. The echo brings back the original event, though, reshaped or refigured, thereby returning sound and rendering it a spatial object. (LaBelle 2010, pp. 6–7)

We might consider then that the echo of *Deuxième projet pour la Bibliothèque du Roi* is a signature of the notion of the grand, of "bigness," given that the walls and the space become heard, they become tangible and understood through a speaking back to us of our sonic interventions. In this sense, we would truly assimilate into the architecture, into the architectonic. This would then further satisfy the notion of "bigness" given that the auditory complement to the vast volumes would have an impressive immensity and consequently "a power 'over our senses.'" (Baek & Shin 2015, pp. 52–53) But Boullée's notion of the gigantic in regard to the anechoic chamber as a site that seemingly negates any definitive acoustic "impression of space" might be further uncoiled in light of the notion of critical listening. In spite of the notion of the silent room as a "free-field" condition lacking in any dimensions aurally, it simultaneously alludes to an impossibly small or miniaturized box, one that has been internalized. We might conclude that the containing box of architecture then collapses, hardens and desiccates into the box of the human body through a heightening of sensation. Such a state, and such a scalar, may in fact be conceptualized as sitting on a Möbius strip of variable size in which Le Corbusier's *Modulor* maps to the object's surface and is twisted and stretched such that it becomes self-enclosed and continuous yet infinite in both directions. As one end of the scale stretches out, ever growing as the dimensions of the strip itself increase, the counter end superficially shrinks, as smaller and smaller integers appear to collapse at its edge.

There is a suggestion of just such a warping of space when considering the effects of communication through direct sound sources within an anechoic chamber. Cage's sit in silence revealed the containing box as infinite in its apparent physical dimen-

THE THIRD POLICEMAN
Flann O'Brien

Figure 20. First-edition cover of Flann O'Brien's *The Third Policeman*

sions, given the lack of any acoustically activating interaction with the room. But Cage listened in "silence," that is, without intentionally producing sounds. Given that such a chamber is a filter that enables only direct sounds to perpetuate, having a conversation in such a space, or in fact encountering other introduced non-reverberant sounds, would take on those qualities that suggest, not just an intimacy, but moreover, a radical diminution of the physical dimensions of the box. The apparent size of the acoustic arena diminishes markedly as there is no confirmation of an exterior space. Experiencing only direct sounds provides a particularly discomforting notion that the box has not only disappeared, but its presence will never be actually perceived, nor is it even perceivable—that somehow it has been absorbed into us. The crisis then is the dissonance and warping, the folding back of the *Modulor's* ends such that what is presented is an acoustic paradox, a collision between the scale of the imperceptibly small and unimaginably large.

Certainly, as Mark Burry notes, it is this type of curious collapsing of dimensionality that drove much of the narrative in the work of Irish writer Flann O'Brien, whose expansion "of time and space" is akin to the work of a skilled animator. (Burry 2011, p. 134) In one of the most captivating passages of O'Brien's novel *The Third Policeman*, we encounter the narrator of the novel, who, after finding himself in a seemingly altered world of unpredictabilities and other strangeness, comes upon a police station, itself possibly existing in multiple unknown dimensions given its apparent lack of discernible edges. Residing (perhaps eternally) within the structure is an exceptionally peculiar policeman who has crafted a series of small chests over the course of his natural life. The narrator gradually discovers that each chest has another inside, and as each is exposed using ever-smaller tools for the handling of the precious objects, the final chests are revealed to be imperceivable, and indeed have not yet been seen by anyone. Though these smaller chests are unknowable to the eyes, the policeman uses invisible tools for their construction and handling. What follows for the narrator is perhaps the effect of a metaphysical violence on the senses in which a sudden realization, a *satori* by way of Zen scholar Daisetz Suzuki (1974), that space-time has gained some quality other than it should have, or some deeper terrifying truth, has been forcefully explicated:

> At this point I became afraid. What he was doing was no longer wonderful but terrible. I shut my eyes and prayed that he would stop while doing things that were at least possible for a man to do. (O'Brien 1967, p. 64)

The anechoic chamber is perhaps also capable of producing such disquiet given its seemingly twofold paradoxical state. Such spaces are renowned for causing physical discomfort, feelings of unbalance and psychological distress. They are, in one instance, of an infinite acoustic scale, like Boullée floating above the world, a room without aurally perceivable walls, while on the other, practically of the subatomic, a complete interiorization of auditory sensation where the walls are similarly not perceived yet manifest somehow within us at a much smaller scale than is outwardly grasped.

For Andrea Mina, these powerful types of disruptions, this intrinsic ambiguity, similarly provided a fertile ground for interrogating the meaning of architectural scale and our reading of it. Mina's intricate and highly detailed architectural models are made from dust, scraps and found objects and are often no larger than what can be placed in the palm of a hand, though labeling them as "scaled" models is counter to his intentions:

Figure 21. Andrea Mina's *Model 30*, architectural 1:1 model

> "Miniature" is both a misleading and useful word to describe or attempt to contextualise these objects as the word offers an intriguing ambiguity in interpretation ranging from re-presentation on a small scale, with the implication that an "original" exists prior to the production of a representation of "it" to "the art of action," originally that of a medieval illuminator, of painting portraits on a small scale ... The latter interpretation is the more useful application as the inference is that the "miniature" is the original, it is neither a reproduction nor a stand-in for something else but it has a presence and integrity of its own. (Mina 2006, p. 159)

Mina's architecture too it seems seeks to reconcile and redefine notions about the connection between scale and proportion to the human body—between boxes within us and outside us. He offers up the experience of the architectural miniature as a potential to become enveloped within the apparent scale of the structures, as an interiorization by which we become projected into them. The box then is one that maps an intersection, or similarly enables us, like Gaston Bachelard, to act out daydreams that "as invitations to verticality, [create] pauses in the narrative during which the reader is invited to dream." (Bachelard 1969, p. 162)

Perhaps the anechoic chamber is, as Serres might have imagined, much like Mina's models: an interstitial two-way structure that demarcates sensation. We become projected into the box as an architecture of containment, yet at the same time, the box becomes doubly projected into our bodies, it becomes fused into us. The chamber itself may well be a type of "black box" that resists any forms of controlled scalar interrogation, yet from within it flows a sense of relative dimension, a sense even of envelopment. As Serres argues, "sensation is held in a black box, and functions like one. Both the former and the latter precede knowledge, just as each, misunderstood, comes after, envelops or punctures it. Through sensation the hard becomes soft. Sensation protects and guides us." (Serres 2008, p. 145)

The need for openness, or what I envisage as the call for a critical listening in architecture as "the construction of the largest white box of all," acutely reminds us of the dichotomy of the anechoic chamber. Like Mina's models, the question of the relation is paramount. For critical listening this is extended to encompass the relation between the notion of architecture as an articulation of space and its auditory dimension, which is duly the confirmation of that articulation. This apparent delimiting of the subject–object distinction, of the potential of two radically different states of interpretation in the anechoic chamber, becomes a catalyst for driving a new and constitutive thought experiment, much along the lines of the classic conceptual precipice proposed by Erwin Schrödinger's 1935 paradox: the cat in the box.

Schrödinger's thought experiment calls into question the classic problem of scale in regard to the relationship between quantum mechanics—that which is concerned with the nonlinear and the exceptionally small scale—and regularly occurring objects at the human scale which ostensively obey the laws of classical mechanics. Of interest to Schrödinger was the Copenhagen interpretation (Peres 2002) of the state of particles and the so-called ψ (or wave function), which postulates that the state of any particle, such as the spin of an electron, can only be known at the point of its interaction with another particle, or indeed the direct observation of the particle itself. Thus, until either of these situations eventuates, it is said to exist in both states simultaneously, but collapses into one of the states at the point of observation. Hence what is known about such a system is often framed as a series of probabilities about the possible states of the constituent elements of the system. Schrödinger however sought to extrapolate out this peculiar quality, to scale up, so to speak, the paradox into a real-world situation:

> One can even set up quite ridiculous cases. A cat is penned up in a steel chamber, along with the following device (which must be secured against direct interference by the cat): in a Geiger counter, there is a tiny bit of radioactive substance, so small, that perhaps in the course of the hour one of the atoms decays, but also, with equal probability, perhaps none; if it happens, the counter tube discharges and through a relay releases a hammer that shatters a small flask of hydrocyanic acid. If one has left this entire system to itself for an hour, one would say that the cat still

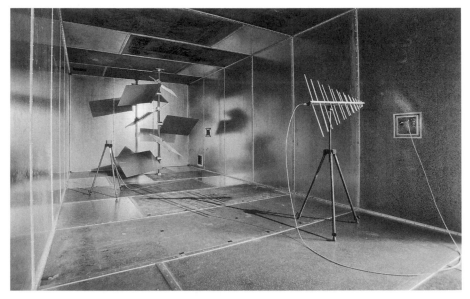

Figure 22. The reverberation chamber at IETR laboratory, Rennes, France

Material	125 Hz	4000 Hz
Glass fiber	0.7	0.9
Fiberglass	0.3	0.75
Painted concrete	0.1	0.08
Gypsum	0.25	0.04
Plaster	0.14	0.03
Linoleum	0.02	0.02
Thin carpet	0.05	0.4
Wood	0.15	0.06
Glass	0.35	0.04
Chalkboard	0.01	0.02

Table 2. Sound absorption coefficients (as % of the total energy of the wave) for common building materials showing variability between 125 Hz and 4000 Hz

lives if meanwhile no atom has decayed. The psi-function of the entire system would express this by having in it the living and dead cat (pardon the expression) mixed or smeared out in equal parts. (Trimmer 1983, p. 157)

What is important here is the fact that, according to the Copenhagen interpretation, the cat is both dead and alive until the moment of somebody opening the lid on the box to observe the state of the cat, at which point the wave function would collapse and the cat will be either dead or alive. Here, the box then is a containment of a nonlinear system in which two states are coexistent. Similarly, we might think of the anechoic chamber in a homologous state of dissonance where though there is a definite spatiality that bounds the physical dimensions of the chamber, there is at the same time an acoustically infinite space that pervades through the lack of reverberation. The chamber is thus both infinitely large and finitely described at the same time. To take this analogous conceptualization to its limits, we can further deduce that the collapse of the ψ function within the chamber is the point of auditory observation, of critical listening, at which the room either becomes infinitely large (that is, on noticing the complete negation of reverberation) or infinitely small (on noticing the phenomena of only direct sounds).

Dimensions

What then of the anechoic chamber's contrary acoustic condition? As might be expected, the reverberation chamber is also a room of unusual acoustic qualities. Instead of the presence of only direct sounds as found within an anechoic chamber, the design of the reverberation chamber is one in which a hyper-diffuse acoustic state is sought through the use of exceedingly hard surfaces on the walls, ceiling and floor, as well as the potential for other reflecting panels placed at various points within the space. The objective of such an acoustic typology is to generate a maximum number of reflections from sound waves, such that the sound field becomes homogeneous and isotropic—that is, it is completely uniform in all orientations. Speech intelligibility is particularly affected in such rooms, where the absolute diffuse nature of the sound field reverses the emphasis from hearing direct sounds to hearing the secondary and tertiary reflections. This in turn produces a nebulous washing out of the sound field that quickly envelops everything. To avoid the potential of standing waves, which in turn produce room modes that may amplify particular resonances at certain points within the box, the walls, ceiling and floor are often intentionally skewed, thus ensuring that sound waves reach all parts of the chamber through reflections. Instead of the direct, dry sounds of an anechoic chamber, in the reverberation chamber, everything is wet.

Furthermore, whereas the anechoic chamber is often used as a box in which to record sounds sans room, for example the testing of loudspeakers, or sampling of musical instruments, one of the functions of the reverberation chamber is to test the sound absorption qualities of materials. Given that the reverberation time is known within the chamber, the recording of the interaction of sounds with materials, and thus the reduction in the reverberation time, can give a measure of what percentage of the energy of the incoming wave of known sound pressure level the material has absorbed, which may vary considerably according to frequency band. A curious artifact then that sits contrary to the anechoic chamber is the notion of the box as an iterated object. The reverberation chamber is an amplification of the sense of the containing box in its auditory dimensions. Whereas the anechoic chamber is *anti-room*, the reverberation chamber is *über-room*. Though there is a finite spatial demarcation of the box, its highly diffuse nature and wet auditory qualities when filled with sounds give the impression of a much larger space, a space that might be described as swimming in sounds. Though this impression is not limitless, as is found at the other end of the continuum with the anechoic chamber, there is certainly an expansion outwards beyond the walls as visual articulations—a type of iterative scaling. Even a relatively small reverberation chamber may have a reverberation time in excess of four seconds, the type of acoustic broadening one might expect in a Gothic cathedral. But this sense of iterative scaling is in fact, as De Landa suggests, evident too in structures in natural phenomena, such as the shape of trees, from twig, branch to trunk, that produce continual scalar iterations: "there is a recurrent part-to-whole relation, in which wholes at one scale become parts at the next larger scale." (De Landa 2011, p. 16) This scaling up of objects by direct iterative means is one of the more intriguing devices masterfully exploited by filmmaker Charlie Kaufman in *Synecdoche New York* (2008).

Here, the main protagonist Caden spends the latter part of his life writing and staging a theater piece by constructing a 1:1 replica of New York City inside a warehouse. But as the fantastic nature of the piece becomes more complex, and the demand for a greater realism emerges, Caden eventually constructs a warehouse within that warehouse and so on through a continually unfolding scalar iteration. It is during this obsessive period of recursive grandeur that Caden's estranged wife, an artist, who begins the film painting miniatures, pursues a path leading to the other end of the *Modulor*. Towards the end of the film, her paintings are so small they require specialist magnifying glasses to view, while Caden's theater work is already at a point in which actors are playing other actors performing a role, and the set has reached literally cosmic dimensions. As Richard Deming notes, the magnitude of Caden's final project pushes the viewer's conception of time and space into the nonlinear, into the indeterminate given that "the relative scales are constantly shifting." (Deming 2011, p. 195) The film then is a particularly erudite examination of architectural tropes and those scalar relationships born out of considering the interrelations between recursions of parts to a whole and a whole to its parts.

The auditory experience of the reverberation chamber then sets into action a similarly progressive model of the sense of an ever-increasing auditory spatiality. This arises from the fact that the physical dimensions of the box itself are not indicative of the sensation of the accompanying auditory space, which itself seems contained within a larger box, seemingly sitting outside the experience of the dimensions demarcated by the chamber—much like the warehouses of Caden's universe, in which there is always another box to be encountered as soon as one steps "outside." Thus from this particular auditory experience, of the reverberation chamber as an ever-present

Figure 23. Warehouse within a warehouse, still from *Synecdoche New York*, Charlie Kaufman, 2008

über-room, the ostensive silence of the anechoic chamber is a stark reminder of an exceptionally diverse auditory continuum. It ranges from the sense of an interiorization, of the box becoming assembled within us at the level of the anechoic chamber (in one interpretation), to that of exteriority—of an outwards scalar iteration beyond the walls of the box with the reverberation chamber. The approach of critical listening then is perhaps the recognition of this acoustic continuum in its numerous manifestations and occupying shades within architecture as habitable space.

It is too, in both formal and informal approaches, a consolidation of what Geoffrey Scott deemed as the universal in architecture, that is, the experience of the form and substance of architecture as not a retreat into pure visual aesthetics, but a sensorial empathy with architecture:

> The concrete spectacle has done what the mere idea could not: it has stirred our physical memory ... We have looked at the building and identified ourselves with its apparent state. We have transcribed ourselves into terms of architecture ... The whole of architecture is, in fact, unconsciously invested by us with human movement and human moods. Here, then, is a principle complementary to the one just started, we transcribe architecture into terms of ourselves. This is the humanism of architecture. (Scott 1914, pp. 212–213)

We might also just as poignantly say that we not only look into, but also hear into the building, and identify in ourselves a scale we attribute to Serres's box—a box built on sensations housed within the human body. There are then myriad incarnations, or a multitude of sensations, that arise between the paradigms of the anechoic chamber and its opposite condition, the reverberation chamber. Indeed, the potential to map this continuum, or at least to have the capabilities of reproducing any number of different degrees or acoustic states between the two extremes, was an exemplar characteristic of the spectacle of the German spherical auditorium at the 1970 Osaka World's Fair.

The involvement of visionary composer Karlheinz Stockhausen as technical adviser for the specifications and the design of the auditorium brought him into a working collaboration between architect Fritz Bornemann, acoustician Fritz Winckel, engineer Max Mengeringhausen and artist Otto Piene. The result of this extraordinary collabo-

Figure 24. German pavilion and spherical auditorium, Osaka World's Fair, 1970

ration was a striking, partially submerged blue spherical auditorium based on Buckminster Fuller's geodesic dome. The physical structure of the dome was constructed from a steel truss "space" frame, and the electroacoustic infrastructure located within included over fifty loudspeakers positioned above and below the audience, as well as a lattice of light sources (designed by Piene) all controlled from a single command desk.

The theme developed by the German planning group for the pavilion, *Gärten der Musik* (gardens of music), was manifested through Bornemann's initial ideas for the architecture and a complete usurpation of modern technology:

> I wanted to create no building at all. I would rather have had radar-frozen air, but we are not yet capable of that, so I tried the next best thing ... People suggested that we could save a lot of money by setting up our location like a football field with a cheap fencing made from hardboard at each end, at the place where the goals would have been. Visitors would enter at one end, receive audio-visual helmets, and float across the other end, they would be relieved of the helmets and leave with the idea that the German pavilion was the most unbelievable thing in the world. (Van Wesemael 2001, p. 600)

In Bornemann's final design, the pavilion became a series of five underground circular spaces with the only discernible topological feature sitting aboveground being the striking blue dome of the auditorium. The notion then of the "planting" of the pavilion as a garden was realized through the auditorium being the most significant "sprout" to emerge from beneath. But Bornemann envisaged the initial form of the auditorium as a standardized amphitheater containing a central orchestra podium around which the audience would be seated. After the West German Fair Committee invited Stockhausen in 1968 to participate on the project, he convinced Bornemann the same year at a meeting at the *Summer Courses for New Music Darmstadt* to develop the auditorium's capabilities further, and to utilize a dome instead of a canonic shoebox form. (Bornemann 1970, p. 1492)

With the auditorium becoming the focal point of the landscape aboveground, under Stockhausen's stipulations, the interior would house enough loudspeakers to create an immersive sound field that relied on utilizing rings of loudspeakers that extended well above and below the seated position of the audience. Loudspeaker layers could be controlled via a rotation mill at the control desk, which also allowed any geometric combination of loudspeaker groups (i.e., as circles, spirals or through diagonals) to be utilized. The resulting capabilities of the system produced an immersive audiovisual experience, a common theme of *Exp. 70'*, where dramatic movements of sound and light literally produced *Klangbomben* (sound bombs) in all directions in space. The intrinsic spatial processes of manipulation, movement and transformation in Stockhausen's earlier magnetic tape works such as *Telemusik* (1966), *Hymnen* and *Gesang der Jünglinge* (1955–56) became a compositional prototype for the total integration of sound within architectural space.

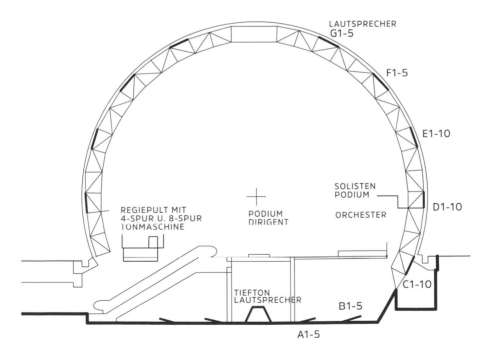

Figure 25. Section of spherical auditorium at Osaka

On Auditory Scale

59

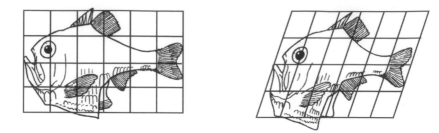

Figure 26. The transformation of *Argyropelecus olfersi* into *Sternoptyx diaphana* by applying a shear mapping

What could be achieved then at the spherical auditorium of the German pavilion was the design of myriad sound-spaces given the large electroacoustic and technological infrastructure available. Given the interior was also near-anechoic, with heavy acoustic insulation, sound-absorbing panels and an acoustically transparent mesh floor, practically speaking, any acoustic typology between an anechoic (or near-anechoic) chamber and a reverberation chamber could be simulated and experienced. Though the interior of the auditorium would have suggested otherwise, and indeed the program of the space was exclusively for the playback and performance of contemporary German art music, nonetheless, any number of architectural typologies could be re-created through the spatial playback of sound sources, giving the auditorium the option of becoming a museum for sound-space.

In fact, the process of morphing between sound-spaces with such infrastructure operates in much the same fashion that D'Arcy Wentworth Thompson famously advocated vis-à-vis the shape morphology of organisms being a function of physical and mechanical influences from the environment. Thompson's structuralist approach to understanding biological changes in organisms was famously demonstrated through his simplistic usurpations of mathematical transformations such as shearing, in which one organism could logically morph into a related other. Take, for instance, the form of the deep-sea fish *Argyropelecus olfersi*, which through a shearing transforms into *Sternoptyx diaphana*. Here, there is an emphasis on not only the parts of the organism, the jaw, fins and tail of the fish, but their relation to the whole, as demonstrated through the literal stretching of the corners of the grid. Indeed Thompson was adept at suggesting how much more general rules could account for the changes in organisms as a whole as well as the role of self-organization as a foil to Darwinian natural selection. As Winther acknowledges, "structuralism's commitments to emergence, complexity, and nonlinearity are in contrast with the atomism, reductionism, and additivity of adaptationism." (Winther 2014, p. 471) Indeed within the grid of the acoustic space of a spherical auditorium such as at Osaka, such deformations and transformations could also be undertaken within acoustic space, and perhaps most interestingly, in a manner that equally satisfies Greg Lynn's new properties of computational design, that of "topology, time and parameters." (Lynn 1999, p. 20) It is not surprising then that Lynn identified in Thompson's approach a means by which the architectural body might be overcome through deformable geometries, and in doing so, presents a challenge to the perceived rigidity of the organism of architecture as a whole. The concept of architectural form as fluidity, as a malleable object, also gave rise to Lynn's notion of a Thompson-inspired architectural system that self-organizes such that it allows for the merging of segments, thus highlighting how space must be considered a deformable entity:

> Geometry is no longer a static measure of invariant and unitary characteristics but what Gilles Deleuze and Félix Guattari have referred to as a "plane of consistency" on which differential transformations and deformations occur. (Lynn 2004, p. 38)

Indubitably, acoustic space is equally as malleable. With the simple addition of artificially generated forms of reverberation, any room and the sources appearing from the loudspeakers within it may suddenly change and morph in time, giving the impression of the box changing its dimensions. Added to this are the modern capabilities for sound specialization or the ability of sounds to fly about the space, such that the notion of the parameters of architectural containment, of the dimensions of the physical box, need not be understood as absolute, nor grounded along one particular axis, or along one particular footprint. Like Thompson's shearing of *Argyropelecus olfersi*, the transformation of the underlying acoustic grid, in either a time-contingent linear or non-linear fashion, could invoke myriad new orientations and listeners' positions. In regard to the topology of such a space, the seemingly fixed auditory aspect of the listeners can be radically shifted (without the physical movement of the listener), and moreover, in rapid succession. Here, the traditional static grounding of seating arrangements is, from the auditory viewpoint, able to be twisted, thrown upwards or downwards, or, from one moment, to be contemplating the earth as passenger in Boullée's balloon, to the next, violently experiencing that which Smith nominated as the "hardening of architecture," the "fleeing from sensation" and the instantaneous reduction of Serres's box to a minuscule prison located somewhere inside us.

REVERBERATION UNIT
EMT 140 TS

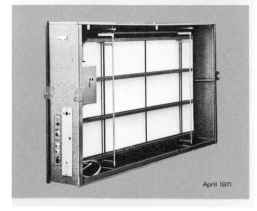

April 1971

The possibility for such malleability of sound-space, of the dimensions of the auditory, and the manipulation of expectations and sensation presents a particularly radical type of architectural event. There is suggestiveness about such a proposal that would seemingly satisfy too what Bernard Tschumi understood: "that there is no space without event, no architecture without program." (Tschumi 1996, p. 139) In fact, in spite of the underlying musical program found at Osaka, the inherent notion of such an auditorium as a potential realm for an unseen architecture built with sounds brings to the fore its ostensive connections to the box as an architecture of containment, and the box of the human body as a purveyor of sensations. These types of manipulations of auditory space, and of the architectural

Figure 27. The *EMT 140* artificial reverberation unit (1957) generated reverberation through a large metal plate. The source signal was fed into the plate, causing it to vibrate, and microphones captured the results.

experience, no doubt challenge too what Kuniichi Uno argues as architecture's grounding in the earth, its immobility and its inseparability from sedentary life, which consequently marks for it a crisis in terms of the conceptualization of its oft-professed dynamics. (Uno 2001, p. 1017) Indeed, when Paul Virilio reflected on his work with Claude Parent in the late 1960s, and spoke on challenging the notion of the body (as architecture) as a classically conceived "static entity" that must be redrawn in light of the "dynamic age of the body in movement," he may well have also been addressing the possibility for a shape-shifting of auditory manipulations, of auditory trajectories:

> The objective of our research was to challenge outright the anthropometric precepts in the classical era—the idea of the body as essentially a static entity with an essentially static proprioception—in order to bring the human habitat into a dynamic age of the body in movement. In our work, the traditional stability (habitable stasis) of both the rural horizontal order and the urban vertical order give way to the METASTABILITY (habitable circulation) of the human body in motion, in tune with the rhythms of life. The space of the body became MOBILE. The limbs of the individual became MOTIVE. And the inhabitant effectively became LOCO-MOTIVE, propelled by the (relative) disequilibrium created by the gravity of planet earth, the habitat of our species. (Virilio 1996, p. 13)

To consider then Virilio and Parent's theory of the oblique, of the push towards an architecture of motive instability and disequilibrium, of their desire for an abandonment of the traditional orthogonal grid of the vertical and the horizontal, brings to mind the types of possibilities afforded to the procreation and fomentation of acoustic space. We might also adjudge the circumstance of architecture as a system paired to an auditory agent that will tend towards a state of least energy, that is, the anechoic chamber. In this conceptualization, the metastability of Virilio's notion of the oblique can also be read as embodied in those numerous states of auditory activation that map out the anechoic–reverberation continuum. As Teyssot suggests, metastability is a system "that has not yet exhausted its potential difference by increasing order or information." (Teyssot 2013, p. 44) The metastability of auditory states and acoustic qualities is thus an inherent feature of an architectural system in which the maximum and minimum states of information, or energy, describe the extremes—echoic and anechoic. Metastabilities arise in the auditory continuum as various "in-betweens" of the extremes in which myriad acoustic typologies found across a range of historical periods, spatial programs, buildings and habitats assist in defining architecture as an auditory system.

But what Lynn identified in regard to the "plane of consistency" is also worth considering. Perhaps in a manner akin to what Jamie Murray acknowledges as the dynamic nature of the concept does a true sense of the dichotomy of the anechoic–reverberation continuum and its various metastabilities emerge: "in the plane of consistency all virtual differences and events are brought together and new connections machined between the differences and events, and old connections are continually dissolved." (Murray 2013, p. 18) We may think then of the auditory continuum between these two extreme states, and their numerous shades and typologies found in myriad architectural contexts from the domestic to the public, the grand to the intimate, the secular to the religious, the artistic to the scientific, as examples of the continuing

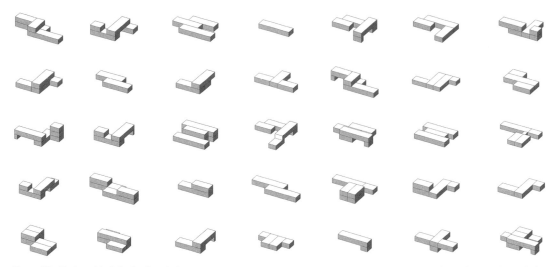

Figure 28. *Modern Modular* by Resolution: 4 Architecture, NYC. A combinatorial approach to generating volumes through the free merging of seven individual types.

unfolding of an acoustic experience. In these encounters, new spaces recurrently emerge as old ones dissipate, and the shifting auditory dimensions of the box merge inside us and between encounters, thus congruently pointing towards Scott's humanistic architecture, an architecture that becomes transcribed in our bodies. This is perhaps the most striking and erudite aspect of the Osaka auditorium: that it could, in real time, explore numerous acoustic states as metastabilities, and through various manipulations of entropic scaling, continually machine new relations between the sense of the architectonic as an articulation of habitable space and the agency of the resulting auditory experience.

Continuum

It is important then to not so readily dismiss the function of the extreme spatialities of the anechoic–reverberation continuum as merely states of otherness, as they are a reminder too of how the modularity of form is also a template for understanding the connection between space and how sounds behave because of the articulation granted by architecture. Auditory scale is perhaps easily envisaged not only through the anechoic–reverberation chamber continuum, but also as an incredibly subtle shift in auditory perception between the shapes of different volumes and the important impact of materiality in regard to sound absorption and the reflection of a sound wave's energy. In the work of the architecture practice Resolution: 4 Architecture, we find a simple yet elegant reminder of the subtle shades of acoustic variety, of acoustic signature, in their *Modern Modular* mass housing project.

Here, the notion of the "modular" is not so much an attempt to place the human form at the center of architectural scale, of architectural proportion, but more a usurpation of "how modern home design can be transformed to take advantage of the economical, environmental, and structural benefits of standard, proven modular construction techniques." (Resolution: 4 Architecture, 2016) Le Corbusier's vision of the human body as a standard of measurement is thus surpassed by a notion of a standardized volume, again the return of the empty box. Approaching design as a combination of volumes, of boxes, is as a means by which to reduce production and fabrication complexities, in addition to allowing for an opting of the client to co-design "off the plan." Here, the elements, in what might be read as an algorithmic approach to design, are seven individual volumes or types: *Single Wide Series*, *Double Wide Series*, *T Series*, *L Series*, *Courtyard Series*, *Triple Wide Series* and *Z Series*. Through their various combinations, orientations and groundings within a site are any number of constituent elements of an exceedingly vast taxonomy of the house available.

Though *Modern Modular* is much less complex say than Lynn's *Embryological House* (Bird & LaBelle 2010), whose mission was to secure a distinct morphology through the conception of architectural form as a fluidity of states, nonetheless, *Modern Modular* unknowingly showcases the foundational notion of *WYSIWYG* (what you see is what you get) as a fundamental driver of architectural conceptualizations and architectural modeling. Unlike the seeming fluidity with which architectonic ideas can be exploited, worked, arranged and, in the case of *Modern Modular*, corralled into an elegant taxonomy of possibilities, the prediction and representation of auditory space is bound to a number of physical parameters that cannot be simply reduced to a single parameter: the volume as a box. What Jeremy Till describes as the "vanity of form" (Till 1999) in architecture enables the concepts, aesthetics and perhaps even politics of *Modern Modular* a direct currency, literally, what you see is what you get—single story, multiple story, split-level, courtyard, tower. This immediacy of the ocular, its ability to communicate living aspects and imagined programs, is delivered in a particularly lean manner in *Modern Modular* through the combinatorial formation of volumes.

Auditory space and the imagined behaviors of sounds in space are somewhat more complex and rely on a greater suite of parameters that must be acknowledged before one can begin to understand the types of immediate spatial potentials so readily understood in the visually modeled taxonomy of *Modern Modular*. As James D. Foley observes, in *non-WYSIWYG* computer graphic systems, "users must translate between their mental image of the desired results and control codes. Confirmation that the control codes reproduce the mental image is not given until the coded input is processed." (Foley 1996, p. 396) Here, we can ideate control codes as representing the architectural program and materiality, the knowledge of the type of sounds that will proliferate inside, and how their textures, dynamics and structures will together produce distinct auditory signatures. From these signatures arises a notion of scale, and the situation of the acoustic qualities as metastabilities locatable somewhere within the anechoic-reverberation continuum. These control codes are considered and processed, which to the point of a usurpation of critical listening can allow for a greater depth of auditory awareness. Certainly within contemporary architecture, a computer-aided simulation of acoustic qualities as "a time-ordered sequence of states" (Parker 2009, p. 486) is often sought, though these approaches have traditionally been post-design rather than enmeshed within, or during, the onset of the design process.

The connection then between the visual, as an architectonic gesture, and the acoustic qualities and thus auditory experience of architectural space is not a simple 1:1 relation when reduced to the single parameter of considering a volume. The combination of two *Single Wide Series* types may have an obvious communicable meaning in terms of spatial program, of footprint and of the size of the volume to be further resolved, though in regard to its auditory complement, much less is known until other parameters are factored. Whereas one form may suggest a complete visual openness, its acoustic conditions will rely on the resolution of the box through a generated meta-stability. The auditory then becomes an agent defined not only by the articulation of the architectonic but similarly through materiality, program, texture and structure. Numerous seemingly unlikely combinations of boxes then may share common acoustic behaviors due to factors that push against their geometry, against their containment. This means then that there may be a hidden secondary taxonomy that pairs, groups and articulates boundary conditions in which the visual family of volumes of *Modern Modular* is further divided according to acoustic typologies.

Indeed if Le Corbusier saw his *Modulor* as a utility in which to give what Vitruvius named as the three requisite principles of architectural design—commodity, firmness, delight (Wonton 1970)—a fundamental and grounding metric, then it might also be reasoned that the acoustic conditions of architecture must equally abide by these and indeed other metrics. We might approach then the invitation to "delight," "firmness" and "commodity" as a chance to qualify an attention to, or even a restraint towards, the loss of sensation, or the slippage into a "hardening" of architecture. But as Hanno-Walter Kruft suggests, as Scott did too, what becomes most relevant of the architectural virtues of Vitruvius is that each of them "cannot be sacrificed to the exclusive advantage of one or the other. This means above all that 'delight' [beauty] must not be turned into a mere function of 'commodity' [functionality] and 'firmness,' [structural soundness] but must contain a value of its own." (Kruft 1994, p. 343) Appropriately, there are implications in this reasoning for the auditory experience of architecture and for critical listening. Thus there may be a cost for overemphasizing the ocular within architecture at the price of developing a truly multisensory dimension to the spatial experience. To embrace critical listening then is perhaps to also embrace Scott's architectural humanism in that listening to the building is essentially transcribing the building into *architectures of sound*.

3
Dumb Holes and the Acoustic Horizon

Grid
Form
Materiality
Program
Texture
Structure
Hole

Dumb Holes and the Acoustic Horizon

Grid

How are the dimensions of auditory space defined? Given the containment of architecture, its articulation of a site and the tangible embodiment of its boundary conditions, visual space and the visual horizon represent our immersion in an environment. Auditory space, however, is not always immediately restricted by the architectonic, by the localized environs or by the image of a resolute interiority. Auditory space may be equally defined, challenged and articulated through other forces, conditions and influences. For light, there are always inherent boundary conditions that create boxes and territories that map out the limits of visual sensation. Indeed, the role of light in the construction of the visual horizon and its boundaries can be most readily perceived, especially in architecture where form becomes materialized, identified and known. Visual space, produced through the interaction of light on surfaces and other objects, produces continuities that are seemingly ever-present. For sounds and acoustic space, however, there are numerous "breaks" in auditory perception such that we engage with sound and its ability to embody or suggest space through its shifting territories and its inherent discontinuities.

Those boundary conditions that assist in structuring acoustic space, in generating a sense of its shape, form and scale, in many instances exist outside the containing box of architecture, outside the known, the tangible or the predictable. Indeed, when Stephen Hawking first provided a theoretical argument for the presence of measurable amounts of radiation emanating from black holes, he described the architecture of the event horizon as an unseen plane through which light or any other object may only pass into the hole (Hawking 1974) — from the known to the unknown, the finite to the infinite. As a boundary condition, the event horizon is not a tangible articulation, not an architectonic manifestation of form, or even a sensation, but rather, a condition of a threshold for which movement through the hole is understood as the difference between experiencing the vectorial as opposed to the omnidirectional. This type of directionality was predicated by Hawking, given that radiation should be produced from the black hole because of the process of vacuum fluctuations. Here, the curious phenomenon of particle/antiparticle pairs occurs in which any particles close to the horizon will cause a virtual negatively charged ghost to appear. These fleeting virtual particles, however, will inevitably only experience a directional vector of movement that herds them forthrightly towards the horizon and into the black hole. In order to keep the equilibrium of the total state of energy in the universe, however, it is always the negatively charged particle that is lost to the black hole. With the *Doppelgänger* shadow then disposed of, the other particle seemingly escapes, freely, and in any direction, away from the event horizon.

In slightly more real-world contexts, the gravitational analog to the black hole is the dumb hole, or sonic black hole. Though only created recently in the laboratory by Oren Lahav and colleagues (2010), a dumb hole is of interest for its potential to reveal Hawking's prediction of the emergence of radiation on or near to the event horizon. Interestingly, though, rather than finding, say, positrons (the antiparticle of the

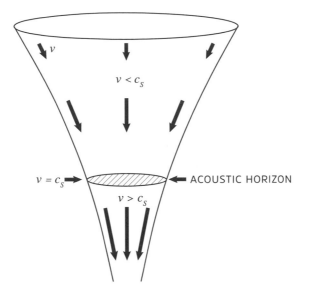

Figure 29. Diagram of the acoustic horizon of a theoretical dumb hole. Arrows indicate a liquid flowing at initial velocity, v. As arrows grow in size, so v approaches the speed of sound, c_s. The acoustic horizon is reached when $v = c_s$, and as the liquid increases velocity beyond the horizon, such that, $v > c_s$, any sound perturbations occurring beyond the horizon will not escape the cone.

electron), a dumb hole's antiparticles would be virtual phonons (collective excitations in condensed matter), and thus the measurement of Hawking radiation in a dumb hole as created by Lahav would be through the tactility of escaping sounds. The virtual becomes the heard as vibrations from beyond the threshold escape the box and the limits of audibility—the dumb hole will potentially speak. The event horizon then of the sonic black hole is an acoustic horizon, a construct that can be envisaged most simply through the model of the flow of a perfect fluid (a fluid without viscosity, heat conduction or shear stress). Imagine a funnel in which the perfect fluid is poured onto its interior surface. Given the ability to speed up the fluid rapidly in its descent into the funnel, its increased velocity past the localized speed of sound produces an acoustic horizon, a space or limit by which sounds cannot pass back out. As Lahav explains:

> This sonic black hole contains regions of subsonic flow, as well as regions of supersonic flow. Since a phonon [an excitation in the perfect fluid] cannot propagate against the supersonic flow, the boundary between the subsonic and supersonic regions marks the event horizon of the sonic black hole. (Lahav et al. 2010, p. 1)

The horizon describes an intangible plane in which given acoustic perturbations occurring in the liquid, those that occur within any part of the liquid up until it reaches the local speed of sound, may in fact "escape" upwards, out of the funnel and out of the hole. Any sound vibrations occurring within the liquid at a point in which the liquid is traveling equal to, or faster than, the speed of sound will be contained, the invisible horizon demarcating a limit. The acoustic horizon then acts as a mesh, a transparent threshold, yet porous in only one direction, and for which a limit is given for contain-

Figure 30. Architectural context and the acoustic horizon. An observer can see to the visual horizon as a bounded fixed area (yellow highlight). Sounds emanating from points A, B, C, D that are heard by the observer lie outside the visual horizon (E and F can be seen and heard), thus producing a sensation of the presence of another layer of meaning.

ing all acoustic phenomena. It represents perhaps a type of model of what Brian Massumi recognizes as an inaccessibility of the virtual to the senses beyond those fleeting appearances manifested in the multiplication (by way of images, representation) of its effects. (Massumi 2002) Though the event horizon can never be seen, touched or formally measured, instead existing as perhaps a disputed territory, its effects are known and, moreover, knowable. It is a space that invisibly suggests a boundary, and demarcates a limit, yet remains ostensibly hidden from our senses until its effects are decisively revealed.

What then are the implications of the acoustic horizon of a dumb hole in terms of architecture? Though the dumb hole produced by Lahav and colleagues was formed in a Bose-Einstein condensate of rubidium atoms cooled to near absolute zero (–273.15°C), what is pertinent is perhaps not the novelty of the condensed matter state as medium required for the experiment, but the notion of the limits that any medium provides, and thus the metric which may describe these limits. Sound waves are a disturbance in a medium; whether they exist as photons in supercooled rubidium or vibrations in air, water or the liquid of the cochlea, we are privy to the experience of them as the limits of the medium allow. Barry Blesser and Linda-Ruth Salter have recognized this too, as the medium of hearing is usually the atmosphere, and therefore the acoustic horizon as a sensation is an intimation regarding the outward extent and bounds of acoustic space:

The concept of virtual sonic boundaries leads to a new abstraction, the acoustic horizon, the maximum distance between a listener and source of sound where the sonic event can still be heard. Beyond this horizon, the sound of a sonic event is too weak relative to the masking power of other sounds to be audible or intelligible. The acoustic horizon is thus the experiential boundary that delineates which sonic events are included and which are excluded. (Blesser & Salter 2007, p. 22)

In a similar manner, Barry Truax describes the acoustic horizon as a production of auditory space where "incoming sounds from distant sources define the outer limits over which acoustic communication may normally occur." (Truax 1999) Thus while acoustic space is often the confirmation of architecture's containment, it functions also as an agent such that the alignment or coherence between the visual horizon and the acoustic horizon may often be at odds with each other. As a qualitative metric then, the acoustic horizon, while describing the farthest distance over which a sound is heard, also enables a conceptualization of the dimensions of auditory space, and similarly, its omnidirectionality.

The representation of the three-dimensional onto a two-dimensional plane is perhaps an avenue in which to further conceptualize the omnidirectional nature of the acoustic horizon and its dynamism. It has been well established that from at least the Italian Renaissance, numerous artists had developed approaches to representing a plane or flat surface of the world in much the same way as looking through a window. As Leonardo da Vinci speculated, "perspective is nothing else than the seeing of an object behind a sheet of glass, smooth and quite transparent, on the surface of which all the things may be marked that are behind this glass; these things approach the point of the eye in pyramids, and these pyramids are cut by the said glass." (MacCurdy 1955, p. 992) In 1435, Alberti presented via a mathematical context the notion of geometry as the underlying tool for generating a perspectival representation of objects on paper. Here, the perspective image of a plane figure is "the intersection of the picture plane and the pyramid, called the visual pyramid, which has the figure as base and the eye point of an observer as vertex." (Andersen 2012, p. 7)

Figure 31. Brook Taylor's illustration of Alberti's mathematical model of perspective. The cube *ABCD* is depicted as abcd on the picture plane. The visual pyramid of vertex *O* originates at the eye and intersects the vertical plane *EFHG*.

Imagine then the plane that extends outwards beyond us, and indeed the continuity of the visual horizon that affronts us, as a grid of varying dimensions. Indeed the use of grids, particularly by Jacques Aleaume and Étienne Migon in their *La perspective speculative, et pratique* of 1663, as a coordinate system provided a secure means by which to depict the shapes and sizes of things in two dimensions, relative to how they appear in the three-dimensional world. Imagine then a Cartesian plane of infinite breadth and width, moving outwards in Euclidean space in all directions, something akin to what Lynn identified in the "plane of consistency" of Deleuze and Guattari—a completely deterritorialized state in which "there is

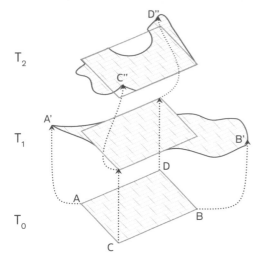

T_2

T_1

T_0

D"

C"

A'

B'

D

A

B

C

Figure 32. Diagram of the visual and acoustic horizons. At T_0 we assume that both the visual horizon and the acoustic horizon are equally defined (represented as grid on the plane *ADBC*). At intervals T_1 and T_2, the acoustic horizon transforms the shared mesh such that it becomes deformed and juxtaposed yet finitely contained.

not structure, any more than there is a genesis." (Deleuze & Guattari 2004, p. 266) We might consider that the visual horizon exists as a subset of this plane, or at least becomes an organized territory within the plane given our movements across space. Thus the local dimensions of the grid change, though it remains always a proper subset of the plane, even in some cases a self-organized territory. The acoustic horizon might similarly exist on this plane, though in relation to the grid marked out by the visual horizon, its territory may shift, seemingly independently of the visual horizon, and holes or punctuations occur that shift its aspects and form, creating discontinuities. But inevitably there are occasional coherences between the two grids, they become superimposed, fused by the architectonic and its auditory articulation—a discontinuity dissolves to become a continuity, the intangible becomes the tangible and the infinite becomes the finite. At other times though, and in particularly rich environments, full of artifacts and sensations, the grids decouple, even possibly separate, while dancing across the plane in subtle shifts of slippage.

The grid then, grounded on the plane, maps out both the visual and acoustic arena. Located within the grid, we are privy to a sense of visual and acoustic space, and though these two boundary conditions may not always find equivalence with each other, or share an edge or corner, they are conditions locatable on the infinite plane. But the shapes and forms that the grid takes, its boundary conditions, might also be seen in the same manner that Tim Ingold describes the "mesh." Here the mesh is not taken to be an architectural analog, a network of point-to-point connections as surface; rather, Ingold argues for conceptualizing the lives of people as lines that continually cross and inscribe the plane and thus produce places. From this density arise knots, meeting places of events, sounds and activities such that "every strand is a way of life and every knot a place. Indeed, the mesh is something like a net in its original sense of an openwork fabric of interlaced or knotted cords." (Ingold 2009, p. 37) We might envisage then the boundaries of the acoustic horizon and its grid as formed and influenced through this mesh in which lines of sounding objects (people, animals, machines, interactions) congregate and produce knots that articulate a point on the plane. These points are then the attractors that displace or produce limits to the acoustic horizon and thus assist in demarcating the acoustic arena. We hear then within the grid: on the plane. But the grid binds a mesh of interwoven complexity. This arises because of the temporal unfolding nature of auditory phenomena being continually in flux. As Sam Elkington asserts, "the lines of [Ingold's] meshwork are not connectors—rather, they are the paths along which life is lived, and it is the binding together of lines, not the connection of points that constitutes the meshwork's form and feel." (Elkington 2015, p. 31)

We might further consider then the specific forces that are at play from which the acoustic horizon and the dimensions of auditory space, the acoustic arena, become defined. What metrics exist that construct, influence and curate the acoustic horizon? To begin such an interrogation is to perhaps acknowledge what I consider five important architectural facets that assist in the shepherding of auditory space: form, materiality, texture, program and structure. Though each in itself does not represent an overwhelming factor, that is, an absolute or indeed completely dominating influence for the definition and construction of auditory space, when taken as a whole, they provide a particularly useful metric. Furthermore, they can be directly understood in terms of the architectonic, of the box, and of sensation. The notion of critical listening then is the awareness of these facets, and moreover, how their interrelations and composite synthesis influence the perceivable dimensions and sensation of auditory space as architectures of sound.

Form

Perhaps one of the most singularly important problems that has faced architecture is the notion of form. In light of the digital age, and of assisted computation, the rise of optimization strategies and the increasing importance of the language of mathematics as mediator between engineering solutions and architectural visions, form continues to be of pressing concern. Together with the structural design of a building, architectural form convalesces the texture of materials, their superimpositions, and, as Pierre von Meiss contends, can be counted as a "measure and order [of] the design of space, light and place." (von Meiss 2013, p. 168) That sounds or the auditory dimension are missing from this characterization is not unusual given that, as Rudolf Arnheim suggests, "when architects discuss form, they are generally content to describe it as physical shape." (Arnheim 1977, p. 225) But quite obviously, if form is but a measure of the order of a design, it is just those physical shapes and geometries that assist in the ordering of the acoustic space, in the creation of an acoustic signature. The question then of the relationship between form and technique arises, and the manner in which the building seeks to deflect what Konrad Wachsmann noted as the ever-present "material struggle against the destructive forces of nature," (Wachsmann 1961, p. 170) or the idea of stasis in a building: that its grounding and sedentary nature is in fact a dynamic set of relations that are constantly energized as a measure against its collapse, against its entropic reversion to a state of least energy. Thus the notion of the technique of form generation, or perhaps what Heidegger referred to as *techné*, a type of revealing of the essence of things, is a reminder of the difference between the crafting of a thing (discovering its essentiality, its *techné*) and the simple production of an object (the *pratakton*). (Heidegger 1977, p. 13) Whereas *pratakton* refers to the practical, technical or perfunctory matters of making, *techné* is a means by which a conception of the making as a manufacturing, as well as an aesthetic positioning, is preconceived. Heidegger's concept of "bringing forth" resides in the process of *techné* in that it is a means to reveal the essence of things: the quintessential phenomenological notion that crafting is a way of realizing meaning in an artifact. As Andrew Feenberg explains:

> The idea of the artefact is not arbitrary or subjective but rather belongs to a *techné*. Each techné contains the essence of the thing to be made prior to the act of making.

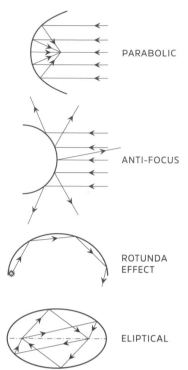

PARABOLIC

ANTI-FOCUS

ROTUNDA
EFFECT

ELIPTICAL

Figure 33. Diagram of typical behaviors
of sounds regarding various geometries

The idea, the essence of the thing is thus a reality independent of the thing itself and its maker. What is more … the purpose of the thing made is included in its idea. (Feenberg 2004, p. 1)

Louis Sullivan's most oft-cited notion that "form must follow function" because of the apparent "pervading law of all things organic and inorganic, [and] of all things physical and metaphysical" (Sullivan 1896, p. 408) seems a pertinent argument to consider here given the frequently de-emphasized role of the auditory in architecture. This is in spite of its important connection to the geometry of form, and indeed the notion of the *techné* of the acoustic signature of a space as pre-purposed into the very idea of a building as a type of functioning auditory system.

Feenberg's argument for conceiving *techné* as something existing before the act of making, before the act of crafting the design response, is a poignant insight into the design intervention that Bernhard Leitner took in his augmentation of the Danube temple at Donaueschingen, Baden Württemberg, Germany. Leitner's career has been one of an experimenter and interrogator of the interstitial spaces between sound, music and architecture, for which his work in the 1970s is particularly known for its innovative architectural exploration of sound through the use of loudspeakers and sound sculptures, as well as numerous architectural interventions that both highlight and manipulate auditory space. Of these projects is the particularly notable 1987 collaboration with Bernard Tschumi at the *Parc de la Villette* in which Leitner's *Cylindre Sonore* sound installation is housed in a double-walled circular pavilion of three-meter-high, perforated cast concrete sections. But unlike many of these earlier works, which have in many ways followed a parallel path to those types of total media spaces such as the Osaka auditorium of 1970, Leitner's temporary intervention at Donaueschingen was in its most pure terms, a masterly use of form for the purposes of un-silencing the narrative voice of the small neoclassic temple that marks the headwaters of the mighty Danube river.

At the foot of the temple a small spring emerges with water flowing out and into the surrounding pond (the Brigach) before joining the Breg River downstream in Donaueschingen and tackling a nearly two-thousand-kilometer journey across ten countries before reaching the Black Sea. The orientation though of the temple places the visitor some two meters directly above the hidden source for which a vista of the small pond and watercourse of the river are the primary focus. *Wasserspiegel* (Water Mirror), Leitner's temporary architectural intervention commissioned by the 1997 Donaueschingen Music Festival, saw the installation of a reflective acoustic dome positioned under the ceiling of the temple that acted as a parabolic reflector to greatly amplify the sound of the hidden spring at the temple's feet. As Leitner comments:

By suspending a flat metal vault between the four columns, the sound of the water falling into the Brigach is focused and amplified. The Danube itself, its very *raison d'être* is projected and reflected into the temple. Naturally filtered rushing sounds, without microphones, amplifiers, loudspeakers, electronics, shape the water temple. In the metal arch, which also reflects the optical refractions of the undulating water surface, various frequency ranges are filtered from the deeper-lying, rushing sounds of the Danube. Through the searching, scanning, listening movements of head and body, the person wanders in the frequency fields of the vaulted ceiling. A dance-like dialogue with the Danube floating above one. (Leitner 2016)

Suddenly the temple's ubiquitous neoclassic form and its situation on the watercourse gains a deeper meaning as the communicative power of the sound of water springing forth literally amplified the architectural narrative. Here, although the spring itself cannot be seen, it is heard and brought to life, for which the semiotics of the temple as an architectural monument to the river become most forcefully communicated. The use of a curved surface for the purpose of reflecting sounds is perhaps a fundamental example of the inherent connection that architectural form and geometry have for the basis of creating acoustic space, or producing particular acoustic signatures. Within a hard, reflective surface of a parabola, all wave fronts that enter the dish will be reflected back out through the focus of the parabola (and vice versa). Depending on the steepness of the curvature, the focus is a point often found at some distance removed from the interior space of the dish. This ability to converge waves occurs regardless of the initial incidence angle of an incoming sound signal, or where on the completely smooth surface the wave strikes. Thus, unlike a spherically curved dish, which tends to diffuse sound in all directions through primary reflections, the parabolically curved surface possesses an ability to produce an auditory image that is object-like, almost tangible, and one that may literally project down into our heads.

Indeed, the notion of head listening or the ways in which in some situations sounds become part of our bodies has fascinated Leitner, who often conceptualizes the idea of sounds becoming internalized phenomena, and thus also able to craft new interiors within us. Perhaps a return then to the architectural humanism of Geoffrey Scott in which Leitner's notion of headspace is indeed the transcription of the architectural into us, or even the transformation of our internal listening space to take on architectural dimensions and proportions.

Figure 34. *Wasserspiegel* (Water Mirror), Bernhard Leitner's temporary architectural intervention commissioned by the 1997 Donaueschingen Music Festival

Dumb Holes and the Acoustic Horizon

Here then is an expanding of the grid within our heads through the pushing out of the acoustic horizon into other territories, into other dimensions.

But if Leitner's *Wasserspiegel* is a particularly erudite and masterly synthesis of form, geometry and the identification of an underlying *techné* at the Danube temple, there are numerous other manifestations of architectural form that have been purely the results of chance, or a visual seductiveness, yet have caused particularly unique acoustic signatures to emerge. Any curved surface represents a potential for a number of acoustic behaviors to emerge. Generally, non-parabolic surfaces that are reflective (that is, hard) are exceptional objects for the diffusing of sounds, for the anti-focusing of sound reflections. Thus, columns and other cylindrical objects are akin to large devices for the homogenization of sounds within a space. Though if sound encounters the concavity of a curved surface, the inverse shape of the column, the result is often a rotunda effect.

Here, sound waves follow the curved surface around its radius. This effect has given rise to numerous "whispering galleries," perhaps the most well-known at St. Paul's Cathedral in London. The gallery under the dome is circular and composed of typically hard stone surfaces. Sounds cling to the walls of the gallery, such that even a quiet conversation on one side of the gallery can be clearly heard at the other side when facing the wall. An even more seemingly unlikely whispering gallery can be found at the magnificent Art Deco-style Cincinnati Union Terminal Station, in Cincinnati, Ohio. Within the cavernous interior, replete with marble and smooth stonework, a giant arch of the front-facing window is adorned with decorated flues that effortlessly straddle the divide between its bases. The flues, though perhaps conceived as purely decorative in their function, and very typical of Art Deco ornamentation, act as sound channels such that even in the acoustic chaos of the completely diffuse and highly reverberant space, two people standing thirty meters apart at the base of each arch, while outside each other's sight line, can conduct a private conversation with minimal effort.

Figure 35. *Headspace*, Bernhard Leitner

Materiality

Materiality then represents an important aspect of the defining of such unique acoustic signatures, where the construction of an acoustic horizon, the demarcation of the expanse of the grid, is a function of the architectonic—whether planned or unplanned.

dB level	Direct Sound
140	Jet takeoff
130	Jackhammer
115	Rock concert
110	Dance club
105	Shouting voice
100	Factory
80	Busy street
70	Restaurant
60	Conversation
50	Average suburban home
30	Quiet whisper

Table 3. Typical SPL (sound pressure level) of common phenomena

The architectonic and its materiality then present a type of resolute flattening to the auditory dimension of Ingold's concept of the mesh. Architecture, as a demarcation of space, through its form, structure and materiality, provides a filter to the sounds of the meshwork and its knots and traced lines. Though at the same time, this filtering through tangible demarcations creates new territories and allows other types of knots and meshes to emerge from within the containment of the box—seemingly like an excitation upon the grid, or more simply, a sleight of hand produced through a shift in focus. Thus the materiality of form, in auditory terms, presents itself as of utmost importance in the influencing of what we hear, the distance to sound sources, and thus what knots might be revealed, encountered and lived through.

In the work of artist Paul de Kort, we find how even in large open, free-field environments outside the boundaries of the architectonic, the influence of materiality plays heavily in the construction of the acoustic horizon and the attenuation of knots as auditory encounters. Within an 81-acre open field close to Schiphol Airport in Amsterdam, an opportunity arose to address the problem of low-frequency noise and those associated disturbances from the constant air traffic for a nearby housing estate. Like the situation close to all airports, noise disturbances are particularly prevalent during takeoff, when all available power of an airplane is in use, and the consequent sound pressure levels exceed the physically painful threshold of 120 dB. Moreover, lower-frequency sounds travel greater distances without feeling the effects of attenuation from the absorptive properties of the air and are thus more adept at both penetrating architectural facades and indeed diffracting around obstacles. According to the inverse square law of sound, for every doubling of the distance from the sound source in a free-field situation, the sound intensity will diminish by six decibels. In spite of this drop in sound pressure, because of the high energy of the sounds of jet engines, and indeed their wide frequency band, their sounds perpetuate across a wide area.

This posed a particularly difficult situation for the design of de Kort's Buitenschot Land Art Park of 2013, carried out in collaboration with H + N + S Landscape Architects. Meeting the challenge required a completely new and innovative rethinking of the connection between soft materiality, landscape form and acoustic experience so that the field could take on the large-scale role of becoming a giant sound sponge. Studying the 18th-century work of Ernst Florens Friedrich Chladni (1756–1827), who invented a technique to visualize the various modes of vibration active within a solid, de Kort integrated the same types of patterns Chladni discovered when he drew a violin bow across a metal plate dusted with sand.

The incorporation of these patterns into the landscape was initiated through the generation of 150 straight and symmetrical furrows, each around two meters in height. Assuming the same type of form found in the walls of an anechoic chamber led to

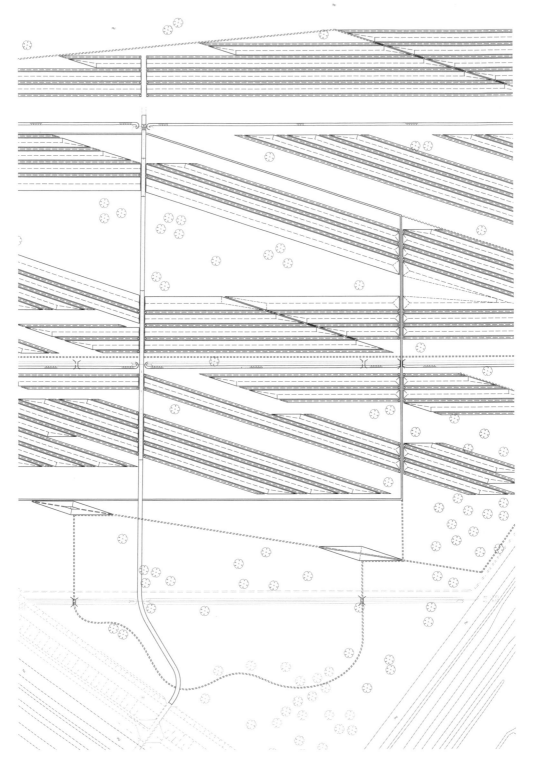

Figure 36. Detail of landscape design of Buitenschot Land Art Park, Paul de Kort and H + N + S Landscape Architects

a similar acoustic result: the absorption, diffusion and containment of sound waves. But the furrows also drew on traditional farming techniques of the Haarlemmermeer area, for which the large voids between the furrows became used for mini parks, accessible by bike and also littered with art objects, including a number of parabolic dishes that allow for moments of concentrated listening to direct sounds within a very small area of the park. But the furrows' alignment represents more than just a purely visual aesthetics of patterning borrowed from Chladni, as their distribution across the field cut the noise levels in the surrounding area from the airport in half. This is not only because the shape and spread of the furrows effectively deflects the low-frequency sound waves away from the local estate, but similarly, the small pockets and rough mowed earthen topography is located at such a distance from the sound sources that it can make an auditory impact through dissipating all energy from incoming waves via absorption. The acoustic horizon then experienced at the local housing estate is significantly affected, pushed inwards and retracted such that those sounds that are occurring locally and within the estate take precedence and tend to mask and overwhelm any of the exterior sounds from Schiphol that arise due to wind effects or other atmospheric conditions.

Figure 37. Drawing of Chladni's technique for visualizing vibration modes in a solid

But the attenuation of sounds through materiality is also a common technique for not only affecting the acoustic horizon but also providing a greater clarity to an already fixed and established acoustic arena. At the neurological level, our hearing functions much like the frame rate of a film or other moving image. When sounds arrive at the pinna that come directly from a source, they are, after a short period of time, supported by secondary (and even tertiary) reflections from objects and physical articulations of space around us. But this supporting framework of the direct source and the early reflections is contingent on the "flicker rate" of hearing. Reflected sounds that approach the pinna within five milliseconds will enhance the sense of the direct sound, while those that appear later will increase the sense of reverberation and thus reduce the sense of clarity. Thus the sense of acoustic clarity and indeed ambience are

> determined by a sequence of events beginning with the arrival of the initial signal, followed by a continuing series of room reflections that gradually dissipate because of losses experienced at the boundaries and in the air. The strength, time and direction-of-arrival characteristics of the reflections, in connection with the relative strength of the direct signal, determine subjective impression. (Cavanaugh et al. 2010, p. 137)

The challenge within any interior space then is the consideration of the amount of reverberation gained through reflection, and thus materiality, in relation to the con-

Dumb Holes and the Acoustic Horizon

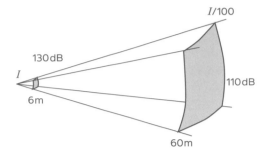

Figure 38. The inverse square law indicates that if a sound of 130 dB occurs in a free-field condition 6 m from a source of intensity *I*, then at 60 m away the intensity will fall by a factor of 100 due to its 100-fold increase in surface coverage. This equates to a drop of only 20 dB in this case: that is, from roughly the level of a jet engine to the level at a rock concert.

current needs for maintaining a sense of clarity and a favorable acoustic impression. This is, of course, more pertinent in spaces primarily used for human speech.

The approach taken then by Hodgetts + Fung Design and Architecture to improve the acoustic qualities of the presentation space of the Auditorium of the Southern California Institute of Architecture (SCI-Arc) in Los Angeles was through the integration of an absorbing ceiling. The seemingly inverted landscape utilizes not distinct furrows as found in Buitenschot, but undulating waves in which a topography is created that suggests just the type of visualization of optimizing forces of the weighted models that Antoni Gaudí utilized in his designs for the Church of Colónia Güell and the Sagrada Família. (Huerta 2006) The Hodgetts + Fung ceiling is described as an XSS—Experimental Sound SurfaceCeiling in which the catenary undulations and form are a function not of a wholly predetermined digital model of topological fitness, but rather, as in Gaudí's upside-down hanging chain models, a result of the natural weight of the 16 mm industrial wool felt which is fixed via a specialized upholstery studding to a lightweight aluminum frame. The curves and volumes then of the inverted topography are self-organized according to the density, malleability and weight of the fabric. But perhaps in a most innovative fashion, the ceiling attends to the difficulties of adjusting the acoustics in larger rooms

Figure 39. *XSS*—Experimental Sound SurfaceCeiling of the Auditorium of the Southern California Institute of Architecture (SCI-Arc) in Los Angeles by Hodgetts + Fung Design and Architecture

Figure 40. Sound profile of Royal Park and vicinity, Melbourne, Australia

primarily for speech where for the increase in clarity, reflection paths need to be short-ened. The heavy absorptive qualities of the wool felt in addition to the perforations within the surface enable sounds to essentially become diffused and dissipated in the air pockets, thus removing the ceiling as the sixth surface reflector of the box. This then reduces the reverberation time and increases the likelihood of early reflections from the sidewalls and floor, so important for the pellucidity of verbal communication.

Program

Program perhaps divides then what must be seen as the knowledge of the types of sounds that will be occurring within a site. As such, it is concerned with what archi-tectonic interventions will be most appropriate for generating an acoustic signature, for the defining of the boundaries of the acoustic horizon. In common parlance, the architectural program refers to the requirements of a building, its list of utilities, an indication of its internal and contextual relations, and what Bernard Tschumi nominates as a potential for "the relation between program and building [as one] that could be either highly sympathetic or contrived and artificial." (Tschumi 1996, p. 147) But program must also refer to the acoustic space, its potentials, qualities and dimensions and, more poignantly, exactly which sounds are to be commonly expected. To read the approaches of the examples I have so far explored as a synthesis between form and materiality also alludes to the fact that they are situated in environments in which the particulars of the sound world, of the sounds themselves, are specifically accounted for and known in advance. This is not always the case, and in some situations, the types of sounds to be heard and their composition become an element for the driver of the program of the site. What becomes evident then is that a site is either already in possession of or will gain a sound profile. By this I mean a taxonomy of anticipated or observed sounds that will define its acoustic signature, its acoustic arenas and the limits of its acoustic horizon.

In addition, though, to the sound profile is that of the act of a critical listening, of a close consideration of the sound profile as an unfolding in time, and via a multitude of sources: that is, the range and shape of its taxonomy. Though conceived within a musical rather than a spatial context, David Dunn's 1997–98 work *Purposeful Listening in Complex States of Times* asks similar tasks of the performer, who actively becomes reappropriated and reconfigured to take up the expertise of a close listener. Tracing an arc from the act of performance as "non-action," as found in Cage's 4'33", Dunn simply asks the performer to engage in various modes of listening, that while attentive to the sound environment at hand, and the shape and distribution of the sound profile, the performer also becomes fused with typical dichotomies of the exterior and interior, memory and fantasy, past and present, being and nothing. The types of parameters that Dunn nominates to define the listening modes include level of attention (sky, body, ground), direction of attention (left, right, forward, behind, all around), proximity of listening attention (adjacent, near or distant) and time of event listened to (present, past/remembered, future/imagined, nonspecific). Thus, unlike the "empty" score of 4'33", the score of *Purposeful Listening in Complex States of Times* is highly detailed, for which an internal structure delineates durations of the various listening modes as well as transitions and tempos. It appears then that the precedent of Cage is used as a point of departure from which to more completely realize the act of listening as a highly specific role, a function of a definitive action that goes beyond the casual notion of the passivity of simply hearing something. From the "performance" then must come new types of engagement with the program, given the site-specific nature of the score—indeed one could argue the opposite, that the score is completely site-specific and a total immersion in the spatial qualities of a site. Ultimately then, Dunn's work serves to only accentuate how the program of a site is by its very nature a collection of sounds, but similarly a collection of different listening modes given the potentialities of numerous auditory aspects, intersections of acoustic arenas, fluctuating acoustic horizons and tapestries of the sound profile.

But in the case of the generation of the sound profile of a site for the complementation of an architectural program, the work of Lars Spuybroek (principal of NOX Architecture) presents a particularly telling case of innovation. In particular are the

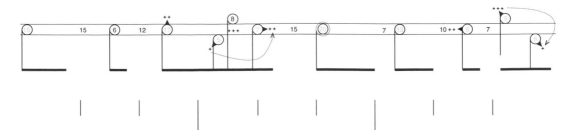

Figure 41. David Dunn, *Purposeful Listening in Complex States of Times* (1997–98), page 19

multimedia projects *Son-O-House* and the *Water pavilion*. As a technologically maximalist complement to Leitner's *Wasserspiegel*, and perhaps what Marcus Novak might eagerly consider a species of *archimusic* (Novak 1994, p. 66), the *Water pavilion* was a collaboration with the sound artist and composer Edwin van der Heide. Like the Danube temple, the *Water pavilion* is a monument to the forces and concept of water, though unlike Leitner's handling of the sounds of water as an already integrated feature of the program, as an intrinsic element of the sound profile, at the NOX *Water pavilion* can be found a program activated through a multisensory onslaught of sound and light. Dedicated to the experience of water, it arose from the desire to create a communicating architectural environment in which the encounter is one of a sounding building rather than a building of sounds. Thus, the sound profile of the building serves to build and communicate the narrative, to imbue the architectural program with a tangible and, moreover, a semiotics of the heard.

The interior of the pavilion uses electronically generated sounds, actual moving water, lighting effects, sensors and video imagery to augment intersecting nonuniform surfaces that immerse, wrap and revolve around the visitor. The hard metal surfaces and concrete flooring recall the environment of a reverberation chamber and only assist in generating a complete feeling of immersion, of perhaps even drowning in sounds that are as perceivably wet and as amorphous as the flowing water visitors found occasionally lapping their feet throughout the interior. If the architectural program of the building is one that is a reminder of what Tschumi described as "the definition of architecture as simultaneously space and event," (Tschumi 1996, p. 22) then it is through the sound profile and the acoustic signature that the program becomes delivered and indeed discretely communicated. But the sounds too are designed not only to inhabit the pavilion as fixed or continually repeating structures, but also to behave autonomously, by which the notion of immersion arises as a consequence of the constantly changing acoustic arenas of the interior—essentially an acoustic of emergence. Here then, Spuybroek and van der Heide seem particularly drawn to the concept of an autonomous architecture of sounds that inhabit the box and assist in shaping the notion of the scale of the interior through varying the dimensions of the numerous acoustic arenas. Here then, the grids of the visual and acoustic horizons dance around each other across the plane as the fixed visual articulation of the containment of the architectonic, of the box, is supplemented with an acoustic horizon that is shifting through emergent structures and thus forcing us to consider ever new auditory perspectives.

A second collaboration as an interrogation between sound as program and architecture as an articulation of habitat is found in the pair's *Son-O-House*. Here, the structure

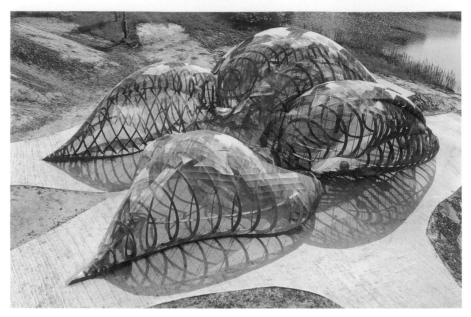

Figure 42. *Son-O-House*, a collaboration between NOX and sound artist Edwin van der Heide

of the pavilion is derived from a series of choreographed movements of bodies at three scales originally developed from a paper model composed of strips with various cuts that become revolved and offset to produce volumes that were then digitized, elaborated and resolved. The pavilion is described as a house where sounds live, and its connection to the analog paper model imbues the conceptualization of the house as an "arabesque of complex intertwining lines," in regard to both the movement of bodies and the movement of sounds. Indeed, its structure is thus a reference not only to the body, but to the nature of movements that accompany human habitation. But as a house in which sound resides, it is also an interactive installation equipped with twenty loud-speakers for which

> twenty-three sensors are positioned at strategic spots to indirectly influence the music. The sound generation system is based on spatial interferences and dynamic standing wave patterns resulting from the combination of speakers. As a visitor (slowly becoming an inhabitant because this structure will stay in its place forever) one does not influence the sound directly, which is so often the case with interactive art. One influences the landscape itself that generates the sounds. The score is an evolutionary memoryscape that develops with the traced behavior of the actual bodies in the space. (van der Heide 2016)

The notion of the sound profile of the pavilion and the architectural program then become fused so that the compositional strategy behind the sound layer is such that the influence and presence of visitors directly contributes to an ever-evolving taxonomy of sounds that constitute its acoustic signature. As van der Heide suggests, because the sensors are constantly analyzing, quantifying and updating the spatial information obtained from a rudimentary tracking of temporary inhabitants, the sound profile of the pavilion "challenges the visitors to re-interpret their relationship with the environment." This challenging of an interpretation of the environment is effectively delivered through the ways in which the sensors attempt to influence behaviors. As van der Heide explains, "the more activity on one location the faster the sounds transform in that region. On the other hand the system will try to attract the visitors to visit the opposite locations or 'push' them away from the current location." (van der Heide 2016)

We might say then that the program arises equally from the communicable power of the sounds as artifacts of human occupation, of fleeting habitations, and from the idea of the structure as a type of ephemeral abode, a pavilion of manifested ideas about the body. Perhaps then the pavilion is a means by which a sonification of the "complex intertwining lines" occurs, something akin to the making audible of Ingold's notion of the knots and lines that form the mesh. The paths, lives and intersection of lines of people and their temporary occupation of the pavilion as a knot provide the spatial and temporal information required for the sound profile of the pavilion to act out, renew and regenerate and produce an auditory précis. But furthermore, the sound profile of *Son-O-House* is not one that can be completely accounted for. By the very programming of the compositional layer, of the sounds that emerge from the embedded loudspeakers, only a statistical knowledge of the possibilities exists. These possibilities are inhibited or encouraged by the human occupation of the house, such that the encounter of the site is an encounter with the very notion of sound functioning as a program.

Texture

As one of the five nominated metrics of auditory space that define the acoustic horizon, texture becomes useful here in that it is a means by which to eruditely examine the qualities of sounds themselves. The knowledge of the types of sounds that form the taxonomy of the sound profile of a site, of an architecture, is an important token in considering the variety of the taxonomy, by which an understanding of texture provides a utility for a deeper engagement in the notion of sound as a phenomenon that produces particular sensations. As Robert Erickson suggests, though texture may be primarily considered a description of the feel of an object, the imagined or tangible interaction of sensation regarding its materiality with our bodies, it is also a means for describing the tactility of sound worlds:

> Texture always denotes some overall quality, the feel of surfaces, the weave of fabrics, the look of things. Words from visual and tactile sense modalities are often appropriated for descriptions of sounds and their combination: sharp, rough, dull, smooth, biting, bright, brilliant, brittle, coarse, thick, thin, dry, diaphanous, airy, finespun, flaccid, fluid, gauzy, glittery, grainy, harsh, hazy, heavy, icy, inchoate, jagged, limpid, liquescent, lush, mild, murky, pliant, relaxed, rippling … (Erickson 1975, p. 139)

In addition to the description of sounds in such poetic terms, we might also consider the most basic ways of describing their properties in terms of relative amplitude (soft vs. loud), frequency (high-pitched vs. low-pitched) and duration (sustained vs. pointillistic). In this case, sounds are obviously relative to other sounds regarding their frequency, amplitude and duration. Here, the usefulness of an audiogram as a basic

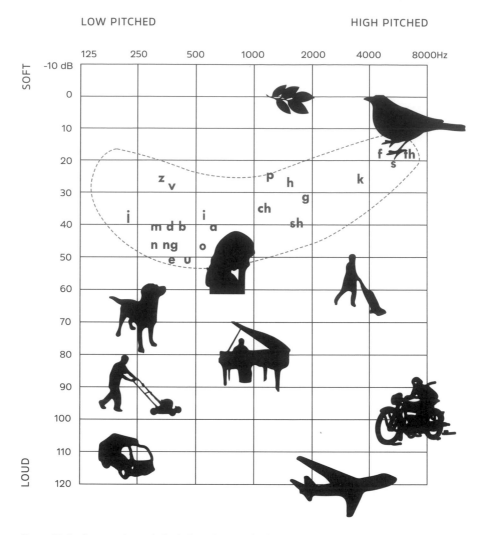

Figure 43. Audiogram of sounds (including phonemes) relative to pitch (Hz) and loudness (dB) with pictorial representations. Sounds represented include: rustling leaves, birdsong, crying, vacuum cleaner, dog barking, piano, lawn mower, truck, airplane at altitude, motorcycle.

visualization of the common relations between sounds regarding their loudness and pitch highlights their place in the activations of the human auditory system (Figure 43).

The relatively wide frequency distribution of common sounds, and indeed the myriad sound pressure levels that are found between each, means that the auditory experience of any rich sonic environment is one in which masking frequently occurs. Masking is the ability of some sounds, through either their frequency (pitch) distributions or their energy or amplitude levels (loudness), to conceal other localized sounds. Thus as Blesser and Salter noted, the boundaries of the acoustic horizon are greatly affected by the ability of some sounds to be heard and to mask other sounds. The high-pitched and loud pointillistic interjection of a car horn will always mask any birdcalls of the same frequency spectrum. Indeed, recent research has suggested that the impact on urban wildlife from the mechanization of cities and the numerous introduced electronic sounds has caused new animal behaviors to emerge. In 2011, Dominique Parris and colleagues found that the species of small bird *Zosterops lateralis* had significantly changed its pitch and tempo calls in urban environments compared with its rural cousins. (Potvin et al. 2010) As a significant evolutionary adaptation, the ambient background noise of traffic and other city sounds was found to be inhibiting the birds' ability to communicate within their auditory niche, thus requiring them to sing higher and slower to be understood.

But the qualities of masking are not simply a product of twentieth- and twenty-first-century urbanism. Even at the height of the Roman Empire, the ability of falling water and, in particular, water fountains to mask the sounds of iron-rimmed chariot wheels on cobblestoned streets was known and masterfully exploited, given the calming and aesthetically pleasing visual spectacle of a fountain. That falling water contains such a large frequency spectrum and similarly, through careful design, may produce rhythmic heterogeneity is a discovery that was similarly exploited in Japanese garden design. (Fowler 2015)

We might consider the texture of sound not only as a quality that assists in masking and thus demarcating an acoustic boundary, but similarly, as both an interior and exterior element that helps to define the qualities of the atmosphere of an acoustic signature. Consider then the texture of the sounds of Boullée's *Deuxième projet pour la Bibliothèque du Roi* (Figure 19). Here, the diffuse and soft murmurs of human voices together with sharp rhythmic footsteps and the extremely subtle sound of the turning of pages of ancient books combine to produce a particularly subdued family of textures. The sound profile of the site sits in a remarkably heightened contrast to the "bigness" of the space at hand, its surface textures of hardness and resoluteness, and its focus on the intimate as something born from the subtlety of the sounds at hand rather than the absolute visual spectacle of the void of the interior volume. To consider the acoustic signature of architecture is also to consider the texture of sounds, and those most common examples of the canon in architectural design in regard to room acoustics. The design of a concert hall is thus an anticipation of known sound textures and the taxonomy of a particular sound profile. All efforts of the acoustic design are thus aimed towards satisfying a series of parameters for listening that are tied to the frequency and loudness of the expected sounds of music.

The notion of the ability to be immersed either literally through a particular listening aspect, a seating arrangement within an auditorium or other space, or conversely, as composer and architect Iannis Xenakis considered, simply through the fact that sounds themselves are capable of producing space, of producing "sonic surfaces," (Harley 1998) places the notion of the texture of sounds then as a commanding characteristic of auditory space. For Xenakis, the types of experimentation found in his *Polytope de Montréal* (1967), the first of a series of temporary architectural structures that accommodated light and sound projection, were a chance for the "musicalization of space." (Sterken 2001) This was achieved, like that at the spherical auditorium at Osaka, through highly considered and composed-out sound and light trajectories. But in addition to this infrastructural capability, it was, in particular, the mediative qualities of the textures of the sound which, when synthesized with the architectural structures, emphasized their complex, nonplanar geometries. Again, the use of loudspeakers in such structures enables a sense of new types of space to emerge that could

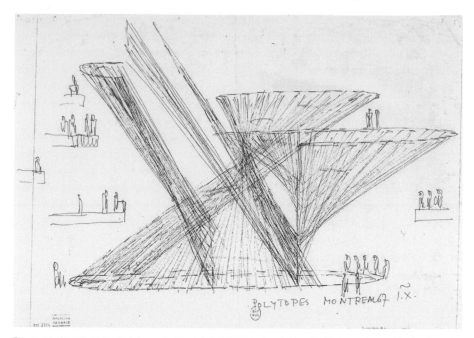

Figure 44. Sketch of the *Polytope de Montréal* of 1967 by Iannis Xenakis that was located in the French Pavilion of *Expo 67*

be a function, not only of the simple spatialization of sources, but more subtly, of the textural composition of the sources themselves.

As composer Barry Truax also suggests, certain approaches to electroacoustic composition that are based on what I have nominated here as texture are similarly concerned with generating three-dimensional space. These approaches then, "may be thought of as shaping the space within the sound, that is, its perceived volume." (Truax 2007, p. 141) But perhaps an under-investigated typology for such consequences of the effects of texture as a device for creating immersion arises in a far more unlikely source—the Japanese *Pachinko* parlor. Though an improbably "designed" auditory experience, the consequences of such spaces as environments of total immersion arise from their telling sound profiles and fortress-like immobilities. The game of *Pachinko* is believed to have originated in Osaka Prefecture in the 1920s and is thought to be a corruption, or in effect a Japanization, of the popular "Coringth Game" of Prohibition-era Chicago. The game is played at an upright machine that resembles the ubiquitous Western slot machines and involves propelling numerous small steel ball bearings through a maze of pins. The propulsion of the balls into the machine is today managed by a large bulbous knob for which it is debatable if there is any skill or physical influence from the speed or sensitivity used in the turning of the knob to affect the initial travel of the balls. After the balls enter the machine, they are "free" in the sense that there are no more external interactions with their inevitable gravity-fed movement towards the numerous holes. The aim of the game is to collect as many balls as possible through jackpots. But there is a certain resignation about the game too, a passiveness or mute or dumb quality that Yoshio Sugimoto describes as indicative of a cultural trait of the Japanese:

One may also argue that Pachinko attracts so many Japanese partly because it is essentially detached from direct human interaction … to the extent that mass culture points to daily realities which the masses wish to evade, the non-interactive quality of Pachinko games indirectly testifies to the intensity of group pressures and constraints on the working and community lives of the Japanese. (Sugimoto 1997, p. 226)

What is perhaps most intriguing though about the *Pachinko* parlor, outside of the fact that over 50 million Japanese profess to be regular players, is that if there exists a passiveness regarding the playing of the game and in the attitudes and motivations for people to play, the sound profile and textures that accompany the play are utterly raucous, at times ear-splitting and, because of the textures, completely immersive. Unlike their ancient, genteel cousins, the machines today emit noises and electronic melodies (pentatonic and Japanese in flavor), synthesized words of encouragement and other artificial feeding sounds. That the noise floor of such parlors is highly elevated is only exacerbated by the metallic sounds of the balls themselves and their travels across and through metal pins. Given that parlors often contain only one brand of machine, there is a vast iteration of the textures and an unending layering, like a musical canon of infinite voices. Of the sounds themselves, one experiences a total amplification and multiplication of sensation, one that rises to a crescendo that only ceases with the sense that one is not in the space, but rather, of the machine: as if one was one of the balls.

The texture of the sounds in a *Pachinko* parlor then gives rise to a sense of space generated purely through the amplitude and homogeneous, layered and seemingly polyphonic nature of the frequency content. Speaking or conversations in such parlors are rarefied sounds which are in any case completely masked by the overwhelming textures of the balls and colorful interjections and language of the machines—all attempted exterior disruptions to the acoustic signature are subsumed and exactingly overwhelmed by the textures of the sound profile in a surprisingly forceful and non-passive manner.

Structure

By structure, I mean that which describes the periodicity or a-periodicity of sounds, or their temporal and rhythmic qualities as influential demarcators of the acoustic horizon. Thus, unlike what is commonly considered within architecture and building as "the part of a building which resists the loads that are imposed on it," (Macdonald 2007, p. 1) structure is here a consideration of the temporality of sounds, and indeed not the sense of their resistance to a cause, but rather their very visceral embodiment of time within an architectural environment. Sound is an unfolding in time of the vibrations in a medium. Hence to speak of the sound profile of architecture is to also acknowledge ebb and flow, and a larger-scale rhythm in which sounds appear and disappear. They may display regularity or non-regularity, seasonality or non-seasonality yet may also contain predictable structures. Thus, when Tschumi speaks of the event and argues that "there is no architecture without events, without actions or activity," his proposition naturally leads to the notion that buildings possess an ability to respond to and intensify the activities that occur within them, and that events alter and creatively extend the structures that contain them. In other words, architecture is not defined by its "formal" container, but rather by its combinations of spaces, movements, and events. (Tschumi 2016)

What is perhaps most overlooked in such a position is that the events that assist in defining architecture inevitably consist of auditory components that effectively mark out the momentary nature of such events on the grid through their temporal structures. This is true of the most common architecture for the delivery of musical content—the concert hall—in which events are distinguished by their auditory content and their ephemeral yet reoccurring nature. The structure that defines a concert hall then can be defined in auditory terms at the largest scale as a calendar of concerts, which through an ever-decreasing lens of interrogation reveals shorter periodicities: from the individual concerts themselves, to the musical works on offer, the individual movements of the works, and finally the individual sounds within the movements themselves. All of these concentric circles of temporality are events in auditory terms, and similarly sum to define the architecture of sounds that the building assists in curating. Structure then is the accumulated temporality of a sound profile in which a framework for reoccurrence and remerging events becomes mapped against the expectations of the program.

An aid then to the revealing of auditory structure as an experiential rather than purely scientific pursuit is the work of acoustic ecologist and composer Hildegarde Westerkamp. Those measurable structures that concern sound have been the traditional domain of signal processing, whose investigations utilize the tools of mathematics and physics in order to pursue sounds for formalities of regularity, rhythmic content and other statistical pointers. Divergent then is Westerkamp's use of the soundwalk as an attempt, perhaps like Geoffrey Scott, to retrieve and rescue sound from the objective hands of determinists and empiricists, in order to capture new humanistic ways of knowing and hearing. (Westerkamp 2006) Westerkamp's practice of soundwalking involves a group of technologically unmediated listeners whose pre-planned walk through an environment is enacted in silence and without interpersonal communication so as to foster a heightened auditory awareness and thus allow for a deeper understanding of the connection between listener and place. (Jeon et al. 2013) The practice of soundwalking then is one that seeks to both identify and experience the ephemeral nature of sound as unfolding in time, and perhaps sound as a new type of metric that assists in describing the lived qualities of time. When the soundwalk becomes a repeated ritual, following continually over an agreed path, over days or months, or punctuated by longer breaks or pauses (once every month, six-monthly, yearly), whether it be exterior or interior to the demarcation of architecture, it then becomes an action in which Tschumi's notion of the event is reconciled to not only visual or social phenomena, but equally to auditory ones.

In fact, for Frances Crow and David Prior of the architectural practice Liminal, the urban development of Warwick Bar in Birmingham (UK) was examined via the lens of soundwalking as a way in which to scrutinize auditory phenomena as temporal agents enfolded within a place. Crow and Prior integrated soundwalking as a means to embed themselves not only within the acoustic dimensions of the project site, but also

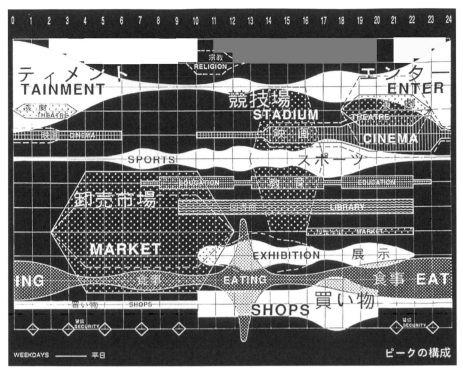

Figure 45. Part of OMA's 1992 *Masterplan for the city of Yokohama*. Here spaces are diagrammed in regard to flows of activities over a 24-hour period.

to enter into the same type of relationship local residents have with the site. (Crow & Prior 2016) Soundwalking then became a means to aurally investigate the sonic character of Warwick Bar and raise the status of its auditory history to a level that would actively influence the development of the masterplan. But it also provided a way in which to educate the partner project architects (Kinetic AIU) as well as the general public on the site's rich acoustic qualities. Additionally, the use of a questionnaire to construct a noise/tranquillity indicator from the local soundwalkers became integrated into the existing Birmingham City Council noise maps of local traffic patterns to generate a predictive acoustic model that tracks the impact of any new architectural or landscape interventions within the site.

That the structures of sound are inevitably tied to site and place is directly revealed in one of the iconic original diagrams of OMA's 1992 *Masterplan for the city of Yokohama*. Representing the mapping of the flow of activities over a 24-hour period, the diagram befittingly displays how the relation between site and event can also be promptly conceived as an auditory proposition, as a mapping of fluctuations in the structure of sound-space. Here then, auditory structure is intimately bound to the program and activities of the sectors of the diagram that represent market, entertainment, eating, etc., and thus can be immediately imagined, perhaps conspicuously heard, as a wealth of acoustic arenas, many overlapping, existing and influencing the myriad acoustic horizons such that the temporality of the activities is similarly a mapping of the ephemerality of a number of sound profiles. As OMA elaborate:

The proposal is for a continuous and formless project which engulfs the site like a kind of programmatic "lava." Three layers of public activity are manipulated to support the largest variety of events with a minimal amount of permanent definition. Noticing that the peak hours of the market fall in the early morning, we propose a complementary spectrum of events, which would exploit to the maximum the location and its existing infrastructure, to create a 24-hour "peak" composed of a mosaic of heterogeneous 21st century life. (OMA 2016)

To compose a programmatic "lava" of events is to also influence and guide auditory structure, to create a diversity of acoustic arenas and thus ultimately to compose a series of architectures of sound that assist in producing both a sense of place as well as temporal continuity, a sense of the unfolding of 21st-century life through 24-hour sound profile cycles.

Such ephemeral cycles of structure revealed through the overlaying of new programmatic "lava fields" need not be completely tied to social or economic forces, or even premeditated design interventions. As is the case at the *Beetham Tower* (Manchester, UK) where the weather provides an activating force for the mapping and revealing of the temporality of sounds, of the inherent ephemerality in their structures. Though a completely unforeseen result of the design of the extremity of the building, where a high wall of glass louvers punctuates its upper profile next to the cooling infrastructure, the turbulence caused by the movement of wind through the wall produces an unearthly singing. The louvers essentially act like "fipples" or the type of thin wedge-shaped inserts that because of the effect of a wind stream across the surface allow flutes, recorders and whistles to produce sounds. At the *Beetham Tower,* the fipples are activated such that the air stream hitting the leading edge also becomes split, causing turbulences at both the lower and upper edges. Because of the voids between the louvers, enough of an air column is created such that the pulses produced from the fipples are amplified and become heard as resonances, as a humming tone centered around 250 Hz that audibly fluctuates in its amplitude with the relative wind speed.

Even after some "correction" to the perceived fault of the design through an attempt to dampen the materiality of the glass louvers, the presence of wind still tends to activate the fipples, though nominally at much higher wind speeds. But this only adds perhaps to the nature of the building's voice as a harbinger of an approaching storm, as a reminder of the nature of weather as a cyclic and ever-repeating episode. Structure then is revealed as the singing of the building in anticipation of a change in atmospheric conditions, as a warning of nature approaching, as a testing of the fortitude of its stasis and its resistance to

Figure 46. Beetham Tower, Manchester, UK

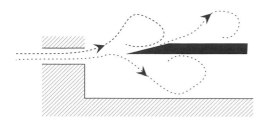

Figure 47. Turbulence generated across a fipple as found in a recorder. The resonant air column of the interior of the recorder provides the amplification for pulses generated by the turbulence.

the ever-present force of entropy in what Konrad Wachsmann noted as a building's struggle against the coercion of nature. But the sound too is quite audible from the street, even at some distance removed, such that to hear the building sing brings a new semiotics to bear about the traditional notion of the architectural facade as essentially indifferent to the exterior conditions—it may be instrumental but rarely acts out through a cybernetic paradigm.

At the Beetham Tower however, the facade is activated in a very particular way, such that the building itself becomes a sound structure whose fluctuations between stasis and activity are a product of the immediate environment, and similarly influence the immediate sounding environment. Thus, unlike David Byrne's *Playing the Building*, in which human occupation and manipulation of the building's surfaces and structural framework provide the elements of the sound profile, and thus the "performer" determines the structure, at *Beetham Tower*, weather and the natural environment are the forces that play the building, that reveal and direct the auditory structure of the resulting sounds.

Hole

To consider then the dumb hole as the contextual framework by which the acoustic horizon is a metric that distinctly describes the threshold qualities of the hole, then it is the interplay between structure, form, materiality, program and texture that represents the metric that can best describe the acoustic horizon in the context of architecture and of critical listening. In contrast to the experience of the acoustic horizon as an everyday phenomenon, the dumb hole represents a specific yet intriguing case, an optimized model in which the movability of the horizon can only be achieved through a radical reformation of the surface of the hole itself, through a manipulation of the boundaries and materiality of the hole's host as a demarcation of space. As an analog to the black hole, which is a puncture within the fabric of spacetime, the dumb hole is a puncture within a state of a perfect fluid—both conditions then satisfying the seemingly reducible notion of a type of negative space being encountered. (Hoffman & Richards 1985) Indeed, as Roberto Casati and Achille Varzi suggest, holes are "not abstractions but individuals, although they are not made of anything but space." (Casati & Varzi 1995, p. 6) Toomas Karmo has countered though that the very notion of a hole may also be considered as a type of disturbance, for which the ensuing implications are that the hole is itself but an immaterial part of a material host:

> A disturbance is definable as an object or entity found in some other object—not in the sense in which a letter may be found in an envelope..., but in the sense in which a knot may be in a rope, a wrinkle in a carpet, a hole in a perennial border. (Karmo 1977, p. 147)

In the case of the dumb hole, the acoustic horizon is the metric that describes the size and location of the edges of the funnel, of the punctuation, or of the slide. Its threshold state as an immateriality thus acts as the foil to the material "sides" of the funnel or host as primary object. But to consider the acoustic horizon as an auditory experience of the built environment, we may be better served to reconsider again Ingold's conceptualization of knots. If the sounds that occur around us that define our acoustic horizon are conceptualized as knots, that is, sonifications of the lines of activities, people, machines, nature and sundry, we might also consider them as proxy representations of the types of disturbances on the grid, functioning in the same manner that Karmo describes the disturbances of the "negative" or immaterial space occupied by holes. We might then consider these disturbances as ones occurring on the grid of the infinite plane, and moreover, as ones paired to sounds—themselves auditory confirmations of the knots and meshwork. But rather than being fixed to a seemingly immovable or static material host, such as we find in the dumb hole, the host here, space and the medium of air, is potentially infinitely reconfigurable. Thus auditory space, intimately connected to a medium and the notion of the grid, is as J. C. R. Licklider suggested, not sharply defined but rather diffuse and, moreover, dynamic. (Licklider 1967, p. 141)

What then of the interplay between structure, form, materiality, program and texture as the metric that defines the acoustic horizon? They are perhaps best regarded as facets of the metric in that the relationship between the whole and its parts is not simply through a sum of the facets. What exists within each facet then is a capacity, such that the relation between the capacities accounts for a greater force when considering the metric as a whole. Thus, the properties of the individual facets themselves, of the qualities espoused by structure, form, materiality, program and texture, do not directly become aggregated at the level of the whole, but it is instead the interaction between and because of their capacities that produces the metric that in turn defines the limit and scale of the acoustic horizon. This is a condition that was similarly described by Deleuze and Guattari as an *agencement*, or as DeLanda explains, "a theory of assemblages, … [which] was meant to apply to a wide variety of wholes constructed from heterogeneous parts." (DeLanda 2006, p. 3) For Deleuze and Guattari, the assemblage was a complex collection of objects, bodies, things, qualities, expressions, territories and the like:

> What is an assemblage? It is a multiplicity which is made up of heterogeneous terms and which establishes liaisons, relations between them, across ages, sexes and reigns—different natures. Thus the assemblage's only unity is that of a co-functioning: it is a symbiosis, a "sympathy." It is never filiations which are important, but contagions, epidemics, the wind. (Deleuze & Parnet 2007, p. 69)

That the acoustic horizon is but a metric, defined by the relations between the facets or parameters of structure, form, materiality, program and texture, is also a reminder of how critical listening seeks to extend the idea of architecture beyond its articulation of form, of its flirtatious and constant remittance to the currency of the visual, by attempting to establish the notion of a whole-to-part configuration that synthesizes these senses and points towards the capacities of one to influence the other. Critical listening then is not singularly a theory of architecture, but instead a framework for both analyzing and imagining the auditory consequences of architecture, in terms of both its indigenous theories and its resolute applied practices.

4
The Taxonomy of a Meta-theory

The Taxonomy of a Meta-theory

Sound-space

Space in sounds or sounds in space? It is just this notion of whether sounds themselves, perhaps like light, can be simply located in space by their relationship to objects, interactions with surfaces and architecture, or conversely are creators or generators of a lived space through their dynamism, texture and structure that has come to define the two recent theories on sound, Barry Blesser and Linda-Ruth Salter's aural architecture and R. Murray Schafer's soundscape. That these two theories in particular are of interest to the aims of this book is nominally tied to the perceived utility that aural architecture and soundscape are envisaged to possess by their advocates and creators. Indeed, it is because of those alleged aural deficiencies of the discipline of architecture that aural architecture and soundscape theory have been positioned as potential catalysts for providing a paradigm-shifting fracture within architecture—the inheritance of which, in the ears of R. Murray Schafer, will be a future as acoustic utopia.

In anticipation of such visionary acoustic futures, the numerous ideas forwarded by aural architecture and soundscape theory are widely gathered interrogations and usurpations from the neighboring disciplines of musical composition, acoustics, sound studies and ecology. Such a synthesis of threads and ideas is envisaged as a viable and interdisciplinary alternative to what is the undying hegemony and disciplining of visual modes used in the design and representation of the built environment. But what has actually been overlooked in this promise of the amelioration of sounding space, of the future urban condition, is the closeness by which both theories operate in terms of their ideas and their positioning of space in regard to sounds—and vicariously, the architectonic. There is then a lack of acknowledgment of where the arc of inscription that represents architecture is found, and in particular, of what the priority of architecture's indigenous discourse is in relation to the realm of the acoustic, and of the multisensory. There is in fact a transparent yearning of both aural architecture and soundscape theory for a recognition beyond the disciplinary boundaries of

Figure 48. Detail from cover of *Bau: Magazine for Architecture and Urban Planning*, Issue 1–2, 1968

sound studies and applied acoustics (which have both resolutely embraced their concepts and methodologies), and furthermore, for a legitimization of the qualities of both theories, their design potentials and their logic by the master of all arts, architecture.

The absolute consideration though of the acoustic environment within architectural design praxis has traditionally been reserved only for those specialized listening facilities such as concert halls or recording studios. But the role of the canon, and of acoustic exemplars, is constantly being challenged through numerous recent theoretical insurgencies such as those from Juhani Pallasmaa, Ted Sheridan, Karen Van Lengen (2003) and Björn Hellström (2003), who have each identified, like Rafael Pizarro, that the seductive immediacy of pure visual articulations of space has slighted the potential for new types of architectural experiences to emerge. (Pizarro 2009) But it is certainly also the willingness of the discipline of architecture to allow for such excursions, and indeed to encourage the seeking out of myriad influences, theories and extra-architectural knowledge, that has created a particularly innovative and robust climate. As radically pronounced by Hans Hollein in his inaugural editorship of the 1968 edition of *Bau* magazine, we may well consider that "Alles ist Architektur" (everything is architecture):

> Architects have to stop thinking in terms of buildings only. Built and physical architecture, freed from the technological limitations of the past, will more intensely work with spatial qualities as well as the psychological ones. The process of erection will get a new meaning, spaces will more consciously have haptic, optic and acoustic properties. A true architecture of our time will have to redefine itself and to expand its means. Many areas outside traditional building will enter the realm of architecture, as architecture and "architects" will have to enter new fields. All are architects. Everything is architecture. (Hollein 1968, p. 1)

This particular embrace, and indeed its recognition of the potential of the acoustic realm, is what Liane Lefaivre has noted as Hollein's desire for "a complete rebooting of architectural thinking, a radical re-categorization of architecture, the elimination of closure in its definition, [and the] removal of all boundaries between it and other fields." (Lefaivre 2003, pp. 1–2) Indeed the cover image selected by Hollein for *Bau*, a block of Emmentaler as a contemporary skyscraper (or perhaps one of Venturi's "ducks") that sagely casts an iconic and perhaps olfactory shadow over Vienna, is an image that seeks to play on the Viennese practice of labeling "bad architecture" as an Emmentaler in the local dialect—if everything indeed is architecture, then one certainly must expect the good in equal proportions with the bad. Indeed, the proposition of everything as an architecture also suggests that the bad might also perpetuate at all scales, a perhaps unforeseen consequence of what Stan Allen argues as the need for architecture to expand its internal boundaries through a "vertical integration of scales" (Allen 2009) among architecture, landscape and urbanism. But the resonances of Hollein's editorship, and what Craig Buckley describes as its emphasis on "the creation of significance through the organization of relations of contiguity" (Buckley 2007, p. 112) via the issue's juxtaposition of myriad images (people, buildings, objects of war, art, advertising, sketches, graphics, etc.), certainly did unhesitatingly communicate a desire for quick transition from the dominant language of the time. Indeed by the 1980s, this current of disciplinary expansiveness had similarly led Jean-Claude Guédon and Botond Bognar to argue that architecture has in fact ceased to occupy a finite domain—its boundaries becoming ever more dissipated as the definition of what architecture is continues to evolve and expand. (Ostwald 1999)

This eagerness to embrace other disciplinary knowledge has for the most part passed over the theories of aural architecture, developed by Blesser and Salter in their 2007 book *Spaces speak, are you listening?*, and soundscape, as posited by Schafer in his 1977 monograph *The Soundscape*. (Schafer 1977) At least since the publication of Schafer's manifesto on the notion of the sounding environment, architecture has been overtly concerned with innate philosophical theories of space and of being. In what Shane Murray sees as the "high theory years" (Murray 2005) of the 1980s and 1990s, with their pursuit of Jacques Derrida's theory of deconstruction, and Deleuze and Guattari's notion of the fold, the more recent proclamations of Patrik Schumacher have given rise to the notion of "parametricism." (Schumacher 2012) These explorations similarly compete with more generalized notions of Marcos Novak, Greg Lynn and other digital provocateurs regarding the possibilities of the *datascape*. But the avoidance of acoustic theory as an augmentation of architecture, particularly as an opportunity for the integration of a semiotics of sound, has highlighted what Geoffrey Broadbent has argued as the common need of architecture to seek out meaning in form. As Broadbent notes, "architects worldwide have been striving again to build meanings into their buildings, yet few seem to know that semiotic principles could help them." (Broadbent 1994, p. 74)

This is not to suggest that there has been little interest in the uptake of acoustic knowledge and acoustic effects and affects into architectural design outside of the concert hall, as is evidenced in the numerous project works explored in previous chapters of this book. What is apparent though, in these experimentations with sounds and architecture, is the seeming intuitive deflection of questions regarding the role of conceptualizing space as in sounds, or sounds as in space, as questions that should ideally arise from the architectural program, from the site context—that is, from a disciplinary-specific position regarding the function of the architectonic and of site-specificity. This distinction perhaps alludes to the restrictions of both aural architecture and soundscape as ostensively firmly based in their respective notions of sounds as capable of illuminating space (as expounded by aural architecture), as opposed to the notion that sounds are wholly capable of producing space (commonly argued by soundscape theory). Here then the fundamental difference, and indeed the limiting canvass to a wider dispersion of each conceptualization into myriad architectural environments, discourses and practices, is the axiom that sounds are either a viable design parameter and available as utilities to augment the architectonic articulation of space (most commonly through the suggested use of loudspeakers), or are architectonic objects in themselves, free to produce ephemeral architectures, programs and an architectural experience as an agency, even at the risk of alienating the context of the surrounding built environment, or even the program of the site.

Aural architecture

As with the pairing of the approaches and ideas of the study of traditional room acoustics with environmental psychology, it is in Blesser and Salter's theory of aural architecture that questions are raised regarding the notion of where architecture stops and where room acoustics begins. The theory seeks to problematize this boundary, this traditional demarcation between design as a composition of spatial elements — of objects, surfaces, typologies, forms — and room acoustics as an analysis of the behaviors of sounds in regard to such compositions, such collections of designed artifacts. This is achieved through suggesting a causal logic that exists between those inherent connectors, materiality, spatial volume and sound sources, and what Blesser and Salter argue as a need for an increased "auditory spatial awareness" among the technologically mediated general population in the Western world. Aural architecture then is a designate of the

> properties of a space that can be experienced by listening. An aural architect, acting as both artist and social engineer, is therefore someone who selects specific aural attributes of a space based on what is desirable in a particular cultural framework. With skill and knowledge, an aural architect can create a space that induces such feelings as exhilaration, contemplative tranquility, heightened arousal, or a harmonious and mystical connection to the cosmos. An aural architect can create a space that encourages or discourages social cohesion among its inhabitants. (Blesser & Salter 2007, p. 5)

Of course, Steven Holl's long-held argument that architecture is an inherently multisensory experience that encompasses all the senses places Blesser and Salter's emphasis solely on the auditory channel as one that might be considered of limited enterprise — a type of phenomenology only for the blind or visually impaired. As Holl acknowledges, "architecture more fully than other art forms, engages the immediacy of our sensory perceptions. The passage of time; light, shadow and transparency; color phenomena, texture, material and detail all participate in the complete experience of architecture." (Holl et al. 2006, p. 41) But to counter such accusations, while at the same time noting architecture's fixation with visual forms, two key terms, active aural embellishment and passive aural embellishment, are introduced by Blesser and Salter as a means to accentuate that fact that architectonic form may encourage particular acoustic behaviors:

> Architecture includes aural embellishments in the same way that it includes visual embellishments. For example, a space we encounter might contain water sprouting from a fountain, birds singing in a cage, or wind chimes ringing in a summer breeze — active sound sources functioning as active aural embellishments for that space. [...] In contrast, passive aural embellishments, such as interleaved reflecting and absorbing panels that produce spatial aural texture, curved surfaces that focus sounds, or resonant alcoves that emphasize some frequencies over others, create distinct and unusual acoustics by passively influencing incident sounds. (Blesser & Salter 2007, p. 51)

Here then are the most acute aspects of the theory of aural architecture. The physical articulation of space and the materiality of form have marked effects on the acoustic behavior of sound sources. Geometry, spatial volume and materiality sum in ways that create unique acoustic signatures that enable definitive auditory experiences given

Parameter	Subjective listener aspect
G	Level of sound (dB)
EDT	Perceived reverberance (s)
C_{80}	Perceived clarity of sound (dB)
LFC	Apparent source width
LG_{80}	Listener envelopment (dB)

Table 4. Common room acoustic parameters: G = sound strength, EDT = early decay time, C_{80} = clarity, LFC = early lateral energy, LG_{80} = late lateral sound level

the function of particular sound sources within a site and the site's program. This is a rather elementary aspect for the discipline of room acoustics, whose field is concerned primarily with the auditory measurement and evaluation of architectural designs. Perhaps the innovative nature of active and passive aural embellishments for architectural praxis then is the simplification of acoustic concepts that can be often lost within the scientific language of assessing acoustic parameters such as T-30 (reverberation time) and LG (listener envelopment). Though the concept of an active aural embellishment as a design parameter that illuminates the auditory qualities of architecture is rudimentary and perhaps somewhat reductionist in scope, it serves the greater purpose of instilling the importance Blesser and Salter place on their concept of a "spatial auditory awareness."

But their argument that aural architecture is a newly founded field is to partly disown the mid-twentieth-century rise in digital technologies, and in particular the shift from acoustic space as wholly a function of the physical articulation of space (that is, sounds in space) to it becoming independent, or a generator of space (space in sounds) through acoustic simulation and the rise of computer-assisted auditory analysis and prediction. The notion of aural architecture as a concept indeed would suggest, as Penelope Dean argues, that "the recent and radical expansion in design activities over the past thirty years" has produced a significant "impact on the identity of architecture itself." (Dean 2012, p. 35) But it is the attempted forging of a parallel discipline to architecture that perhaps most marginalizes Blesser and Salter's theory of aural architecture as an influencing force for canonic upheaval within the discipline. Indeed, the opportunity to extend the conceptual underpinnings of aural architecture as one potentially bolstered through an engagement with the vast edifice of extant theoretical discourse in architecture becomes, disappointingly, a lost opportunity. In fact, the power of such potentials has already been suggested by Jeffrey Kipnis, who using the example of Mozart, a composer who masterfully imported myriad extramusical exotic influences, effortlessly created an unmistakably unique and innovative musical style. (Kipnis 1995) That aural architecture then is privy to its own marginalizing within architecture, yet equally keen to be recognized for its catalytic pronouncements, is also particularly telling in light of how K. Michael Hayes argues that architecture's "primary task is the construction of concepts and subject positions rather than the making of things," (Hayes 2010, p. 1) a commentary that appears to suggest the usefulness of developing new ways of conceiving architecture in light of the auditory.

Given the scope of the rise of recent digital technologies to allow for any number of acoustic spaces to be simulated and experienced via headphone or other multichannel (multiple loudspeaker) listening formats, aural architecture necessarily becomes then a representation of space that moves beyond the purely functional notion of an extant physical environment. Is spatial music then, in electroacoustic or spatialized acoustic formats, a form of aural architecture? For Blesser and Salter, musical space is a subset of the space that aural architecture encompasses, and an important precursor to the appreciation and application of exemplar acoustic qualities to the more tangible articulations within the built environment. The authors nominate those often-cited exemplars of the unification between spatial electroacoustic music and architectural form, such as Bornemann and Stockhausen's Osaka auditorium as well as Xenakis and Le Corbusier's 1958 Philips pavilion at the Brussels World Fair. At Brussels, like the later Osaka multimedia space, Le Corbusier collaborated with Xenakis to create a multichannel, immersive sound, light and filmic experience in which moving images were projected onto the interior surfaces. Xenakis composed the spatial electroacoustic composition *Concrete PH* for the pavilion, which was also accompanied by Edgard Varèse's *Poème électronique* and projected across over 425 loudspeakers in 11 channels that lined the interior surfaces. Xenakis later commented that the effect of the sound projection within the interior was of "lines of sound moving in complex paths from point to point in space, like needles darting from everywhere." (Rowell 1984, p. 241) Le Corbusier had initially developed the plan of the space after the form of a human stomach, for which Xenakis "completed" (or perhaps complemented) the design with an elevation constituted of hyperbolic paraboloids that delivered the building's unique and striking envelope.

As Blesser and Salter allude to, the aural architecture of the Brussels pavilion then seems readily apparent, though one actuated primarily through musically crafted sounds whose spatial projection and compositional form followed the principles of musical aesthetics. The architecture of the pavilion served or facilitated the delivery of

Figure 49. The Philips pavilion *at Expo 58*, a collaboration between Xenakis and Le Corbusier

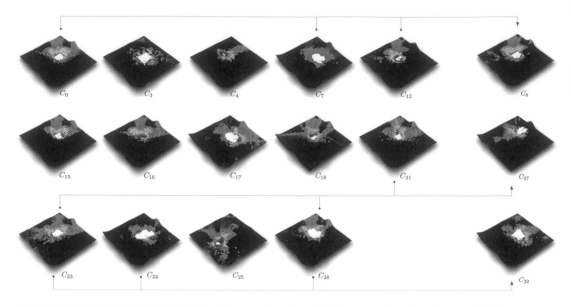

Figure 50. Acoustic simulation and prediction of topographic surfaces. Grid responses for each surface predict SPL (sound pressure levels) for a line source of 75 dB in a free-field condition. Color range of 2 × 2 meter squares from red (high energy/loud) to black (lowest energy/quiet). Given a homogeneous materiality among the surfaces, topographic features greatly influence the listening experience.

thematic content that was bound to musical narratives. Thus the architectonic dimensions and materiality of the pavilion were not in themselves designed to evoke aural architectures. It merely acted as a conduit, or perhaps instrument or vessel for ephemeral electroacoustic events designed by the composers whose works it performed, and subsequently delivered via technological mediation—that is, multichannel loudspeaker sound diffusion. This means then that for aural architecture, designers need to consider the ways in which auditory behaviors might be encoded into architectonic form (with or without technological mediation), such that an imagining of the auditory properties and qualities of a space not yet inhabited or lived in might be perceived from a plan or physical model. What is dutifully required then is Blesser and Salter's call for an "auditory spatial awareness" as tool to fill the gap of the traditional role of the room acoustician. Thus, an awareness is seen as an invitation to generating a framework for listening, which itself is akin perhaps to Pallasmaa's notion of "heightened awareness," in which a sound source, as carrier of a temporal continuum, partners the embedded visual impression of the architectonic articulation. But Blesser and Salter go further by proposing how the specifics of a tripartite encounter of sensation (detection), perception (recognition) and effect (meaningfulness) provide a basis by which an external environment becomes an internalized auditory experience.

Accordingly, this complex set of interactions between sensation, perception and effect cannot be completely premeditated during the design concept stage of architecture as a human-internalized aural image. Perhaps then what sets aural architecture apart from other traditions of design is its fundamental reliance on computer modeling as the true means by which the aural attributes and the aural experience of a space can be predicted and a simulation (or auditory model) consequently constructed. As a pioneer in the development of the first commercially available artificial reverberation unit (the EMT 250 from 1976), Blesser's background here in applied acoustics belies the approach taken in the theory of aural architecture, in which the sociocultural aspects of the formation of acoustic space are read as the measure by which the architectural design ought to respond. This argument is further elaborated through their account of the historical record of designed auditory space, particularly in concert halls, where over centuries a process of trial and error, an almost Darwinian approach, fostered the best designs as copies and slight modifications to the existent exemplars. But the rise of digital technologies and computation has enabled new forms of auditory prediction, optimization and auralization to emerge that have radically changed the manner in which auditory space is conceived and designed. That there is then a necessary reliance on modern computation for designing auditory space suggests that there is also a potential for a dissipation between those traditional spheres of acoustic modeling and architectural modeling: a situation that Michael Ostwald might nominate as an example of the "hybridisation" between acoustic theory and architectural praxis. (Ostwald 1999, p. 61) Indeed, the striking direction that architectural computing has taken on the generation of form, and what Mark Burry notes as the computer's ability to foresee forms that could never have been human-internally visualized (Burry 2011), seems a platform equally poised for the discovery of unknown auditory experiences and thus new meaningful relationships between architecture, site and program. But if the emphasis of aural architecture seems a natural fit to the idea of architecture as an act of spatial composition (at least superficially), whether the materials used are ephemeral or tangible, the question remains of how, and by what means, the traditional materials of the built environment must be summed and combined to achieve an exemplary or meaningful auditory status, and moreover, how will these manifestations address the auditory expectations and listening habits of the intended end-users?

It may seem then that though the focus of aural architecture supports what I have nominated as three of the facets that form the metric (as assemblage) that defines the acoustic horizon, texture (active aural embellishment) and the pairing of form and vicariously materiality (passive aural embellishment), it somewhat deflects the notion of program and structure in favor of a more generalized notion of attuned listening strategies (spatial auditory awareness) and the sociocultural history and significance of acoustic space. But if the notion of aural architecture is a solid embrace of the relationship between sounds and the spaces they inhabit, in soundscape theory, a refocusing on sounds themselves brings us back to a rereading of texture and structure and, to a degree, program.

Soundscape

If sounds then are the illuminators of aural architecture, they are congruently the space-makers of soundscape theory. In Schafer's notion of soundscape, there is an acknowledgment that each sonic environment that can be heard (whether natural, urban, simulated, musical or otherwise) is dependent on the discreet nature of sound sources to generate a particular semiotic schema between source and receiver. Schafer derived the term *soundscape* from the word *landscape* as a provocation against the contention that a landscape constitutes all objects within the visible environment—a soundscape then represents all auditory phenomena within a given environment. But as Blesser and Salter note, "with a soundscape, the sounds themselves are important in themselves [...] [whereas] aural architecture emphasizes sound primarily as illumination." (Blesser & Salter 2007, p. 16) This distinction also gives rise to the fact that Schafer views the constituent elements of a soundscape as an acoustic ecology, and therefore to study the sounds of an environment is to seek to understand that environment's ecological dimensions. But Schafer's focus on sounds of human-made and natural environments as carriers of information, and similarly, as mediators between a listener and an environment leads to the theory's de-emphasis of the spatial context of the sound sources, of its program, form and materiality. This particular de-emphasis of the physical context and refocus on the semiotics of sounds and their texture and structure, particularly in the urban environment, has meant that the discipline of acoustic ecology has forged a unique methodology for the analysis and classification of sounds as a means to better understand how the soundscape helps construct ideas about place.

The alignment of the discipline of acoustic ecology towards the rigorous analysis of the sounding environment would seem at odds with the creative direction of its founder, R. Murray Schafer, an internationally recognized composer and environmental activist. But the ideas of Schafer were a result of a multidisciplinary investigation into noise within the urban environment, first initiated at Simon Fraser University (Vancouver, B.C.) in the late 1960s:

> The home territory of soundscape studies will be the middle ground between science, society and the arts. From acoustics and psychoacoustics we will learn about the physical properties of sound and the way sound is interpreted by the brain. From society, we will learn how mankind behaves with sounds and how sounds affect and change this behavior. (Schafer 1977, p. 4)

Barry Truax has argued that a soundscape then represents not merely the presence of an acoustic environment—which could be natural (located) or simulated (dislocated)—but also the potential of such an environment to communicate information to a listener. (Truax 2001) As the two most prominent theorists active within the field of acoustic ecology, the field that grew out of soundscape theory, both Truax and Schafer have argued that, in particular, natural environments and their acoustic behaviors produce particularly meaningful experiences to auditors, and thus the sounds within them constitute a type of mediating language between listener and environment. Given that the ubiquitous and immersive nature of sonic events perpetuates just about every corner of our daily lives, and that discrete meaning is communicated through a plethora of functional and nonfunctional sounds, is a cause that Schafer argues presents architecture with a pressing, albeit largely overlooked resource.

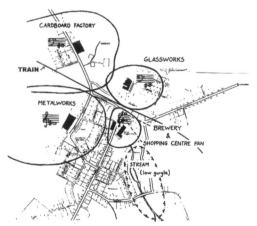

Figure 51. Diagram of the frequencies (as musical pitches) of hums (keynote sounds) heard from industrial sites in the Swedish town of Skruv

The power of soundscape theory then is perceived in its latent suggestion that new modes of communication for architecture exist, and moreover, that there is a potential for generating new and meaningful relationships between people and the built environment. Indeed, Schafer and the discipline of acoustic ecology have attempted to use this firstly as leverage to better understand and classify the urban acoustic environment, and secondly, as a catalyst for a redesign of the urban acoustic environment of the future.

Figure 52. Cover design of the CD *The Vancouver Soundscape, 1973*

Like the theory of aural architecture, the study of a soundscape is a phenomenological study of the environment, though cast exclusively via the auditory channel: as Hildegard Westerkamp notes, a listener is situated *within* the soundscape. Acoustic ecologists categorize this immersion via a new terminology that formalizes the taxonomy of a soundscape—the terms *soundmark, keynote* and *signal* being its primary syntactic communicators. This new terminology attempts to document classes of sounds regarding their semiotics, and these three fundamental classes enable a rather broad investigation into what is being communicated to an acoustic community: that is, those auditors actively listening to sounds and immersed within a particular acoustic arena.

Soundmarks are those sounds that are considered culturally significant or deemed by an acoustic community to warrant preservation (such as church/temple bells, town square clocks, foghorns), while keynote sounds are those which are continuously operable within a site and form a background (e.g., traffic, air-conditioner sounds, Muzak). Sound signals represent foregrounded sounds within a soundscape and thus may dynamically change and include local soundmarks, though as Truax (1999) and Jean-François Augoyard (1995) have noted, within modern cities the increase in the sound pressure level and electronic nature of emergency warning signals is a direct consequence of the increased noise floor level of urban spaces. Truax also argues that within urban environments, because keynote sounds are overwhelmingly generated through mechanical means (and thus occupy predictable frequency bands), they are contributing to the masking of historical soundmarks and thus producing lo-fi (low-fidelity) auditory environments.

The larger goals of Schafer and the acoustic ecology movement have been not only to examine the qualities of a soundscape, but to also use this effort as a means to ascertain whether there are reoccurring patterns that point towards exemplary soundscape designs. The work of Bernie Krause in bioacoustics and his "auditory niche theory" (Krause 2008) certainly provides an important pointer towards the composition of pristine natural soundscapes and their qualities. But for Truax and Schafer, there is a greater desire for the soundscape of the urban environment to become an exemplary auditory design space. This desire for urban planners and architects to utilize soundscape concepts within their design processes has attracted criticism though, and not only from within the discourses of design theory, but also from the field of anthropology.

For Tim Ingold, the question of soundscape as a design parameter within the built environment is not the hairy question so much as is the very notion of soundscape itself. As an anthropologist, Ingold objects to the concept that the landscape should be further divided in "scapes," and contends that the experience of space is a multi-sensory one for which the very idea of a separate agency awarded to acoustic phenomena destroys Schafer and Truax's deeply held notion of the ecological importance of soundscape studies. Sound designer and theorist Sophie Arkette similarly cites their misguided assumption on the nature of silence within the city, noting that

> Schafer and his colleagues are apt to condemn cities for eroding silence. Their ecological approach appears to treat silence as an endangered species; something that must be preserved by maintaining habitats for its incubation and growth. (Arkette 2004, p. 166)

Arkette sees the critique of acoustic ecologists against the elevated sound levels of cities as a complete misreading of the nature of city sounds, the inherent semiotics of city spaces and their dynamics. As such, she read this as a stance based on a romantic idea of the pastoral becoming a stand-in for an auditory utopia in which current technologically mediated space represents a malformed and misshaped entity that requires tuning. Thus the idea of tuning may imply the act of acoustic attenuation or amelioration, an approach that Ursula Franklin advocates through her call for the instigation of "silent commons" within cities. (Franklin 2000) Contending that the appreciation of silence is at stake within the urban environment leads Franklin to note that the impact of technology has created both new opportunities and hazards for the qualities of the postmodern city soundscape. Indeed, there is more than a passing interest in the impact of technology within the discipline of soundscape studies regarding the auditory experience of cities. For Paul Carter though, the notion of silence or the natural acoustic environment as a type of auditory Eden easily attracts the same criticisms as those leveled at Borgmann and his notion of the device paradigm and the need for a return to "focal things and practices" such as reading and gardening. (Borgmann 1984) Carter notes that

> any research program that takes a notion of harmony or reharmonisation as its ground and goal risks recapitulating the nostalgic trope which, already in the early 17th century according to Francis Bacon, characterised the empirical sciences, and which, in repairing fallen appearances, has as its goal the restoration of Paradise. (Carter 2003, p. 12)

Carter's most compelling observation on the discipline of soundscape studies lies in the way in which he reads its use of technology, and how its use has created a fracture, essentially splitting the discipline into two camps. The first contains sound activists whose implicit objective is

> ameliorative, to draw attention to a neglected dimension of the everyday world, and, by appealing to the listener's musical sensibilities, to enlist support for its preservation and protection. Another camp, mainly represented by anthropologists

and historians, regards acoustic ecology primarily as a strategic tool for resisting the visualism of Western analytical thinking. Applied to diverse cultures and historical periods, it unveils dimensions of social and cultural signification that a deaf perusal would inevitably miss. (Carter 2003, p.12)

Perhaps what Arkette and Carter identify most critically about soundscape studies' apparent readiness to present itself as a utility to urban planning and architecture is the discipline's emphasis, and thus potentially alienating stance, on the aesthetics of sound as consumed wholly within a music-centric discourse in spite of its great desire to be ubiquitous within architectural discourse. Indeed, the derivation of the idea of keynote from Western art music's notion of the functional harmonics of a home key or base tonality betrays the ease with which the practice of musical soundscape composition arose. Given the less problematic definition of aural architecture for anticipating novel types of tangible spatial designs potentially contained by the architectonic, a soundscape is, by contrast, any sounding environment. This may include then environments created through piecing together collected field recordings: works also known as soundscape compositions. Many of the electronic and electroacoustic soundscape compositions of Truax and Westerkamp thus function as virtual acoustic experiences in that they suggest acoustic spaces that may never be completely formed, built or realized outside the electronic music studio—space then becomes constructed through the sounds, and potentially acquiescent to a preconceived musical narrative.

It may be surprising therefore that there is a continued effort of the discipline of acoustic ecology to turn towards the generation of soundscape compositions as legitimate products that represent an influential currency for acoustic change in architecture or urban design. Certainly the presentation of such approaches has some tangible effects, especially as a means to enact new modes of listening, but as projective or imagined essays in sounds, they may suffer a fate of being misunderstood, or remaining in the eyes of architecture as ever tied to the aesthetics of a musical discourse from which they are strongly fettered. But given the musical backgrounds of the many active figures within the discipline, such approaches would seem logical. If soundscape composition though has found an assured footing in acoustic ecology, it is certainly the catalyst by which a shift has taken place towards the preeminence of the making of soundscapes rather than the theorizing on soundscapes. But in this deemphasizing of the critical in acoustic ecology and a focus on the making we find a curious parallel to that which Sarah Whiting and Robert Somol have argued as architecture's next great need. (Somol & Whiting 2005)

For Somol and Whiting, the end of architectural criticism, and its ties to a small group of highly influential North American architectural thinkers and practitioners, is a call to embrace making once again, to build a transformative and projective practice. By arguing that the last twenty years of architectural discourse have been consumed with criticality, they set out "to provide an alternative to the now dominant paradigm" (Somol & Whiting 2010, p. 192) by reclaiming design as that which "keeps architecture from slipping into a cloud of heterogeneity." (Somol & Whiting 2010, p. 197) But the incorporation of soundscape theory into modes of practice outside of soundscape composition and into the making of architecture has found a somewhat limited currency. It still remains a surprising advocacy that the fields of acoustics and applied acoustics have in the last half a dozen years become the main proponents for the adaptation of the theory of soundscape into frameworks intended to guide future urban design. (Adams et al. 2006) While the thirty or more years since Schafer's development of acoustic ecology has seen the discipline focused primarily on soundscape composition and the preservation and documentation of important natural and cultural soundscapes, the recent interest by the field of acoustics has highlighted what Truax correctly anticipated as the necessity for assessing not only the physics of sound (through the energy transfer model) within an environment, but also the semiotics of sound (what Truax calls the "communicational model"). (Truax 2001)

This newfound interest has moved the field of soundscape studies into a new territory that relies more heavily on the scientific method that Blesser and Salter outline in their tripartite model of sensation, perception and effect. The most recent work then that utilizes the concepts of Schafer, Truax and others in the field of acoustic ecology tends towards the deployment of metrics to describe an urban soundscape, and the development of predictors for gauging the perception of ideal soundscapes among users of a site. (Yu & Kang 2009) Traditionally, soundscape research has relied on the concept of an expert aesthetic listener, their documentation of an auditory environment and their mapping and description of its qualities. For acousticians, a methodology that investigates the nature of human perception of sound within the urban realm, and among human participants (who are not necessarily expert listeners), has been more of a focus, as have large studies that qualify what are engaging or preferred soundscapes for an acoustic community within an urban environment. (Zhang & Kang 2007)

Much of this research though has been locked up within the discourses of acoustics and applied acoustics, even though to the same ends as the acoustic ecology movement's hotly anticipated rapid dissemination desires, here, too, numerous frameworks and proposals for the immediate uptake of soundscape design guidelines for urban planners and architects have been presented. (Kang 2010) That architectural discourse has yet to fully see these strong postulations from the field of either acoustics or acoustic ecology only seems to highlight deep-felt differences regarding the methods of presentation, the utility of information and the language of dissemination regarding such diverse fields. The traditional separation between architectural design and acoustics has been one forged not only through the function of each discipline (acoustic measurement versus spatial composition), but also through the language and methods by which knowledge is assessed, understood and disseminated within each field.

But for acoustician Bert de Coensel and colleagues' 2010 urban planning project in Antwerp, the theory of soundscape became an ascendant to negate any ulterior reliance on preconceived musical aesthetics that might drive design decisions. By focusing on local residents' perceptions of sound and noise within the project site, de Coensel sought to influence the housing design so as to provide for a future idealized soundscape that meaningfully connects residents to their built environment. Here, soundscape theory became a valuable directive to guide the earliest stages of the project. By using a range of approaches including end-user site questionnaires, noise maps (Figure 53), acoustic modeling and SWOT (strengths, weaknesses, opportunities, threats) analysis, a series of design scenarios were proposed for the housing estate that sought to greatly influence the quality and presence of particular sounds that were important to residents. (de Coensel et al. 2010) Other design measures that were

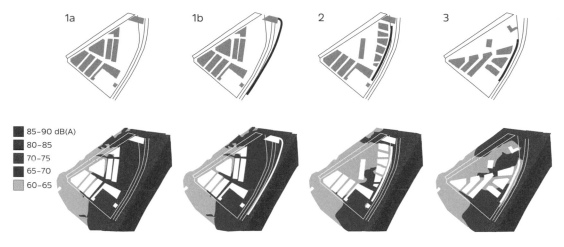

Figure 53. Bert de Coensel's four projective planning scenarios (1a, 1b, 2, 3) for a housing development in Antwerp with corresponding SPL noise map calculated for sounds from a nearby freeway

suggested included the concept of a quiet side to the housing estate optimized through the geometry of roof shapes and facades covered with climbing plants combined with planted green roofs so as to improve acoustic insulation and limit acoustic diffraction. Similarly, a nearby urban park was earmarked for various types of greenery and ground coverage as well as optimizing topography as a means for spectral fine-tuning of the soundscape of nearby transport infrastructures.

Critical listening

What then of the role of critical listening? As I envisage it, its role here becomes one of mediator, as it is covertly conceived as a working meta-theory that positions both aural architecture and soundscape as part of the taxonomy that is created by its formal ontology. That is to say that what both aural architecture and soundscape abide by and possess is an explicit, and at times implicit, focus on listening as a fundament of the architectural experience. Listening is a vessel of sensation and of Serres's boxes and is thus enfolded in architecture, the architectonic and all other lived environments that articulate space. We experience these sensations through Ingold's knots, the acoustic horizon, the acoustic arena and those disturbances on the grid of the infinite plane. As a meta-theory (that is, a theory of theories) of perhaps the two most important conceptualizations of sound and space to emerge in the later half of the twentieth century, critical listening is but a framework that unobtrusively unites ideas inherent in both aural architecture and soundscape. Though they seem superficially at odds with each other, their common espousal of new modes of listening is only offset by the intransigence each seems to possess regarding where to locate architecture within them—if indeed there is a core for which one can locate a discipline. Perhaps this is what has hindered each the most, that somehow they are envisaged to be rightly juxtaposed onto architecture, rather than to grow from within the architectural discourse. Critical listening is a proposition then in which a deeper examination of sound and space only serves to accentuate how aural architecture and soundscape theory are born from the same root. It explicitly seeks out such a path by questioning exactly where the

Figure 54. The 1923 version of the *Bauhaus Teaching Diagram*

architectural is located within the two theories, as both overtly claim to be in correspondence with the discipline of architecture, yet seem ineffective communicators of their reputed persuasiveness, particularly in terms of the promise of new models of design. Congruently, critical listening also seeks to provide a more direct interface with architecture, its acoustic typologies, its architectonic features and the notion of sensation by attempting to engage in the theory of architecture and of architectural discourse.

Interestingly, there is a certain parallel that has played out between what Hollein sought in his editorship of *Bau*, and what Blesser and Salter have argued as the ubiquity of aural architecture and our influence over it. Though it was Le Corbusier who had firstly claimed in 1931 that "Tout est Architecture," (Le Corbusier 1988, p. 111) it was in the magazine format that Hollein saw *Bau* as "a vessel for desires that looked to exceed the confinement of contemporary architecture altogether, [by] publishing manifestos that looked to radically expand architecture's definition." (Buckley 2007, p. 109) The parallels to Blesser and Salter reside in their similarly counter attitudes to the status quo as a forthright goal of their theory. As the authors acknowledge, "in a very real sense, we are all aural architects. We function as aural architects when we select a seat in a restaurant, organize a living space, or position loudspeakers." (Blesser & Salter 2007, p. 6) It might seem then that the everyman aspect of aural architecture is equally capable, or indeed destined, to produce the Emmentaler of the auditory—which is certainly what Robert Woodbury has suggested in his assessment of the divide between designers as "amateurs" in regard to developing useful and reusable strategies in design computation and programming. (Woodbury 2010, p. 9) Indeed, the ongoing difficulties of producing a world-class interior acoustic to match the striking innovations of the facade of the Sydney Opera House attest to the fact that the Emmentaler need not be confined to the rise of the amateur. (Taylor & David Claringbold 2010) If then for Hollein "Alles ist Architektur," we might also believe that this "everything" also creates a subsequent aural architecture—of which we are all agents for its manipulation (regardless of skills or acumen). But what then of the somewhat marginalized notion of program in regard to aural architecture and soundscape theory? Though the divide between the two theories can be explicated through the nominated facets of texture and structure (favored by soundscape theory) as opposed to form and materiality (emphasized by aural architecture), it is through program, and indeed, most importantly, the idea of the assemblage of these facets that critical listening primarily operates as meta-theory.

To consider though the meta-theory of critical listening as a centering between architecture, the concept of the grid and its sonnified knots of disturbance, and similarly the metrics of the assemblage that defines the acoustic horizon, finds a curious parallel in Zeynep Çelik Alexander's reading of the 1922 *Bauhaus Teaching Diagram* of

Walter Gropius. The diagram served to present the pedagogical approach of the early design school in which at its core was architecture (*Bau*). The first six months concentrated students on both fine and applied arts and consolidated this through the activity simply named *Gestaltung* (design). But following on from this was a three-year course that offered

> hands-on experience in the workshops, a valiant attempt—informed by the aesthetics of Gottfried Semper—to radically reconfigure artistic fields in accordance with materials and techniques—stone, wood, metal, weaving, color, glass, or sound … (Alexander 2012, p. 85)

What is intriguing here are the ramifications, or albeit the opportunity of perhaps usurping Çelik Alexander's mistranslation of *Ton* as meaning sound. In one instance the meaning of *Ton* is sound, as in *Tonmeister* (sound engineer) for example, but within the context of the Bauhaus diagram its other meaning of "clay" (as one of the seven nominated materials) is more obviously correct. But rather than seeking to find a critique in such a slight typographical error, it provides somewhat of a more instrumental avenue to consider, even within the confines of the diagram itself, of the relationship between clay and sound and the context of how materiality and the other facets within critical listening as meta-theory can be further codified.

It may indeed seem almost logical to present *Ton* as relating to sound in the context of the other materials of the diagram—stone, wood, metal, *Gewebe* (textiles), glass—given that *Farbe* (color) is also included. This perhaps reinforces then the position of soundscape theory: that sound is like a material, it is like clay in that it can be formed, composed and, moreover, enables the generation of spaces through its dynamic qualities and its semiotics. Thus the focus on texture in soundscape theory through the production of soundscape compositions reminds us of the qualities of the visceral connections we inhabit in our encounters with materials such as wood, stone and metal. That *Ton* as sound might hold an equal right to be represented within Gropius's pedagogical diagram alongside other more common materialities is suggestive too of the relation between architecture (*Bau*) and those materials in which it embodies myriad articulations of space. If a building can articulate its presence and typology through brickwork, so too can it generate an acoustic typology through its sound profile and the acoustic arenas that it curates—we might then truly perceive an architecture of sounds.

But if sound might be considered in the same way as clay, in which the facets of texture and structure bring to it the capacity for the temporal, for an unfolding, sound might also be, as Blesser and Salter allude, simply considered as sound. That the linguist Ferdinand de Saussure had similarly identified the "mistaking [of] the written image of a sound for the sound itself" (de Saussure 2011, p. 30) provides a useful and analogous construct. As distinct from soundscape theory, aural architecture concerns itself less with the sound as an image unto itself, and more with the context it unfolds in and interacts with. The function of critical listening then is as Johanna Drucker asserts in her assessment of Saussure's argument: it is a common approach to place "these two domains … into a relation of dependence," and in fact, "each can and does, in many situations, function independently, preserving its own autonomy and specificity." (Drucker 1997, p. 20) Whereas Saussure was concerned with the notion of the written image of a sound and the sound itself, the domains of critical listening then are the semiotics of sounds and the architectonic or environmental context in which they are found and within which they unfold.

We might consider that aural architecture is thus contingent on the separation of the domains in which sounds as objects, as self-referential agents bound to a sign, a meaning, are somewhat dislocated in favor of a consideration of their contexts and that which influences their propagation. As a meta-theory, critical listening thus identifies the two modified domains of Saussure's model as the sound which possesses a meaning and is communicated through the program and sound profile (of which its taxonomy can be described in terms of texture and structure) and the architectural or environmental context replete with appropriations of form and materiality that produce particular acoustic signatures and typologies. Crucially, critical listening positions these two domains as generating interactions, a symbiosis, and an interpenetrating influence towards each other, while still potentially unfolding independently. These two fundaments can be understood as the use of sounds as simply to accompany architecture, as opposed to the design of sounds or a sound world that is of architecture or of a site—that is, site-specific or program-specific. This brings to the fore then the idea that the addition of sounds to a site may have an alienating effect on the experience if the sounds themselves do not partake in the very idea of the program. Thus the notion of an integration of nominally introduced sounds within an architectural context produces a hindrance towards any attempt to produce coherence between sound forms and architectural forms when the sound profile becomes an element that is post-rationalized.

But even from this position we find still a valuable conceptualization in Gropius's diagram. Sound, in one instance, as an illuminating presence then places the emphasis back towards the materiality and form of the core of the diagram, architecture as *Bau*. We can thus conceive the relationship between *Ton* and its behaviors regarding its neighboring sectors of materials on Gropius's wheel. From the reflective presence of reverberation from glass or stone to the absorbing qualities of *Gewebe*, the behaviors of *Ton* are contextualized both around the ring of materialities and through a direct contact to the core of the diagram. The meanings of sounds are thus contained within each *Ton* and may of course change given a reconfiguration of the ensuing architectonic containment, of the materiality and form, but are also agents unto themselves.

To reach an end, if that is a goal of any meta-theory, is perhaps to reach a point for which those conceptualizations and notions about structures of a system, of a theory, can be understood in holistic terms, or in a manner that elucidates predilections and characteristics of the investigated structure. As Michael Kimaid asserts, a meta-theory should ideally function to elucidate "a consideration of theoretical foundations, practical forms and functional utility." (Kimaid 2015, p. 26) It is through these types of assertions that particular types of investigative problems have arisen, for which interrogations into what Geoffrey Hunter describes as "the consistency, completeness (in various senses), decidability and independence" (Hunter 1973, p. 10) of the notions of a language, theory or system are commonly appraised. Consider then a diagrammatic representation of the relations between the notions of critical listening, aural architecture and soundscape theory (Figure 55). The figure, as an undirected acyclic graph, is also a partially ordered lattice (Willie 1982), in fact, it is a formal ontology that describes the taxonomy that is critical listening. The nodes (circles) of the diagram represent the formal concepts of the ontology (as a closed universe under investigation), with the apex occupied with the superconcept of critical listening. The two subconcepts located below and found through connecting vertices are the theories of aural architecture and soundscape theory. In the lattice too are objects (sitting directly beneath the nodes), which are connected to the formal concepts and produce local subsets of concept + object(s) that are again connected through vertices that indicate the larger subsets of the lattice. (Wolf 1994) Accordingly, the objects of {keynote sounds, signal, soundmark, structure, texture} are objects that are part of the subset that form the formal concept of "soundscape." Similarly, the formal concept of "aural architecture" has the single object of {passive aural embellishment} as its immediate element. Accordingly, then, the lowest objects of the lattice {acoustic arena, acoustic horizon, active aural embellishment}, because of the two vertices that connect them to the subconcepts of "soundscape" and "aural architecture," are common or shared elements of both concepts, and thus vicariously of critical listening. The notions of an active aural embellishment (that is, any heard sound), the acoustic horizon and the acoustic arena are of equal relevance to both soundscape theory and aural architecture. These objects are the intersecting elements between the two subconcepts, but similarly are also objects that fall under the superconcept of critical listening.

Of interest too perhaps are the uppermost objects that form the subset of critical listening as the superconcept of the lattice. The objects of {form, materiality, program} are not formally named in either the theory of aural architecture or soundscape theory as codified notions, as newly named terminologies, yet are implicitly present in their approaches to conceiving sound-space and are thus located sitting above, yet part

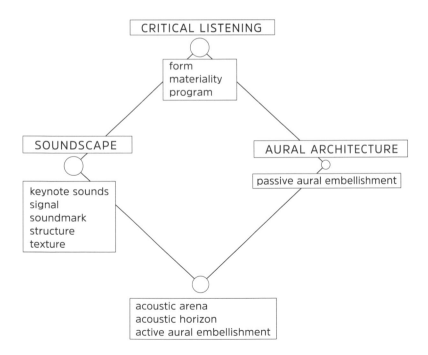

Figure 55. Diagram 1: Representation of the taxonomy of the meta-theory of critical listening

of, the subconcepts. Thus through the vertices leading upwards from both subconcepts, there exists a relation of hierarchy as {form, materiality, program} are of the powerset (the set of all subsets) of the lattice, and together with all the other objects map the complete taxonomy. (Priss 2006) To understand critical listening as a meta-theory then is to identify the objects of {form, materiality, program} for their distinguishing role in the hierarchy of the lattice while at the same recognizing that the facets of texture and structure, though conceived as part of the assemblage of the metric that defines the acoustic horizon, nevertheless have a shared relation to the analytic methodologies used by soundscape theory.

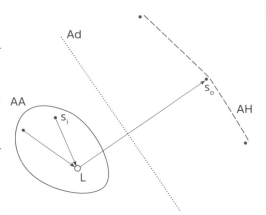

Figure 56. Diagram 2: On the relation between the acoustic arena and the acoustic horizon in terms of the architectonic demarcation of space. The presence of sound sources s_i (interior) and s_o (exterior) in relation to L (listener) points towards the perception of both an AH (acoustic horizon) and the immediate AA (acoustic arena) through the potential of an Ad (architectonic articulation of space).

Though I have not explicitly introduced here the reading of both the acoustic horizon and the acoustic arena for aural architecture and soundscape theory, as this was discussed previously, a diagram that visualizes its structure within the meta-theory of critical listening should suffice (Figure 56). While both theories lay claim to the importance of understanding, identifying and conceiving both the acoustic arena and acoustic horizon, both constructs are not explicitly addressed in terms of metrics, architecture, or the idea of the importance of site and program. As a meta-theory then, critical listening seeks an attendant inquiry into site, into program and into that which Stan Allen identifies in this way: "architecture—in both its artifacts and its practices—is uniquely tied to place in ways that other art forms are not." (Allen 2012, p. 83) But perhaps even more resolute is the consequence of conceptualizing critical listening through what K. Michael Hays argues as architecture's primary task as "the construction of concepts and subject positions," an obvious reference to what Deleuze and Guattari asserted in their final collaborative book, *What is Philosophy?* As Miguel de Beistegui alludes, the ultimate purpose that affords philosophy is, accordingly, that of

> posing the right problems and developing the concepts by means of which such problems can be solved. In this respect, concepts are valuable only to the extent that they allow us to designate specific problems and not mere generalities, events nor universal rules or essences. They must allow us to delimit and define situations that are themselves singular. (de Beistegui 2000, p. 5)

If, as Deleuze and Guattari argue, philosophy, and by proxy architecture, is but the creation of concepts, it thus distinguishes itself as a field because science then becomes concerned with the creation of functions on a "plane of reference." This may assist in conceptualizing how the uptake of much of the methods and terminology of soundscape theory has found its way into the science of acoustics, its discourse, and those functions of application (as rules, planning stipulations and remedial urban acoustic strategies) that are firmly situated on the plane of reference. Here then is how the meta-theory of critical listening might be perceived. Working as a concept itself, critical listening is a way of interrogating architecture and the architectonic in the sense that it seeks to examine the discourse of architecture as a currency by which the notions of architecture and its theoretical constructs can be challenged. Thus the "problems" of architecture as a generator of concepts are those oft-marginalized auditory aspects, the experience of hearing a building, or a yet-to-be-completed diagram of a future or speculative design. If architecture is itself about the creation of concepts rather than solely about the making of things, in deference to Whiting and Somol, it must also be about the imagined auditory experience of space as both are inseparable. To think then of architecture not only as an articulation of place, but similarly, as the production and curation of auditory space and of sensation, is to acknowledge that the edges of architecture do not end at the envelope of the building, whether this is a tangible or intangible border.

5
Re-hearing Icons of Architecture I.

Notation
Tuning
Pause / Play
Ad infinitum

Re-hearing Icons of Architecture I.

Notation

What is the sound of an architectural representation? We might consider that the traditional role of the architectural drawing—the sketch, plan and section—as representations of that which is to be constructed. They are guides that suggest the structure of the envisioned building: its form, scale and atmospheric qualities. They have traditionally been somewhat analogous to the musical score in that they are like a self-referential set of projections (or speculations perhaps) for what is to be made, as well as an overall impression of what the building will appear as. Like the score they disregard the materiality of the media on which they are inscribed, paper, parchment, an electronic collection of binary numbers that, when interpreted by a computer, enable a visualization of the drawing, of the vision. But as a set of projections, imagined or virtual perhaps, rather than explicitly named as existing wholly in the world, the architectural concept drawing or diagram does not require of itself a specificity in the way that an assembly drawing clearly maps out its constituent parts and the manner in which the elements are to be brought into synthesis. The architectural plan and section are instructions in the sense that they suggest what complexities may be required in the construction of the form and the structure. Yet they are also presented as a means to provide the idea of the building's visual conveyance, its countenance, its narrative, and a feeling for how the building will impress itself within the site, the context and the interplay between its forces and articulations of space and those in which it becomes embedded.

There are parallels then between what occurred in music in the early postwar period regarding new forms of representation in the musical score and those later architectural drawings, particularly by Daniel Libeskind and Bernard Tschumi, where

Figure 57. Excerpt from *Chamber Works, Architectural Meditations on Themes from Heraclitus*

the notion of drawing itself and its relationship to architecture became problematized and shifted. In Libeskind's twenty-eight drawings *Chamber Works, Architectural Meditations on Themes from Heraclitus*, we do not find any overt suggestions towards what an architectural outcome from an interpretation of the drawings might be, perhaps only what Libeskind describes as a "feeling" or atmosphere that they discretely embody. But if there are not any singular suggestions as to the nature of them as representations of future architectures, of habitable space, they are nonetheless composed of a nomenclature and a language of figures, lines, music-like symbols, checkerboards and other inscriptions that seem inherently architectural, given the manner in which they are combined and developed and populated across the page. James E. Young describes the twenty-eight drawings as intimately connected to the graphic experimentations of composers such as Arnold Schoenberg and John Cage in which "music, art, architecture and history all formed the interstices of these compositions. In these drawings, a complex of lines give way to empty space, which comes into view as the subject of these drawings, meant only to circumscribe spaces and show spaces as contained by lines." (Young 2001, p. 188) For Libeskind then, it is drawing and the inscription of the line that is the foundation of architecture. Robin Evans similarly identified the importance of this and indeed the notion of the compositional act of architectural representation as a core fundament:

> And it is true that the imaginative work of architecture has for a long time been accomplished almost exclusively through drawing, though manifested almost exclusively in building. The great peculiarity of architecture as a visual art (a peculiarity it nevertheless shares with orchestral, choral, operatic works and, to a lesser extent, film) is the considerable distance between the process of composition and the thing being composed. By truncating architecture and disposing of building, an intimacy between a way of designing and the thing designed is achieved. (Evans 1984, p. 94)

Here, the line and the drawing represent a discrete form of what Libeskind identifies as a type of knowing. But this type of knowing seems exposed or perhaps is brought out as an exposition in the *Chamber Works* in the manner that Evans identified as the intimacy of the act of drawing and the object being designed—by removing the specifics of the building, of a tangible or intended articulation of space, we are left with the innate power of the act itself. The architectural drawing is thus read not simply as a form of representation or proxy as a utility that points towards the instruments of building, of drawing, but is as a stimulus in and of itself. It becomes a means in which to question ideas and notions about the nature of architecture and of architectural representation. This might be considered too in terms of what Hyungmin Pai describes as the necessity of the diagram, as essentially a modern phenomenon, in which the subject exercises control over an object of knowledge. For Pai, the genius of the diagram, which can be traced to the myriad requirements of scientific management, "lies in the invention of a discursive code that organizes reality in order that it may be both visible and useable. Instrumentality rather than resemblance, is thus the essential criterion in defining a diagram." (Pai 2002, pp. 163–64) Thus to consider the *Chamber Works* as diagrams in such a paradigm is to also acknowledge that, while they provide both visibility and a certain usability, they similarly call on numerous ambiguities and a

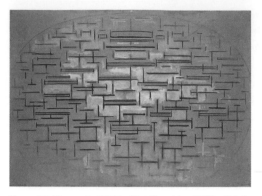

Figure 58. *Ocean 5*, 1917 by Piet Mondrian (1872–1944). Charcoal and gouache on wood-pulp wove paper, glued to Homosote panel.

dissolving of the traditional scientific notion of the separation of knowledge from practice in order that such knowledge, when abstracted within the confines and logic of a diagram, could essentially control practice.

Parallels are found then too within the early experimentations of the composer Earle Brown, particularly in his collection of scores titled *FOLIO* (1952–1954). Perhaps the most cited example of an early purely graphically notated musical work, *December 1952* (for any number of players) is composed wholly of lines, both vertical and horizontal, that given their differing widths and lengths, are suggestive of a not altogether homogeneous sound world to be created, or perhaps even a space for sounds to emerge from. Oft compared to Mondrian's mixed media work *Ocean 5*, it shares a similar approach in that the abstraction and use of lines points towards a "natural" or real-world source, in the case of Mondrian, the ocean, for Brown an imagined instrumental sound world. Indeed, in Brown's notes to the work, the composer suggests that the performer(s) consider the two-dimensional representation of the score as an invitation to inhabit a three-dimensional sound world, to create and produce a space from the score. This approach no doubt has its basis in Brown's acknowledgment of the importance of the radical formulations of composer and theorist Joseph Schillinger, whose system for musical composition and analysis was based on the thesis that music itself is a type of movement. (Schillinger 1949) Thus like Mondrian's representation of the waves and the atmosphere of the sea and of water in *Oceans 5*, the abstracting of the notation explicates how "the signs for the source have been reduced to their most essential pictorial form." (Flint 2016) But if Mondrian's work is a still representation of the fluidity of water, for Brown and *December 1952*, the performer is expected to directly engage and perform within the imagined fluidity of space created. Perhaps in a similar manner to the drawings of Libeskind then, Brown turned to the abstractness of the line as a means in which to present a fundamental notion, in this case, of an ensuing sound world that is purely suggestive by its avoidance of a prescribed method of realization:

The use of line drawings in my work goes back to my attempts in 1950 and 1951 to produce pieces in which decisions as to the validity and rational function of details, such as pitch and vertical correspondences (in general, the editorial aspects of composing), were minimized as much as possible, and the qualities of spontaneity and immediacy were considered to be the most direct and essential aspects of the work. It was an attempt to realize graphically the essence of the piece, the initial intuitive conception, before it was molded to conform to technical and aesthetic concepts of structure, form, continuity, art, beauty, and other acquired habits and prejudices of taste and training. (Brown 2004, p. 190)

What the *Chamber Works* and *December 1952* then share is not so much a common or imagined sound world, but the potential for the line, and the graphic representation as a language, to question the very approaches and canonic structures that have defined both the purpose and manner in which architecture and music have each been read, understood and independently conceived. In fact, Alessandra Capanna asserts that in the *Chamber Works* we find "a kaleidoscopic collection of lines and symbols that represent the same double axial structure of sounds; melody and/or chords, horizontal and/or vertical structure, regulated by the common principle of liberal variation," (Capanna 2009, p. 258) a similar reading that led Kurt Foster to call the drawings "spatial music." (Libeskind 1991)

This novel approach to redefining meaning in the architectural drawing is not dissimilar to what Frederick Kiesler argued: that there is a stasis and confinement in the standardization of activities and that, rather than approaching Louis Sullivan's much-flaunted paradigm of form to follow function, function should follow vision and vision follow reality. Thus the notion of functionalism as a deterministic structure, whether found in an architectural drawing or graphic musical score, has a potential to limit somewhat the expressiveness of the medium by restricting the interpretation to adhere to a canonic or routine (that is, expected) role:

> Functionalism is determinism and therefore stillborn. Functionalism is the standardization of routine activity. For example, a foot that walks (but does not dance); an eye that sees (but does not envision); a hand that grasps (but does not create). (Kiesler 1989, p. 57)

If we accept Brown's invitation to explore a three-dimensional world from a two-dimensional representation, we can then perhaps approach the *Chamber Works* in a nondeterministic way, as an opportunity to follow what Kiesler suggested as the "Law of Creative Transmutation," that is, the means by which to counter a stillborn functionalism. To engage in the drawings as open and nonspecific, yet latent with meaning, is to also identify what Evans sees among the passing glimpses of musical notations of crotchets and semibreves in the *Chamber Works* as a focus on the relationship between dashed and unbroken lines and the suggestion of a body, of a *corpus*. This is perhaps suggestive too of what the pre-Socratic Greek philosopher Heraclitus (of Libeskind's title) saw as the need for a unification of opposites. Heraclitus characterized all things as existing through pairs manifested within contrary properties such that no entity may ever occupy a single state at a single time. "Ever-newer waters flow on those who step into the same rivers," so said the weeping philosopher. Evans treads a similar path in his reading of the *Chamber Works* in which both a unity and a fragmentation in the drawings

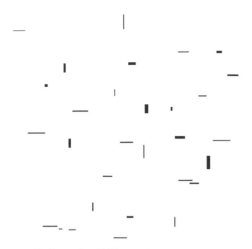

Figure 59. *December 1952*, complete score by Earle Brown (1926–2002)

are identified as representative of "two major contrasted modes of twentieth-century composition in architecture as well as painting." As such, this classic dialectical pair is characterized as "married and bickering ... [and] unable to carry on without each other. The *Chamber Works* do not move towards unity, nor are they subject to fragmentation." (Evans 1984 p. 92)

The suggestion then to hear the drawing is not any different from the approach to *December 1952* in which to encounter the nomenclature of the notation, of the graphics, lines and symbols is to encounter an event, a potential sounding structure that is to be imagined in relation to the space that the drawing or score itself produces. To move through the *Chamber Works* then, to imagine their sound world is to recognize the inscription of the line, much like its use in *December 1952*, as a measure and carrier of an acoustic quality, of an event imbued with texture and structure. This quality is at once drawn out, oft interrupted, coagulated, bunched-up at times and at others broken apart. Sounds then too must follow these lines, or perhaps they are *of* the lines, unfolding across the space of the page, of Bernhard Leitner's *Head Space* and our inner realms, always sounding in relation to each other, and finding ever-new ways of combining, filling out densities and punctuating the silence of the whiteness in which they are embedded.

Tuning

But if Libeskind's *Chamber Works* represent an intentional distancing of the traditional role of representation in architecture and in drawing, we might consider a more resolute pointer towards an imagined architecture of habitation. For Archigram and its political and social concerns about the role of architecture in defining the new technological age of the late 1960s, a period that seemed awakened by the promise of the space race, came iconic collages that speculated on a new type of architectural intervention. These collages and their ideas and transformations of a vision of the urban, and of architecture's future, act much like how Tahl Kaminer describes the function of the diagram in architecture: "The diagram, in turn, is an abstraction that is neither a representation in its traditional sense nor is it reality; it is a 'thing in itself,' a reality in itself." (Kaminer 2011, p. 98) It is in these terms too that Mike Webb described the projects of Archigram:

> The drawing was never intended to be a window through which the world of tomorrow could be viewed but rather as a representation of a hypothetical physical environment made manifest simultaneously with its two-dimensional paper proxy. This is how things would look if only planners, governments and architects were magically able to discard the mental impedimenta of the previous age and embrace the newly developed technologies and their attendant attitudes. (Webb 1999, p. 2)

Indeed, one of Archigram's more iconic projects, *Tuned Suburb* (1968) by Ron Herron for the Milan Biennale, explores just such an imagined future in which the vernacular English housing estate becomes transformed through new technologies. Here the seemingly drab and banal English suburban landscape is populated with all manner of additions—banners, fairground-like props, signage, cooling systems—that are both

Figure 60. Ron Herron's *Tuned Suburb*, collage for the Milan Biennale, 1968

technological and architectonic, and seek to radically transform, activate and invigorate the contemporary suburban condition. This might initially appear in contemporary computer game parlance as the act of "modding" or "the activity of creating and adding of custom-created content" (Sihvonen 2011, p. 37) as it might be applied to the built environment of the suburban dwelling in which material additions complement the vernacular. But as Simon Sadler notes, "ethically and aesthetically, Archigram regarded strictly modular building systems as a mixed blessing, partly an overstated 'demonstration' of prefabrication that might be better combined with other building elements or tacked onto structures already in situ." (Sadler 2005, p. 103)

The notion though of a tuning of the suburb, of a tuning of the architectural environment similarly resonates with the ideals of R. Murray Schafer and the acoustic ecology movement. If Archigram's *Tuned Suburb* is an imagined future environment in which a kit of parts can be applied to existing architectural structures, in turn customizing and breathing new programs and architectural experiences into them, then what Schafer suggests is of equal measure: a future urban soundscape that is adjusted to suit the aesthetic or even utilitarian needs of inhabitants of the ever-growing urban environment. Thus for Schafer, acoustic communities might compose and produce "soniferous gardens" of acoustic delights, they might have complete control over the immediate design and composition of the sounding environment. If, as Sadler notes, "words like 'exchange' and 'responsive' are on hand to affirm the freedoms imparted by the kit" (Sadler 2005, p. 105) regarding *Tuned Suburb*, then we might similarly place Schafer's concept of the amelioration of the soundscape as fostering like intentions, perhaps even through similarly envisaged urban design interventions and customizations. It would seem then that both Schafer's *Tuning of the World* and Herron's *Tuned Suburb* partake in what Peter Cook came to identify as the emancipation of humans from the constraints of the architect (as sound designer too) and the stasis of the architectonic:

125

If architecture laid claims to human sustenance, it should surely have responded as human experience expanded. For architects the question is: do buildings help towards emancipation of the people within? Or do they hinder because they solidify the way of life preferred by the architect? It is now reasonable to treat buildings as consumer products, and the real justification of consumer products is that they are the direct expression of a freedom to choose. (Cook 1999, p. 78)

What then of the sound world of *Tuned Suburb* in light of critical listening? The implications might be obvious in a visual sense, that there are additions to facades and add-ons to rooftops and window boxes, courtyards and front terrace gardens. But for approaching Archigram's concept of a suburb tuned, we might just as favorably invoke a critical listening of its substance and ideas as a means by which to re-engage in the imagined auditory dimensions it clearly maps out. We could well imagine that the inclusion of all manner of artifacts, of the customization of the vernacular, might also bring to light what Archigram envisaged in their quirky use of young, attractive females and other urbanites engaged in activities, however mundane, that are now framed by the excitement of a new type of place in which additions of the technological and of the folly become affixed and transmute the ordinary into the extraordinary. To imagine or speculate on the auditory qualities of a *Tuned Suburb* is to then envisage the assemblage of its acoustic horizon(s), its facets and the grid with its folds and lines of encounters. We may also consider the interaction of the architectonic within the site, what sound profiles abound, and what auditory impacts technological advancements, customizations and "mods" may have for the acoustic signature of the vernacular.

What if such additions, customizations, modifications and tunings though were also capable of the abatement of sounds through their materiality? What if Schafer's keynotes and extraneous postmodernist sonic flotsam so loathed by acoustic ecologists could be quelled, de-emphasized or even silenced? What if the customization of the vernacular architecture also brought about a radical change in the sounding environment such that the warning of the threat of a noisy future itself becomes a new peril because of the ease with which sound might be eliminated at will, by a public hungry for an acoustic bliss—a return to an acoustic Eden? Recall then the protagonist Wang of *Sounding City*, whose built environment is but a whisper in which Archigram's championing of technological refinement and architectural additions and customization may have also assisted in reducing the city's sound profile, its auditory richness, and the scale of its acoustic arenas and capacities of the facets of the acoustic horizon. We might imagine (or more poignantly hear) a city where those sounds which modern society has come to accept, live and imbue are suddenly gone, lost to greater desire for silence, quietude and control.

Indeed, such a negation of sounds of everyday life becomes an important theme in J. G. Ballard's 1965 short story *The Sound-Sweep* in which in a fantastic yet curiously familiar future, the acoustic ecology of our environment is no longer a function of the gradual atrophy of vibrations in air but an ever-present document of past sound-making actions. In this world, sound finds a de facto materiality through its ongoing persistence within a medium secondary to the air in which it was born. As a consequence, the profession of the sound-sweep is a result of the need to recycle and maintain a sustainable acoustic environment that does not become saturated or chaotic. A sound-sweep then combines the responsibilities and tools of a garbage collector with the technical skills of an acoustic engineer. Ballard's future imagines sounds of our everyday lives as burdens and refuse simply given that their normative conditions of ephemerality have been somehow relinquished. Temporal scale within the auditory realm ceases to exist as measurable by a metric relative to the human perception of seconds, or even relative to human life spans. Instead, geological time frames mediate the natural half-lives of audible vibrations, which can be only removed from objects through sound sweeping with a sonovac:

> The Oratory was a difficult and laborious job that would take three hours of concentrated effort. The Dean had recently imported rare thirteenth-century pediments from the Church of St.Francis at Assisi, beautiful sonic matrices rich with seven centuries of Gregorian chant, overlaid by the timeless tolling of the Angelus … Mangon, with his auditory super-sensitivity, was greatly in demand for his ability to sweep selectively, draining from the walls of the Oratory all extraneous and discordant noises—coughing, crying, the clatter of coins and mumble of prayer—leaving behind the chorales and liturgical chants which enhanced their devotional overtones. (Ballard 1965, p.52)

Of course, there is too in Schafer's auditory vision of a future acoustic environment an equal notion of the ability to create a tuned and balanced sound-space and indeed for sounds to persist in the imagination. Though for Schafer, the possibility of sonic detritus is one that is a function of the need for orderly design and an imbuing of aesthetic qualities in signals rather than their extraordinary temporalities and persistence. Nonetheless, in Schafer's notion of tuning, there is an obvious reference to what scientist and occultist Robert Fludd conceived in his *World Monochord* of 1617—both aesthetically and compositionally. Here, Fludd developed a system of tuning (after Newton's observations on the division of natural light into color bands) in which a giant allegorical string instrument depicts the perfect harmony (via musical intervals and spheres of existence) between man and the heavens: naturally God sits at the pinnacle where the purest tones are found. That the sounding environment might be as easily tuned as by the addition of customized parts, sounds or noise-canceling architectonic elements carries with it the potential too that the immediate effects of such additions may be felt outside the confines of the boundaries of the site and thus have ramifications for the larger context—even for the expectations of socially informed interactions. If Fludd considered that the perfection of the tuned

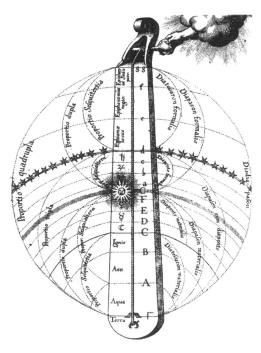

Figure 61. Robert Fludd's *World Monochord*

universe was ultimately in the hands of God, then for Schafer, the toil of mankind and its quest for a more attuned acoustic environment will always be in the hands of society's projective will and aesthetic sensibilities—however fickle, diverse or unpredictable these may turn out to be.

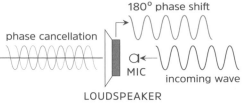

Figure 62. Active noise cancellation of incoming sound sources through 180-phase summation and destructive interference

Pause/Play

Consider then *Tuned Suburb* as a representation of an acoustic scenario, as a future acoustic space in which the urban environment becomes customized through the use of technologies whose role is, for example, the cancellation of sound sources. In fact, these types of technologies are already existent and widely used in industrial settings for noise and vibration control. Through a somewhat simple process that has been eased by the lower latency capacities of more powerful computer processing speeds, sound waves are recorded by a microphone, inverted (or phased by 180) and then replayed back at the incoming waveform to effectively cancel out the noise (or at least severely attenuate it) through a summation of the two waveforms—essentially a destructive interference. Thus rather than passively reducing sound sources through innovative uses of form and materiality, active noise cancellation works at the physical level of waveform transformation. What might be the impacts of such technologies? Colin Hansen argues that in fact such approaches to noise reduction will become much more widespread with applications in the future to target "consumer goods such as refrigerators, washing machines, air conditioners, lawn mowers, personal computers, range hoods, chain saws and vacuum cleaners" (Hansen 2001, p. 6), not to mention cars and other transport systems such as aircraft and trains and of course architecture. What then could we expect from the mass customization of an acoustically deadened city? To borrow from Schafer's musical sensibilities, it would be perhaps like the proliferation of the *fermata* across the city, in which encounters with sound worlds and active spaces were punctuated through "pauses" in the sounds of the urban environment. Traditionally, the musical nomenclature of a pause was notated through the *fermata* sign, a point surmounted by a semicircle. But as David Blumberg explains, these punctuations within musical time are unmeasured and, moreover, indeterminate:

Figure 63. The *fermata* sign appeared as early as the fifteenth century in works of Guillaume Dufay (1397–1474) and Josquin des Prez (1450/55–1521) and commonly denotes a pause in musical time.

Music depends upon the flow of measured time to unfold, yet there is a sign that marks the cessation of time within music. This sign is the *fermata*. It derives from the Italian verb *fermare*: to stop or bring to a halt. Whether of a terminal or more suspensive nature the *fermata* signals the lifting of metered time; a conductor stops beating during a *fermata*, musicians stop counting. The tones or rests over which a *fermata* appears are prolonged according to the context. Its duration is indeterminate; its interpretation intuitive. (Blumberg 1997, p. 595)

Thus to encounter Archigram's tunings of vernacular architecture, of the suburban condition might also be to encounter an auditory

Figure 64. *Fermata City*, after Nono's *fermata* scale of rest values in *Fragmente—Stille, An Diotima* (1980)

contrary, a *fermata* in the sound profile of a site. This suggests then what Toomas Karmo referred to as the negative space of a hole, of an immateriality (Karmo 1977) in which the additions of technology, new materials and facade elements, not to mention Hansen's prediction of innovative and silent consumer products, help to reduce the acoustic signature of the building, its architecture of sounds and the structure of the site. Here then, the program and indeed the structure might be something that becomes severely limited in its active voice, in its natural resolve towards activation. In this scenario of mass customization comes the potential for a pruning of the taxonomy of the sound profile of the city and the built environment. Perhaps to encounter this imagined urban sound world will be something akin to encountering composer Luigi Nono's scale of *fermatas* he used in his 1980 *String Quartet Fragmente—Stille, An Diotima*.

For Nono, the extension of the traditionally notated *fermata* as a single point with semicircle is greatly expanded to include commas, multiple semicircles, substitution of triangle and square brace for the semicircle, as well as a combination of comma and the varied *fermata* sign. This new nomenclature is created in an effort to bring a variety to the notion of silence and of the pause in time and temperament of a musical work. As Blumberg asserts, "the silences [denoted by the *fermata*] are not the negation of sound, but rather part of the continuum between sound and silence as expressed in the scale." (Blumberg 1997, p. 596) By applying a critical listening to such constructs, we might forthrightly imagine the suggestions implicit in *Tuned Suburb* as indicative of a *Fermata City*: an urban environment in which subtleties of auditory emancipation, or the attenuation of the sounding environment, produces pockets, holes or negative spaces

Figure 65. Street view of *Bloch City*, Peter Cook, 1983

of immateriality. Here, buildings and architecture may become customized, decked with new technologies that mask their auditory presence, provide a foil to the surrounding and activated acoustic context. But perhaps even more than masking, they might also actively destroy sounds nearby, sensing and assessing environmental stimulus much like Spuybroek and van der Heide's *Son-O-House*.

This information net of acquired sustenance feeds the system, which reactively throws complementary interference waves to cancel and deaden competing voices in an attempt to bring about a total auditory homogenization. In this auditory world, perhaps all too familiar to the protagonist Wang, a building is a negation of auditory space, not an affirmation or articulation of it—sounds are not in space, and space is not in the sounds, instead what is left is only the void, a new type of disturbance on the plane which is something other than Ingold's "knot" or "meshwork." It is perhaps but a complete negation of the grid itself. Consequently, there must be then a limit to tuning, to the call for quietude in the city, for the amelioration and emancipation of the auditory. Certainly such subtleties of cause and effect have already been leveled at Schafer's own acoustic desires for a greater silence, but to take the notion of a tuned suburb to a dystopic auditory endpoint, we might also fear the complete reduction of all sounds, the negation of the spatiotemporal, as a greater consequence to fear than the threat of a noisy future.

Certainly the lure of music and the musical score as a type of template for the architectonic, as a means by which to construct architecture as a translation of a musical system, has been attractive for numerous designers and architects throughout history. Goethe's now-infamous observation that "architecture is music frozen" (Goethe & Wood 1901) has provided a legacy to notable twentieth-century exemplars such as those by Stephen Holl, Yago Conde, Yoryia Manolopoulou and Garth Ancher, not to mention the Stockhausen/Bornemann and Xenakis/Le Corbusier collaborations. For Steven Holl's *Stretto House*, the usurpation of Béla Bartók's *Music for Strings, Percussion and Celesta* is for a translation of proportional, numeric and textural combinations into architectonic gesture, while Yago Conde and Yoryia Manolopoulou openly sample graphic score-based elements of John Cage's indeterminate work *Fontana Mix* (1958). For Garth Ancher, it is the intangible qualities of Miles Davis's jazz-rock fusion era performances that act as the departure point for an architectural design process as spatial translation mechanism. But this movement of ideas between disciplines has flowed both ways and ostensibly appears as far back as the fifteenth century. Charles Warren (1973) and Marvin Trachtenberg (2001) identify composer Guillaume Dufay's 1436 motet *Nuper rosarum flores* as containing an elegant manifestation of the proportions of the newly completed Florence Cathedral dome of Filippo Brunelleschi, while Claudio Monteverdi's later well-known early Baroque masterpiece *Vespro della Beata Vergine 1610* makes extensive use of the balconies at St. Mark's Basilica for floating brass choir effects that articulate the work's musical structure in spatial terms.

It is perhaps not surprising therefore that for Archigram's Peter Cook, a similar turn towards the musical score, as a type of spatial template, might yield a rich resource for encountering an architecture that is allowed to literally grow out of the page. Cook notes that, "around the time [early 1980s], I had set a series of short projects for students on the idea of 'music' as a direct architecture." (Cook 1992, p. 32) Thus in his *Bloch City*, an architectural transmediation of a short passage from Ernest Bloch's sublime 1938 *Violin Concerto*, we find just such a manifestation in which the very direct usurpation of the notations of music provide the structure and form for a city that embodies a musical representation. But as Galia Hanoch-Roe argues, even conventional musical scores possess a graphic dimension

> which may indicate, without necessity of prior knowledge, aspects such as regularity of pulse, relative tempo, acceleration and deceleration of the pace, density of texture or instrumentation, and formal organization. Such terms also relate to architectural plans, which incorporate ideas of spatial pulsation, density of textures and inner pace. Thus, the conventional score may be translated from linear musical process into fluid architectural or urban design. (Hanoch-Roe 2003, p. 157)

Thus in *Bloch City* we find the note heads of crotchets, semibreves and quavers, in addition to the accidentals of sharps and flats, extruded out of the manuscript, itself a type of template for a plan of an ideal city. Dynamic markings, accents and phrases of the short musical excerpt become walls and other follies while bar lines act as bridges. Here, such articulations and demarcations originally of temporal structure now become transformed in *Bloch City* to connect and unify urban spaces. The five lines of the staff and other ledger lines, so important to geographically defining the musical pitch space of the score, its textures, counterpoints and melodic infusions, serve an equally important purpose in *Bloch City* as the lines of transportation: roads, avenues and access points to the regularly spaced oval skyscrapers. The city then is a system of relations bound to spatial structure that serves equally all elements. Its regularity at the urban scale only becomes more distinguishable as the encounter within and between the buildings belies the logic of the system. Like the *Chamber Works,* we are again focused on lines, connections and events that encourage a traveling through the landscape, the page, the manuscript, rather than a meandering or a de-centering within its territory. It is, as Alessandra Capanna suggests, that

> the idea that the musical[ly] continuous and the spatial[ly] continuous of architecture both have the same nature, described by the same discrete graphical elements, by the same punctuation marks, by the same syntactic coloring. This is evident in this case because the project [*Bloch City*] re-proposes an identical architectural

and musical graphic composition, but it also makes a limit case evident in the correspondence that is obviously realized in the common compositional writing in both fields by using the traits that are characteristic of each. (Capanna 2009, p. 264)

But what might be heard within *Bloch City*? Ernest Bloch's original violin concerto uses Native American and Jewish-inspired melodic themes throughout the work as well as obvious references to the thematic primitivism, orchestrations and martial rhythms of Igor Stravinsky's music. (Newlin 1947) Indeed, to hear the opening of the concerto, we are immediately reminded of the American prairie, the frontier of the West, the cinematography of John Ford, and by the time the opening violin solo hushes us into this imagined and fraught space of history, we already feel an obvious lament for something lost. But *Bloch City* literally cannot partake in such emotive engagements, given its proxy to the original musical inspiration and the intended media of the transmediation. In fact, for Cook, *Bloch City* represents an ideal city in that elements such as vertical gardens, parks and sites for fruit and vegetable plantings seek to provide an environment of sustainability and harmony for urban dwellers. We might imagine then another type of utopic tuning outside of the social, that sits in relief to *Fermata City*, the acoustic hole and the implications of Herron's *Tuned Suburb*, by embracing the polar yet divergent relationship between the loudspeaker and the microphone.

Loudspeakers, which in their most basic structural forms are simply diaphragms (the surface of the loudspeaker's cone) activated by an electromagnetic coil, enable the emission of sound waves as a translation of electrical signals. Recall that the middle ear and the tympanic membrane work in a similar manner in the case of otoacoustic

Figure 66. Elevation view of *Bloch City*, Peter Cook, 1983

emissions. But this system can be simply reversed, given that a microphone (though normally more sensitive regarding frequency response than a loudspeaker) is activated from sound waves that stimulate the diaphragm, actuate an electromagnetic cone and produce electrical signals. This is not at all dissimilar to the manner in which the human auditory system functions. Thus when in 2010, Yoel Fink and colleagues of MIT announced their creation of a new fiber that contains embedded piezoelectric properties (Egusa et al. 2010), not only the chance for materials to detect sounds of the environment suddenly arose, but the curious interchangeable properties of all loudspeakers and microphones: that such materials may not only record sounds, but emit them too. Piezoelectricity is an electric charge that can be generated in certain materials such as crystals in response to mechanical pressure. Commonly found buzzers made of two metal disks that sandwich a crystal are typical as

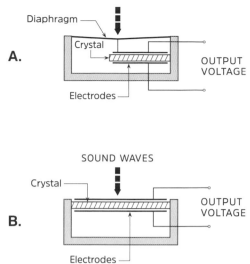

Figure 67. Diagram of two types of piezoelectric microphones in which an electrical signal is generated across two electrodes that sandwich a crystal. **A.** Diaphragm Type (sound waves activate a membrane connected to an electrode). **B.** Directly Actuated Type (pressure from sound waves across an electrode).

small, cheap loudspeakers. The disk can act as a diaphragm when sent an electric current, thus producing sound waves. But they are also capable of becoming microphones when pressure is applied to the disks (contact microphones), which in turn produces an electric current in the crystal that can be interpreted into sounds. Thus for Fink and colleagues, the embedding of such piezoelectric properties into a fabric doubles the capabilities of the material: not only a microphone, but a loudspeaker too—the beginnings of a cybernetic system.

To imagine a future urban environment brought to us by the auditory consequences of thinking through the impacts of the piezoelectric qualities of materials is to identify the potential of sound not only to be immersive, but potentially embedded everywhere and moreover in everything. Perhaps then a critical listening to Archigram's *Tuned Suburb*, in which active noise cancellation produces a *fermata* across the built environment, is only one edge of the anechoic–reverberation acoustic continuum. The other state is the potential of rehearing *Bloch City* as a foil: a city space in which buildings, much like what the protagonist Wang knows of the potential of facades in his world, come alive and breathe and speak sounds. Perhaps what Cook's *Bloch City* lacks in its silent transmediation of the musical score is an obvious acoustic signature, that which would bring the temporal and the sensation of listening (as we normally experience in the violin concerto) to fruition. This is a challenge to Cook's initial thesis of *Bloch City* as a chance to explore "music as a direct architecture" by simultaneously juxtaposing the counter of "architecture as a direct music." Consider then an urban environment in which buildings take on properties as they do in *Sounding City*. They might hum, and sing, not unlike the "design fault" of the Beetham Towers in Manchester. But instead of an erratum to the design, the sounds are instead an exemplar acoustic design parameter of architecture. If there is any more literal interpretation of what Schafer seeks in his "tuning of the world," of Archigram's tuning of the suburb, it cannot be more explicitly delivered than through the notion of a sound world in which the very fabric of architecture resonates and speaks to us directly. If John Grzinich's *New Maps of Time* series of sound workshops (see Chapter 1) are about the amplification of the hidden sound world of architecture as a resonant body, then the opportunity for *Bloch City* in light of the qualities of piezoelectric materials is for a new type of auditory signature, a new sound profile to rise out of architecture itself, yet be fine-tuned to the surrounding landscape, program and events that fall within its influence.

In this scenario, the designed sounds of architecture, whether they be activated electronically (through digital means) or mechanically (through analog means), might be a true function of program in which the sounds themselves emerge out of materiality, out of the form of the architectonic, such that their structure and their texture could be assimilated, processed and consumed from the greater sound-space of the city. We might hear then the urban realm anew, a *Pitch-class City* in which auditory zones are produced from buildings as soundmarks, as auditory systems in which information, space and sounds become interweaved, intertwined and entangled in a dynamic system that breathes, that actually produces an acoustic ecology. To hear the potential in *Bloch City* then is to hear architecture, the architecture of sounds that buildings can produce. Music thus might emerge from such a system, from such a sounding city, when we consider that the individual frequencies, the assignable musical pitches of a facade can be heard as a harmonic event, a melody between buildings and as a series of soundmarks that define a site as a place through sounds—perhaps Schafer's one great hope.

Frequencies then as pitched events can be abstracted, much like what musical theorist Allen Forte proposed in his delegation of the eleven semitones of the equal-tempered octave into pitch-classes. (Forte 1973) Here, and using a mod-12 system, each of the notes of the octave (regardless of which note is chosen to begin the sequence) can be assigned an ascending whole number between 0 and 11. In using modular arithmetic, the integers stand in for the musical pitches and essentially wrap around so that all musical pitches of the same quality (that is, all "C"s or "A"s are equivalent regardless of which octave they are found in (that is, C1=C7). From these, subgroups as harmonies of the aggregate emerge that can be classified and compositionally purposed. In this system then classifications of chords (up to the complete aggregate or eleven-note octave chord) can be mapped. A three-note harmony or trichord of (A, A♯, B) can then be expressed as {0,1,2}, where A=0, A♯=1, B=2. Forte was the first to systematically name all possible combinations of three- to eleven-element subsets of the aggregate with a labeling system. For example, the first and "smallest" trichord is known as 3-1, which is equivalent to {0,1,2}, 3-2, represents {0,1,3}, etc. Thus in *Pitch-class City* we may hear classifiable harmonies as subsets within zones that assist in navigation and allow for other types of information to be communicated (for example, weather, traffic congestion, air quality, etc.). These zones produce an immersion in the urban fabric and might be cybernetic, influencing behaviors, feeding off sonic detritus or unwanted keynote sounds.

They might also approach what Descartes had suggested in his Vortex theory of 1644: that the ether is filled with vortices that produce centers, of the planets, comets, and of stars (another type of tuning perhaps to counter Fludd) which further

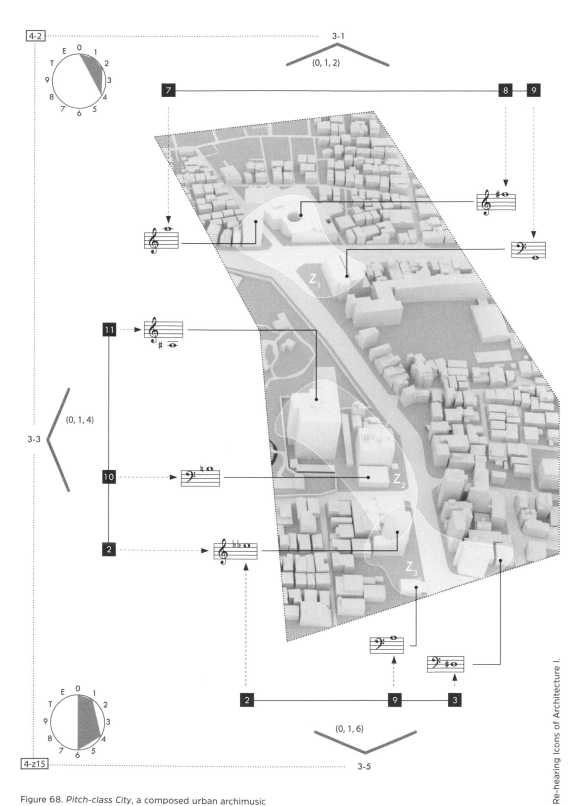

Figure 68. *Pitch-class City*, a composed urban archimusic

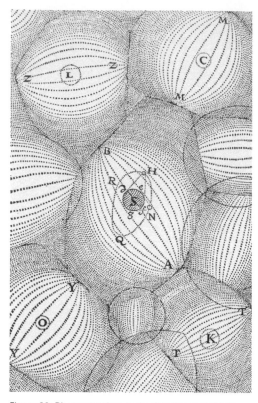

Figure 69. Plenum vortices in the *Principles, Pr III 53*

demarcate territories. Within these territories matter and other things radiate outwards and are in motion due to large circling bands. We might also hear in the concept of *Pitch-class City* similar vortices, not of matter in motion, or of celestial bodies, but of sound radiating outwards from the body that constitutes a building and its facade. These sounds in turn also form territories (an acoustic arena and an acoustic horizon) that can be described and defined through pitch-class information: that is, the texture of the sounding events. The urban environment then becomes much like what Brown sought out in his desire for a performer-led three-dimensional spatialization of *December 1952*: that the lived experience, the movement through auditory zones and events becomes the musical interpretation, the musical experience of the score. The city then might become a score, even more than in *Bloch City* given that with an auditory complement, musical space suddenly becomes habitable space. This space then actively constructs territories and spatiotemporal encounters through its dynamic transmediation of musical concepts into architectural experience, into architectonic form. Navigation within such a built environment takes on new meaning in that sounds are a type of signage, and have the potential to communicate geo-spatial qualities about a site.

Ad infinitum

We might then of course, and with the aid of critical listening, take these consequences again through to an endpoint, another extreme of auditory consequence, a consideration of the auditory continuum in relation to what Andrew Burrow and Robert Woodbury call a "design space." (Woodbury & Burrow 2005) If a city might be a heterogeneous sound-space of musical dimensions in which zones, vortices and buildings act in concert to produce a varied and highly variable auditory experience of texture and structure, we could well imagine the other end of the continuum, another trajectory through the design space. What of the auditory and architectural consequences of a sound world of complete homogeneity? If the city is an auditory construct that is defined through its relations of difference, what could we expect from a built environment of complete stasis, of a lack of discernible acoustic features, of a sound profile that is indistinguishable between sites and places? Such a sameness seems one of the most terrifying elements that pervades the physical model of Archizoom Associati's *No-Stop City* of 1968 (Branzi 2006), where, as Pablo Martínez Capdevila notes, "dioramas of sectors of the city [are] colonized by furniture and objects of consumption in which an illusion of infinity is achieved through the use of mirrors." (Capdevila 2013, p. 130)

It is perhaps one of the more iconic images to emerge from the work of the 1960s Italian design studio of Andrea Branzi, Gilberto Corretti, Paolo Deganello, Massimo Morozzi, Dario and Lucia Bartolini, and is particularly striking given the notion of vastness that seems to play out. The architectural model, housed within a small rectangular area bordered on all sides by mirrors, acts out a particularly radical and somewhat dystopian view of the future city as a perfect, infinite spatial repetition. Architectural volumes, green areas and access roads map out a small corner of a grid, ostensively a point in space that becomes iterated outwards and towards the horizon in all directions. This repetition is achieved in a particularly numbing manner that provides both an insurmountable gravitas while concurrently reducing, silencing even, what Archigram sought in their *Tuned Suburb*: the possibility of an individuality, of a unique space of customization via technology. In *No-Stop City* the notion of a customized space becomes a blanket that is gently yet overpoweringly spread over everything in sight (and site). It is as Pier Vittorio Aureli argues, a project that "poses a radicalization per absurdum of the industrial, consumer, and expansionist forces of the capitalist metropolis in the form of a continuous city with no attribute other than its infinite quantity." (Aureli 2011, p. 19) It seems then that Archizoom use the model as a means to communicate how urban infrastructures can become devices for enacting control, conformity or disorientation on the experience of the urban environment, and similarly, how the urban condition itself is an inevitable function of mass production. Aureli further notes that

if for Archigram technology was a culturally progressive and politically neutral creative device through which to design the iconography of a brave new world, for Archizoom the application of innovative technology to the territory meant a

Figure 70. Archizoom Associati, *No-Stop City*, physical model, 1968

137

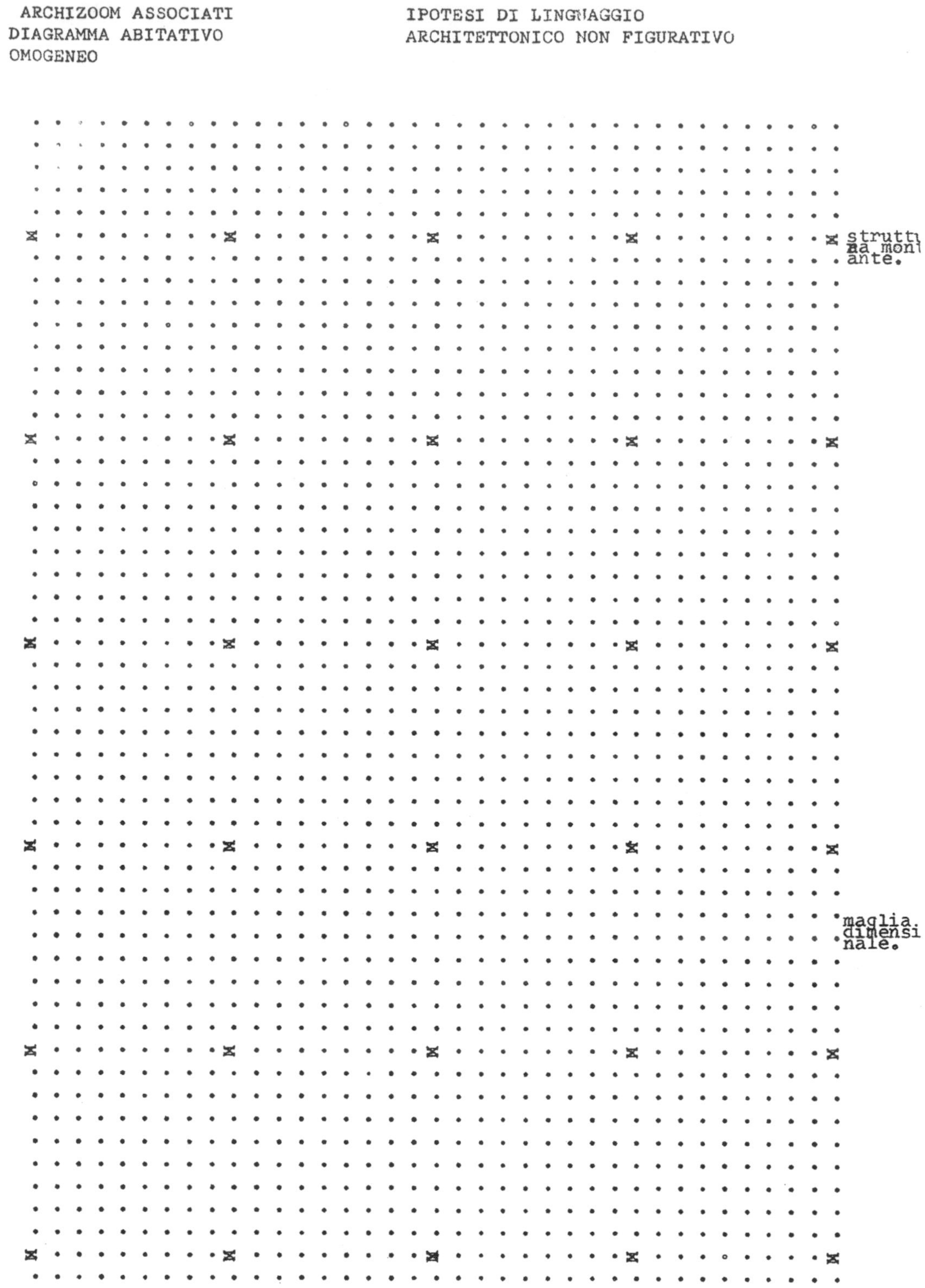

strutt
na moni
ante.

maglia
dimensi
nale.

Figure 71. Archizoom Associati, *No-Stop City*, 1968. Plan of a city produced entirely with a typewriter.

theoretical interrogation of the form of the capitalist city. As embodied in their work, the task of architecture was not an iconic rendering of the city's industrial development, but rather the demystification of urban ideology. (Aureli 2008)

But with this demystification also comes the chance to interrogate the notion of a city in auditory terms, in terms of how the affects and effects of such an infinite expanse of homogeneity might also produce new and necessary forms of navigation and moving through the city. Though, as Aureli observes, there is an isotropic nature to the placement of infrastructure: "an elevator every 100 square meters, a bathroom every 50 square meters." (Aureli 2008, p. 19) There is too the threat of an ever-repeating sound profile, of an encounter with the same types of sounds at every corner, at every street, such that the auditory experience anywhere in the city is indistinguishable from any other place. These concepts of auditory signage, of acoustic waypoints, are particularly important to the blind or visually impaired in that the sounds of a space provide a range of cues about the spatial, temporal and cultural context of an urban environment. What happens when we are thrust into the homogeneity of the sound world of *No-Stop City* in which no two points may have an audible quality that differentiates them? The acoustic information contained in Schafer's keynote sounds, soundmarks and signals, and the perceived dimensions of the acoustic arena and the acoustic horizon serve as a significant set of relationships for nonvisual navigation and orientation. Sound can reveal important aspects about the location and materiality of spatial volumes. It may also indicate the position of objects and of solid structures as well as human activities or potential hazards.

Indeed, for sound designer Lawrence Harvey, this auditory relationship between urban landmarks and nonvisual orientation became the basis for an artistic exploration of sound, materiality and movement used in his *Sound Sites* project. (Harvey 1999) Harvey collaborated with blind and visually impaired individuals, taking spatial sound recordings of distinct auditory features of urban settings and natural environments based on a series of conversations. In his soundscape composition Philip conducts the city, a participant with visual impairments using a variety of different cane techniques on his journey: "Sonic textures roll under Philip's cane as he navigates his way through the city. A rapid montage of clicks, scrapes and clutters." (Harvey 1999, p. 6) The cane and other sensory tools are used to obtain auditory as well as tactile feedback about surface conditions and the spatial context. Indeed, multisensory signifiers integrated into the built environment, such as tactile ground surface indicators (TGSIs) and audio-tactile pedestrian signals, are specifically designed to offer clues and warnings to individuals with visual impairments as well as to the wider sighted community. Their value has been increasingly recognized and included in building codes and guidelines in cities globally, with the Australian and New Zealand Standard outlining that "TGSIs should be installed to provide guidance and/or warning of an obstruction in order to provide cues, which, when combined with other environmental information, assist people who are blind or vision impaired with their orientation." (AS/NZS 1428.4 2002, p. 4)

But what of this "other environmental information"? What happens when we encounter the infinite grid, in which the acoustic sensations and the sound profile of the city is an endless repetition? Take one of the plans from *No-Stop City*, itself produced entirely on a typewriter. Here is a hallucinatory grid of perpetual expansion in which events, things, architectures, are located at intervals, measurable in a predictable metric such that the city is dissolved into an economy of capitalist growth, a never-ending inflationary space that consumes all and itself produces new forms of consumption. Thus we may find that any disturbance on the grid, any complexity or novelty, any nonconformist rhetoric or difference, is cannibalized by the system and its greater desire, its innate process, to succeed. In this expanding universe of a new and dystopic urban order, we can expect that sounds too are reduced to statistical phenomena. The movement through the grid produces no real novelties, but instead can be accounted for through its marked and repeating spatial structures. The auditory experience then of *No-Stop City* is one in which every street corner potentially sounds the same; travel around the block and we encounter the same sounds, perhaps even located at the same relative points in space on the grid. Given the continual repetition of architectural volumes, soft and hard landscape elements, form and materiality assist in only further emphasizing the homogeneous nature of the unchanging acoustic signature. If events, sounds and auditory encounters are ruled by texture and structure, how unique can these be in a city in which they are constrained and encouraged to interact in very specific ways through the repetition of the architectonic? How might a visually impaired inhabitant navigate the city in which everything clings to a sameness, in which the sounds of one block on the grid account for all the blocks?

Evidently, it is this availability of rich multisensory information within an environment that is responsible for what Steven La Grow and Marvin Weessies describe as the fundamentals for orientation. Moving through the spatial environment, whether it is within a city, interior or natural environment, requires

> the ability to establish and maintain an awareness of one's position in space and is dependent upon both the gathering and interpretation of available sensory information. This information may be visual, auditory, kinesthetic, tactile, thermal and/or olfactory … Visually impaired travelers are taught to recognize and anticipate the regularities of the environments in which they travel. Exceptions to those regularities become more informative than the regularities themselves. They become landmarks which a traveler can use to pinpoint his or her exact location in space. (La Grow & Weessies 1994, p. 9)

What then of the movement towards a complete rejection of the balance of opposites, of the smoothing over of irregularities of acoustic experience in favor of a decentralization of structure and of program? Indeed, the fundamental hypothesis of *No-Stop City* was "the evolution of the city towards a much more integrated condition in which not only material production but also housing and education form a unified system devoid of any boundary." (Aureli 2013, p. 144) The removal of exceptions, especially regarding the auditory realm, is perhaps like the presence of streets of the same traffic volumes, of buildings of the same air-conditioning units producing the same hums, the uniform surfacing of sidewalks and roads that produces no audible distinctions underfoot (or undercane), the pedestrian crossings that warn with the same shrill electronic interjections or the building facades that create identical reverberation times on the street and on the sidewalk. This smoothing over of distinctions of the architecture of the city, and what is found in the physical model of Archizoom's *No-Stop City*, are ideologically and theoretically driven, yet provide a rich set of affordances for a critical listening into such a future scenario. As Archizoom elaborate:

> The modern city is born out of capitalism and develops within its logic: capital dictates to the city its general ideology, and this in turn conditions its development and configuration. This general ideology consists of the policy of the "balance of opposites," pursued in relation to economic demands and "produced de facto" in relation to the plan of urban operation. (Archizoom Associati 1970, p. 22)

To find ourselves within a homogeneous city of repetition and of the elimination of auditory irregularities, so important to auditory navigation as points or areas of distinction, might well suggest that a soundwalk (or indeed any goal-based trajectory) through *No-Stop City* be conducted as a random walk. If all amenities might be found at statistical distances from any other point, and if the grand repetition of the architectonic also becomes an influence that curates the homogeneous sound-space of the city, we can consider a soundwalk through the urban environment, and even the movement from one distinguishable point (either architecturally or acoustically) to another, as enacted and guided only by the definition of the desired distance to be walked. By this I mean that any walk from one point on the grid to another is achievable in a given amount of time purely through random decisions: that is, whether to move firstly left, right, forward or backward. Moreover, a random walk conducted in this fashion on the grid will, given an infinite amount of time, cross every point of the grid. This property is also known as the "gambler's ruin":

> The law of gambler's ruin states there is a chance of going broke merely by normal runs of bad luck, regardless of the longer-term expectations. Gambler's ruin is avoided by having sufficient capital to continue to participate in numerous ventures and ride out the bad luck. (Mian 2002, p. 287)

In terms of the grid, and of *No-Stop City* (where the random numbers of 0 or 1 dictate the direction of movement through the grid), "going broke" in this case is the equivalent of a return to the point of origin of the trajectory in the grid. With an infinite amount of time (capital), a full traversal through the grid, to every point (the equivalent of "winning"), is not only achievable, but also probable.

A walk then through the physical model of *No-Stop City* might well be considered as a choosing of a timeframe given that to consider each square as representing the same architectural potential, the same auditory signature, the same availability of an amenity, places an emphasis on the journey and the time taken, rather than the actual structure of the trajectory. Indeed, there are parallels to some of John Cage's later works, in that they were invitations to the audience to question what the auditory materials should be within a musical work. In a piece such as *Demonstration of the Sounds of the Environment* from 1971, the subtle connection between site, silence, audience and new listening modes becomes seamlessly integrated as a social phenomenon. Describing the original directives of the work for three hundred listeners that was conducted at the University of Milwaukee campus in Wisconsin, Cage recalls that:

Through I-Ching chance operations we subjected a map of the university campus to those operations and made an itinerary for the entire audience which would take about forty-five minutes to an hour. And then all of us, as quietly as possible, and listening as attentively as possible, moved through the University community. (Susan McClary 1991, p. 111)

The piece then represents a type of structural précis of Cage's necessity for considering compositions in sound-space as dynamic, social entities. As such, the work generalizes those engaged site interrogations in other works, such as his earlier *Variations IV*. Acting as a generator of a spatiotemporal ontology, *Demonstration of the Sounds of the Environment* defines the relationship between spaces and sound that is found in so many of Cage's later pieces. By generalizing the concept of "site" in the work, Cage manages to point towards the importance of sound as a marker of identity, articulator of space and producer of place. But as a social event too, *Demonstration of the Sounds of the Environment* also highlights the composer's desire for listening within a site to be an interpenetrating consequence of embracing any sound source as a musical event. As Cage describes, the notion of an audience participation in *Demonstration of the Sounds of the Environment* is not something that is channeled or "designed by the composer, but rather [...] of the music that arises through the activity of both performers and the so-called audience." (Kostelanetz 2003, p. 117)

We might see or at least hear then a soundwalk through *No-Stop City* as activated similarly in the manner that Cage sought to explore in *Demonstration of the Sounds of the Environment*. Whether to generate a walk through chance operations or via a random walk, the emphasis is placed on the journey, rather than the objective of moving between two distinguishable points in a certain order or through a pre-mediated trajectory. Of course, in the imagined sound-space of the model of *No-Stop City*, we are given far less information in which to encounter diversity, far less acoustic variety in

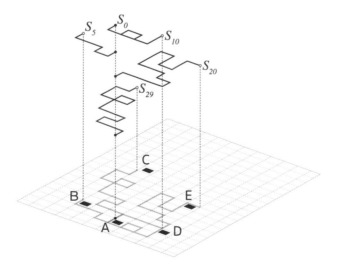

Figure 72. A navigation through the infinite grid of *No-Stop City* via a random walk. *Sn* denotes a random walk of *n* steps which is given by a random number generated output of 0 or 1 that indicates movement in 4 directions from a point A within the grid to point B, C, D or E.

which to distinguish architectonic features that Cage experienced at the University of Milwaukee campus. Thus when we conceptualize a city in which repetition and sameness pervades the entire grid, localized features and geometries lack meaning—so too auditory encounters. A walk through such a city then is a focus on the number of steps that are desired, the length of the intended journey and an attentive listening schedule, given that the route from A to x can be achieved in as little as one step, or one hundred steps: it is only a question of how many other possible points might be encountered between these bookended points, nominally A and B. This of course further implies that there is not any real difference between all points on the grid, that essentially all points are actually iterations of A: A', A'', A''' ... This is perhaps closer to the architectural model of *No-Stop City*, in what looks like a bed, which becomes an infinitely repeatable volume: of this greater space, this infinite city, there is only symmetry, only a reflected image of a singularity mapped to eternity. The garden and plantings, perhaps also critiquing the astute nineteenth-century Italian garden, are perfectly framed in their play between being landscape features while at the same time borders between the model and the virtual. The ultimate question in such a construct then is perhaps how many times we choose to encounter the same auditory phenomena before we decide to bring a journey to its conclusion.

6
Re-hearing Icons of Architecture II.

Continuous
Above
Discontinuous

Re-hearing Icons of Architecture II.

Continuous

If there is a sound of the architectural representation, there is of course an acoustic space that is suggested by it, at least one that can be imagined because of it. If critical listening is a resource for auditory imagination, it is too a type of tool for analytical investigations, particularly into the capacities of the facets of the acoustic horizon and the intimate connection between architectonic form, materiality, site and program. Acoustic spaces are always under the surface, as it were, of the architectural representation, in that they are present as potentialities, as experiences that are born from the composition and enumeration of elements of the representation. Often these aspects, the facets of the acoustic horizon—form, texture, materiality, structure and program—imbue themselves directly within a representation, though they can be overlooked by other, ostensively striking qualities or characteristics of a rendering of architectural ideas.

For the members of the other radical Italian architectural practice of the 1960s, Superstudio (Cristiano Toraldo di Francia, Gian Piero Frassinelli, Alessandro Magris, Roberto Magris, Adolfo Natalini), what can be most overlooked in their extraordinary project *Monumento Continuo* (Continuous Monument) of 1969 is the inherent exterior acoustic behaviors that would play out around such an architectural intervention. This can, of course, be understood in light of the project's radical nature as the ultimate solution to urbanization, in which the very notion of a utopia is averted because of its unattainable nature and indeed its many contradictions. Indeed, as Natalini asserted, the purpose of the *Monumento Continuo* was "manifestly didactic: to analyze and annihilate the discipline of architecture by using 'popular' means of illustration and consumer literature." (Natalini 2005, p. 186) The sense of an Antiutopia then is similarly to be avoided in the hope that a simple Topia, or the extant conditions, might best provide the catalyst for exploration:

> Where do you think you'll end up by taking the Utopian Road? Do you really believe that this is the way out of the mistakes and the misery that surrounds us? Have you forgotten that this road is as long as the existence of man and that no one has ever found a resting place along it. Can't you see that it is illuminated by a false light; that the footsteps you can hear advancing are the sounds of dreams, that the lakes you see from it are a mirage, a shimmering fata morgana provoked by the blinding sun? (Superstudio 1972, p. 93)

In turn, the city and the notion of the heterogeneity of the built environment becomes subsumed into a perfect square form, elongated at times, crossed and intersected, that intervenes, eventually everywhere, to the point of an embrace of the surface of the planet itself. Indeed for Ray Kurzweil, there is an inevitability concerning the future perpetuation of scalar recursion in the built environment. In Kurzweil's projections for the sixth and final epoch of (human) existence, technological infrastructures and the built environment become seamed into an indivisible whole. Here, as "the universe

Figure 73. *Monumento Continuo* (Continuous Monument: On the River) by Superstudio, 1969

wakes up," Kurzweil foresees that because of an imperious need for greater evolutionary momentum, all technological infrastructures on the planet will be swiftly appropriated. The transformation's goal of absolute computational power will require an uptake of all organic and nonorganic substrates on earth for the purposes of creating a planet-sized thinking machine that itself will eventually consume the entire universe. (Kurzweil 2005) But for Superstudio, the function of the box as a secondary type of surface on the planet's surface is not so much for the possibilities latent in its potential for computational routines, but for a greater utopian urban routine. As Douglas Spencer notes, "the neutral monochrome grid of the *Monumento Continuo* formed a mute support for a nomadic utopia. In this liberated environment human figures wandered, played, dined and slept in direct unmediated relationship to one another." (Spencer 2005, p. 103) Here, the solution to the issues of globalization, modernism and the emancipation of the individual from architecture, initially exposed by Archigram, is seemingly dismissed, perhaps even comically, in favor of an architectural order of complete juxtaposition at a truly fantastic scale: is the architectural intervention, the grid and the box, a means by which to assimilate the landscape, or is it to preserve its ecology through an architectonic division? In *Monumento Continuo* we find a not so subtle disillusionment with architecture's evident failure at delivering solutions to the world's problems, its failed mastery of ordering and controlling environments and people. Superstudio suggests that by eliminating everything with one gesture, perhaps the architectural ego will vanish. The drawings that constitute the series the Continuous Monument picture a relentless, gridded, monumental structure superimposed on landscapes and townscapes alike, indifferent to its contexts ... Its varied circumstances are enhanced by virtue of their specificity in relation to its own closed, mute, immutable surfaces. (Pimlott 2007, p. 317)

But are the surfaces of the *Monumento Continuo* actually "mute," actually "immutable" and silent? In the oft-observed nature of their materiality, that of glass panes, or perhaps even as is found in the group's later *Istogrammi di Architettura* (Histograms of Architecture) in which furniture-like objects that are "bare volumetric compositions with neither scale nor program" (Aureli 2014, p. 142) seem to be encased in white bathroom tiles, lies a strong acoustic suggestion. Hard materials, whether glass or tiles, whose absorption coefficients are audibly similar across a range of frequencies, produce very distinct interactions with the sonic environment. Thus when Sander Woertman concludes that the *Monumento Continuo* has "a presence [that] exerts both an attractive and a repelling force," (Woertman 2005, p. 155) we are immediately reminded that indeed the walls of such an architectural intervention are far from mute given their typical environmental contexts. If anything, we might consider the *Monumento Continuo* as built from walls of sound. This is because they are acoustically activating the surrounding sound-space through their hard and reflective surfaces. As sounds that might arise along a river, a wilderness, a small town or motorway reach the walls of the *Monumento Continuo*, they become amplified, they become more present and they produce and increase the reverberation time of the surrounding landscape. This would be particularly audible, and moreover, felt through sensations that suggest a change in the context, a change in the acoustic scale and the size of the acoustic horizon.

In finding the *Monumento Continuo* in a small valley, at altitude, perhaps in the cradle of a rocky ravine, the effect of the glass walls on any sounds coming towards

Figure 74. Superstudio's *Affiche avec les dessins axonométriques des Istogrammi* from 1972 showing the Histograms of Architecture

them is to produce a new acoustic space that did not exist before the architectural intervention. In a sense then, the *Monumento Continuo* is an amplifier of sensation. To find it along a river, an ecology already full of sounds and activities, is also to suddenly hear everything with a greater clarity, to find and experience a new auditory space because of the architectonic intervention. Stand directly the walls and their opaque reflections of light are also the means by which it turns sounds of the environment back onto themselves, it reveals then new sound worlds (or at least those previously unnoticed), and is in fact anything but indifferent to the context and environment that surrounds it. If indeed, as Pimlott suggests, through the box and the grid of the *Monumento Continuo* the ego of architecture is dissipated into the void, it simultaneously distills the auditory qualities of the site, and brings to the fore the concept of an immersion within an auditory environment so often spoke of by Hildegarde Westerkamp and R. Murray Schafer. Through the sound walls and their form and materiality, information regarding the structure and texture of the enveloping sound profile of the context are revealed. If we are at the stage in which the interior of the *Monumento Continuo* is one in which programs have been classified and already considered, what the sound walls allow for is a deeper interrogation into the program of the landscape—its qualities, rhythms, relationships and functions.

close reflections

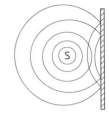

distant source

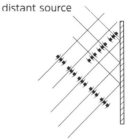

Figure 75. Two scenarios for sound sources reflecting off a glass wall. When the source is close to the wall, the reflections cause an amplification of the sound. A distant source of incoming waves may allow for echo effects as the wave front is reflected at the incident angle.

As an architectural intervention, we can conceive of its presence in the landscape at a level that accentuates and indeed questions the relationship between the artificial and the natural, between earth as a topographic condition and the building as an architectonic articulation. As Terence Riley notes, "the most striking feature of the Continuous Monument is its hard, mirrored surface, which reflects its surroundings, revealing nothing of itself." (Riley 2002, p. 32) Hence there is a starkness and aloofness to the intervention, which at the same time has a strong voice, or echo of the immediate sound profile. As a giant structure that reaches over the surface of the earth, it points not only to the regulated and precise articulation of the architectonic within the seemingly unrestrained topography of the natural landscape, but in fact elevates the sound profile of the natural environment to a new and dizzying acoustic level. This type of juxtaposition, in which an obvious architectural intervention causes an elevation and production of a new type of acoustic space, gives rise to the question of the relation between design and the natural environment, and indeed the notion of environmental sound design. Certainly in spaces such as the Japanese garden a similar dichotomy occurs between the notion of what is naturally occurring and what is designed, particularly in reference to the acoustic spaces that they curate.

In the Japanese garden we find all manner of topographic and architectonic features that sum and function to produce particularly distinct and balanced auditory experiences. As such, the form and the materiality of objects such as ponds, hillocks, dry watercourses, trees, rocks and ground cover are designed to produce and curate particular types of acoustic behaviors and responses. (Fowler 2014) Water is a particularly important element within the Japanese garden (Nitschke 1999), whether it is alluded to through the use of setting stones in the shape of a dry watercourse or virtual waterfall (*karetaki*), or through the placement of rocks within a bed of raked gravel (*karesansui*). Waterfalls are subtle yet highly considered design elements because they are often the loudest element within a garden. Additionally though, they also create numerous acoustic arenas within a garden such that notions about distance or scale can be conveyed through, for example, the muffling of the sound of a waterfall to depict a vast divide between viewer and object. Equally, a waterfall such as the exemplar *ōtaki* at the Taisho-period Kyu-Furukawa Teien in Tokyo has a particular frequency content that allows it to be heard at crucial points within the garden such as at the garden's *karetaki*. The burbling sounds of a brook or small stream are also important sounds of a Japanese garden because they orient the viewer in the visual and auditory scene and are a constant reminder of the sense of a garden as a living ecology.

If, as Aureli argues, "the architecture of the Continuous Monument was determined by one single logic—the grid—and it was conceived as the most abstract and ultimate architectural form possible," (Aureli 2014, p. 142) we might also consider the location of the grid within the natural topography and sound-space of the landscape. Finding the hard, reflective surfaces of the *Monumento Continuo* in relation to particular topographic forms, within the acoustic arena of a watercourse or forest or wilderness, or within a Japanese garden, will greatly impact the perceived amplification of the sounding environment in which it is embedded.

There is a potential then to consider what the *Monumento Continuo* might produce when found not only within a natural environment, but a designed landscape, or designed soundscape. Planar geometries, right angles and surfaces of glass are effective

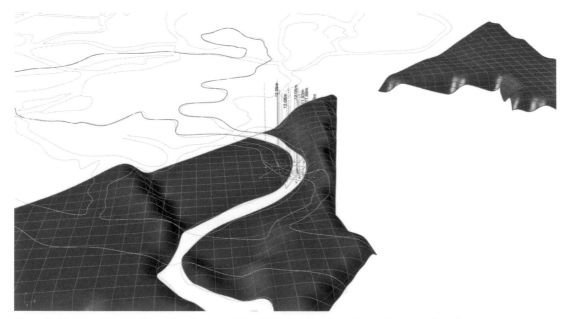

Figure 76. Diagram of the garden of Kyu-Furukawa Teien, Tokyo: topography and acoustic arena of small watercourse

Figure 77. Hans Hollein's *Überbauung Wien* (Superstructure over Vienna), 1960

amplifiers, reflectors and diffusers of incoming sound waves, pushing back the vibrations towards their sources and causing interferences and modulations. Thus these acoustic qualities and inherent behaviors are paired to the visual experience of the *Monumento Continuo*, of the sensation of an architecture that Peter Lang and William Menking describe as "an impossible, unalterable image, whose static perfection moves the world through the love of itself that [which] it creates." (Lang & Menking 2003, p. 130) Indeed in the overpowering visual qualities of sheer glass walls facing falling water, or a forest of trees filled with the cacophony of birds settling down to roost in the early evening, the obvious auditory effects of elongated reverberation times or echo effects become a distinct feature and an acoustic trace of its impact. In the location and site of the *Monumento Continuo*, we may also find the potential for a synthesis and true integration of the architectonic within the landscape: for a symbiotic relationship between what Blesser and Salter nominate as the connection between passive and active aural embellishments. Indeed, as Brian Massumi argues, to encounter architecture is to not only grasp its visual play of light, its perfect articulation of space, but similarly, to embrace an interplay of the senses that produce such an image in us:

> All the sense modalities are active in even the most apparently monosensual activity. Vision may ostensibly predominate, but it never occurs alone. Every attentive activity occurs in a synesthetic field of sensation that implicates all the sense modalities in incipient perception, and is itself implicated in self-referential action. (Massumi 2002, p. 140)

Thus the site of the *Monumento Continuo*, and where it becomes integrated into the landscape, plays heavily, not only on the visual qualities of its orientation, but also on the types of auditory experiences that will be amplified by its form and materiality. We well may consider this as its acoustic legacy. We could easily imagine then a usurpation of topographic or other sounding elements, just like in the Japanese garden, in which a subtle environmental sound design emerges within the landscape because of the care and location of the architectonic articulation of site. Aspects of an

Re-hearing Icons of Architecture II.

environment's texture and structure can be brought to the fore, emphasized and subtly manipulated. The consequences of such are that an environment's sound profile becomes accentuated and amplified so that certain acoustic arenas can be designed and composed to bring us closer to what Schafer envisaged in his soniferous garden: a place of acoustic delights.

Above

But this type of accentuation of the surrounding acoustic environment, whether it be located in the natural or urban condition, is also achieved in a very different fashion when considering Hans Hollein's *Überbauung Wien* (Superstructure over Vienna) from 1960. The form and monumentality of Hollein's vision of a new type of city structure, a mega structure even, came at a period of great upheaval in architectural thinking, which pointed not only to new engagements in political and cultural visions of the future of the urban condition, but similarly, and from the auditory perspective, to a new acoustic space. For Franco Raggi, the notion of a radical architecture, particularly those visions that emerged in the 1960s, was a symptom not only of Hollein's iconoclastic declaration of "Alles ist Architektur," but equally the greater questioning of the canonical status of architecture as a traditional hegemony regarding form and function:

> Architecture, as a concrete art of constructing, presents itself as a form of thinking which offers theoretical and figurative hypotheses. These can represent alternative and definitive answers to the problems of man's relationship with his natural and built environment. Experimental Architecture and Radical Architecture are synonyms of a propulsive attitude, of a thrust beyond architecture's canonical purposes and instruments in order to produce theories, images and elaborated thoughts. Such visions and scenarios may appear to be only future-oriented, but in reality they are bound up with the permanent crisis of contemporaneity. (Raggi 2011, p. 90)

That the *Überbauung Wien* presents an immediate visual conundrum as to its function arises from what Wolf Prix calls its ability to develop "space from the plastic properties of physical forms. The collage *Überbauung Wien* (Superstructure over Vienna) from 1960 tests the results on an urban scale in an effort to overcome the constraints of the present day by detaching from the existing city." (Prix 2004, p. 4) But this detachment is not only from the city, but potentially from architecture itself. As Hollein asserts, the notion of the Superstructure over Vienna is as an entity unto itself, not necessarily as a representation of architecture as habitable space, a building as an abode or a shelter, but indeed as an idea that needs to point to nothing other than its form and where it is to be found:

> In architecture, we are not concerned with beauty. If we want beauty then we want it less in form or proportion than in a sensual beauty of fundamental power. The shape of the building doesn't develop out of the material condition of its purpose. A building shall not show its purpose. It is not an expression of structure and construction, it is not an enclosure or refuge. A building is itself. Architecture is without purpose. What we build will find its usefulness. Form does not follow function. Form doesn't originate by itself. It is the great decision of man to make a building

into a cube, a pyramid or a sphere. Today, for the first time in the history of mankind, at this moment when immensely developed science and perfected technology offer the means, we are building what we want, making an architecture that is not determined by technique, but that uses technique—pure, absolute architecture. Today, man is master over infinite space. (Hollein & Pichler 1963)

Figure 78. Still from episode 49, "The End," season 5 of *The Goodies*, 1975

That Hollein conceived a type of architecture, or at least the representation of an architecture as an idea, as an absolute, finds a curious parallel in the tongue-in-cheek vision of the concrete skyscraper portrayed in the popular British television series *The Goodies*. By the screening of the forty-ninth episode from their fifth season in 1975, titled "The End," the comedy show had come to display a biting wit that had driven the depth and critique of the show into absurd yet socially valuable territory. This reached an apogee in "The End," in which Graeme Garden's character, "Graeme," is the architect of a high-rise housing proposal involving skyscrapers that are simply cast concrete volumes: superstructures without purpose, or an architecture that serves only the concept of architecture. Needing to save money on windows, doors or entrances, the concept of a skyscraper as a pure architectonic object, devoid of program, function or access, points to not only its uniqueness and eerily fantastic qualities, but its function as what Hollein might term "a building that is itself."

But if the *Überbauung Wien* and the poured concrete skyscrapers of "The End" share a resistance to the normal function of architecture in favor of a self-reflective embodiment of the absolute, they also share the notion of a particular type of acoustic interaction with the surrounding sound profile. Accordingly, the seeming detachment from a footing or grounding within the traditions of architecture and its role in the urban context is actually tempered through a particularly close connection both projects display regarding the sound profiles and acoustic behaviors of their contexts. We might consider then, and through the lens of critical listening, numerous auditory aspects that would arise from the *Überbauung Wien*, in terms not only of its location high above the city, but similarly of its form and materiality and indeed what the taxonomy of the sound profile is in the lower atmosphere high above the sounds of the city.

Firstly, we might read the materiality of Hollein's *Überbauung Wien* as of rock, or concrete, or some other formed hard material. Its geometry and form is rough-hewn, pocked with holes and deviations, small interior caves and at times faceted undulating corners and manifolds. The body of the structures sits atop, or even grows out of, pillars, squat legs that defiantly reach up to touch the underbelly of the floating superstructure, both providing a lifting force out of the urban streets below, while concurrently offering a sense that the whole structure might be poised to walk off to another site, to another city. To find such an object, glaringly defiant of the surrounding architecture, also implies that it might function similarly to the *Monumento Continuo*: sounds that approach it being sent back to map out and interact and produce

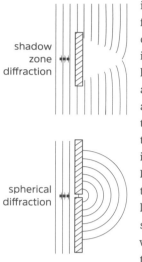

shadow
zone
diffraction

spherical
diffraction

Figure 79. Diffraction of
sound waves around objects
allows sound to be perceived
both behind an obstacle
(shadow zone diffraction) as
well as emerging from a hole
(spherical diffraction).

interference patterns to the extant sound profile of Vienna. We might find curious filtering effects evident within the pockets and small caves located within the superstructure. Indeed, sound has the ability to bend around corners (unlike light) because of its larger wavelengths. Obstacles smaller than the wavelength of a sound contain an acoustic shadow, that is, an arena in which though one might not be able to see through the object, one can hear sounds that emerge from the other side. The phenomenon of diffraction enables sound waves to bend around an object and access this shadow zone. But this bending also occurs when waves hitting a surface find an opening or hole. If the wavelengths are smaller than the width of the hole, they pass through without much bending or diffraction. However, if the wavelengths are close to the size of the hole or larger, standing on the other side of the wall, one hears sounds emerging and ballooning outwards from the hole as if the source was located at the hole. Given then that sound waves are not able to pass through holes smaller than their wavelength, the experience of hearing such a condition is one in which the original source sounds are filtered.

Being located within Hollein's *Überbauung Wien*, in a cavity or a cave or an internal space carved out as a pocket, would enable the sounds of the city to be filtered in ways that brought out particular frequencies, depending on the size of the pocket or opening. Added to this is the hard materiality of the superstructure; low-frequency sounds approaching will tend to diffract around the structure and higher frequencies will be reflected and diffused due to its complex geometry, thus producing a highly reverberant interior space which is active and seeks to acoustically assert its presence. But living atop the superstructure brings yet another type of sound-space to consider: the air, the sky, the weather and the sounds found well above the city streets. Low-frequency sounds travel farther than higher-frequency sounds, so atop the superstructure a filtering of the city hum produces a muffled wash; occasionally discernible sounds may emerge from the amorphous acoustic space below, but a new one is ready and eager to replace it. The wind, birds, aircraft and the lack of any reflective surfaces mean that sounds that leave the top of the superstructure behave in the same manner as the experience in an anechoic chamber (of course without the silence). This means that only the air is available to absorb sounds as they leave the superstructure: like the feeling within an anechoic chamber, the walls seem to be infinitely far apart. The sounds then that originate atop the structure fly out into the air and never return, absorbed only by the sky. Though they are potentially initially reflected by the materiality of the superstructure itself, this condition would seem only to create a reinforcement of the sense of a vastness to the auditory scale. The only ripples, deviations or interjections might arise through the occasional sound of a car horn, siren or rumbling truck far below.

This sense of an otherness to the acoustic space atop Hollein's Superstructure over Vienna similarly plays out in Joseph Kosinski's depiction of the Sky Tower house from the director-writer's 2013 sci-fi epic *Oblivion*. Here the ghosts of Mies and Johnson are awakened, perhaps testifying to Kosinski's training as a graduate of the architecture

Figure 80. Rendering of the Sky Tower house from Joseph Kosinski's 2013 film *Oblivion*

program at Columbia University; sitting atop an impossibly high and impossibly thin spire that sharply pierces the fading atmosphere, a ceiling-to-floor glass-walled house replete with helipad and pool floats effortlessly in sun-drenched beauty among clouds, weather, stars and the improbability of safe escape. From its ultra-sleek monochrome surfaces, all cold and metallic, and its murmuring and humming appliances to its modernist forms of subtle cuboids and curves, we are given a view of the future in which ascetic perfection, simplicity and a complete lack of clutter can only point towards an otherness masquerading as utopia. Indeed Kosinski's *Oblivion* also sets out in rather subtle terms how the exploration and perception of time plays into the relationship between sounds and the acoustic behaviors of architectural spaces, which are inevitably framed and experienced as unfoldings in time—a physical embodiment then of the slogan of the "effective team," a constant refrain used throughout the film. In fact, at the beginning of the film we hear the question "Are you an effective team?" asked by mission controller Sally in a rather folksy Southern lilt to communications officer Vika regarding the status of her and her partner Jack Harper (aka "Tech 49"), ostensively the last humans left on earth. The premise of the film is that humanity is absent from the face of the planet—killed off by invading aliens (the "Scavs") and forced to find a new home on Titan, the largest of Saturn's satellites. The earth has been long ago radically transformed through earthquakes and tsunamis, this terra formation an aftershock effect from the partial destruction of the moon by the invading hordes. This grim situation is initially forlornly described by Harper and visually narrated via a series of strikingly dystopic and ravaged images of the earth, which, because of the presence of numerous fallen, partly destroyed yet readily recognizable nineteenth- and twentieth-century landmarks, seems somewhat familiar though particularly foreboding to us.

But the notion of the "effective team" also plays out in particularly subtle ways regarding acoustic space. The notion of an "effective team" binds not only the social and psychological play unfolding between the characters of the film, but similarly the difference between the acoustic space of the Sky Tower house and that of the surface of the planet, and a hidden and secret log cabin that Jack periodically visits to find solace. The sleek confines of the house, its apparent material transparency, smoothness and ostensive visual connection to the outside environment, has implications for the acoustic signature of Jack and Vika's living quarters. If the living and working quarters are an embodiment of a visual openness, they are also simultaneously an example of a closed-field acoustic condition given the sealed volume and highly reflective surfaces in which sounds are continually perpetuated through the effects of amplification and reverberation. Thus the materiality, program and form of the interior space of the house sum to produce an acoustic intimacy and continuity that defines itself as the dominant auditory experience. Like the view to the exterior, all sounds emanating within the house would be effortlessly perceived regardless of where one is situated within the house. This stripping down of the notion of acoustic privacy present in the sky house becomes an underlying catalyst for questioning the relationship between Jack and Vika, and indeed Jack's frequent sojourns to the surface and his secret log cabin, which is located in a clandestine valley.

As it unfolds within the film, we discover that Jack keeps numerous mementos of his reconnaissance trips to the surface (books, objects and ephemera) hidden from Vika, though he cannot hide the sounds of his tinkering even within the lower-level workspace of the three-level house. But perhaps the deeper semiotics of the architectural and acoustic conditions of the sky house are only more clearly revealed through its foil—or other half of the "effective team"—the ruined landscapes of the surface below and the secret log cabin. At the surface, there exists a free-field acoustic condition in which the lack of any planar architectonic forms together with the sound-absorbing elements of earth, air, sand, grass and ground-hugging shrubs provide a perfect dampening quality for the complete elimination of reverberation. Though on the ground Jack finds himself again within a completely open visual field (as is experienced from within the house), the auditory space at ground level embodies an open acoustic environment such that the notion of an acoustic privacy is ironically overwhelming. With no sense of a box to contain sounds, and much like the experience atop the *Überbauung Wien*, sounds travel into the air to dissipate and become absorbed: there are no surfaces to amplify or reflect them back. Here then, and among the terraformed landscapes that record the defeat of human civilization, a voice in the air can be quickly lost such that a turned back and a low-murmured utterance may be more than enough to generate an acoustic cloak of discontinuity. Unlike the Sky Tower house, the acoustic space operating on the surface facilitates other ways of being, other ways of thinking and other ways of moving. That which cannot be acoustically hidden within the house can be readily hidden on the surface.

The idea of these two realms, of the interior and of the exterior, is exactly that which Michel Serres defines as the acouphene. (Serres 2008) For Serres, there is an obvious mode of contention in which the internal world is separated from the exterior sound world, perhaps like Bernhard Leitner's *Head Space*, in which an individual and their experience is the point of analysis and examination regarding the immersion within an environment. Building on this notion is that of Peter Sloterdijk's phonotope and his concept of the sphere. As Heiner Stahl suggests, the phonotope is a way of creating personal acoustic arenas, or the isolation of the individual from the collective:

The phonotope ... broadens Serres's concept of the acouphene by linking it to the socially generated construction of noise, especially in terms of the blocking out of unwanted sounds. Creating a phonotope, therefore, fosters the insulation of individuals from groups and, in turn, supports the creation of acoustic comfort zones. Central to Sloterdijk's approach to the insulated zones of convenience is the capacity of individuals and communities to filter sound. (Stahl 2014, p. 170)

We might read then the actions of Jack Harper in Kosinski's *Oblivion* as motivated by the overwhelming desire to construct a new phonotope as a means by which to escape the acoustic signature of the Sky Tower house (and indeed Vika); but similarly, as a means by which to continually construct or at least seek out that which Sloterdijk acknowledges as the notion of spheres. Here, spheres are conceptualizations that not only are indicative of shared spaces of human perception, but at both the micro and macro levels represent "the precarious building and break-down of spatial collectivities." (Schinkel & Noordegraaf-Eelens 2011, p. 13) The sphere that connects both Jack and Vika is one that is also defined by the acoustic behaviors of the Sky Tower house, their situation as the last humans on earth as well as their de facto relationship. Thus, when Jack seeks out an alternative acoustic typology at the surface and at his log cabin, he begins to construct an alternative sphere as a filter to these other constructs. As Sloterdijk notes:

The sphere is the interior, shared realm inhabited by humans ... Because living always means building spheres, both on a small and a large scale, humans are the beings that establish globes and look out into horizons. Living in spheres means creating the dimension in which humans can be contained. (Sloterdijk 2011, p. 28)

But this type of separation of acoustic space, of acoustic typologies found in the motivations of Jack Harper, can be similarly read, or perhaps heard, in the proposal *Palmtree Island (Oasis)* by the experimental late-sixties Austrian architectural practice Haus-Rucker-Co (Laurids Ortner, Günter Zamp Kelp, Klaus Pinter and Manfred Ortner).

Discontinuous

If the separation of acoustic space found in *Oblivion* plays out through the diverse acoustic conditions on the surface of the planet, in the log cabin and in the Sky Tower house, in *Palmtree Island (Oasis)*, we find a more obvious juxtaposition: a spatial articulation that allows for an immediate sense of not only a distinguishing between two sound profiles, but subtle suggestions as to the meaning of noise. Indeed, as an instrument for the attenuation of noise, the idea of the dome as a protectorate and demarcator of acoustic space easily allows us to imagine any number of sound worlds that could lie beyond the exterior sources that the dome of *Palmtree Island (Oasis)* divides. But the very notion of a dome, or what Haus-Rucker-Co call a "provisional architecture," (Beyerle & Hirschberger 2006, p. 152) here placed on the Manhattan Bridge in New York, equally recalls Buckminster Fuller and Sadao's "1960 proposal to skin downtown Manhattan with a plastic dome, ostensibly to provide a controlled climate and to economize on snow removal costs, but with an unavoidable implication that the dome could provide protection from nuclear fallout." (Díaz 2011, p. 94) But if for Fuller and Sadao, and perhaps for Haus-Rucker-Co too, the dome became a means to isolate an ecology,

Re-hearing Icons of Architecture II.

Figure 81. Günter Zamp Kelp, Laurids Ortner, Manfred Ortner, Klaus Pinter (Haus-Rucker-Co), *Palmtree Island (Oasis)*, 1971

at the same time it made an idealistic environment differentiated from the exterior yet visible as a potential encounter. Such an approach then also allows for the highly balanced interior space to be one populated only with wanted rather than unwanted sounds. As Stahl argues,

> noise is, first of all, an unwanted sound. Therefore, it can be understood as a loose and flexible, even uncontainable and illimitable arena of social negotiation. Furthermore, noise serves as a projection screen on which yet unregulated acoustic events are related to practices and procedures of filtering, appropriation and scaling. (Stahl 2014, p. 170)

What Haus-Rucker-Co's *Palmtree Island (Oasis)* perhaps represents from an acoustic standpoint is that which Miriama Young sees as the generation of multiple microspheres or "small, pod-like architectures" (Young 2015, p. 158) that modern technologies enable—from the personalized acoustic arenas produced through headphone listening, to specialized listening rooms, quiet cars and even the ubiquitous placement of loudspeakers within devices, computers and appliances that each contribute to create small spheres, bubbles in Sloterdijk's estimation, that create and curate hermetically sealed filters to the exterior sound worlds in which they are inevitably embedded.

Within the dome of *Palmtree Island (Oasis)* lies an otherness of acoustic delights: an auditory experience of the classic desert island, lapping waves and exotic bird calls, the wind through the coconut palms. As an auditory sphere, it is an availability found through what Young has identified in the numerous technologies for listening, particularly those that provide completely sealed pods from the streets of Manhattan. *Palmtree Island (Oasis)* then might just as well be understood as a diagram that represents the potential for modern handheld devices to create such an auditory oasis, but instead of being contained within a literal architectural sphere that straddles the Manhattan Bridge, it is but a bubble that is carried on the person, a containment and filter that is generated and mediated through a phone or a computer. But with the creation of such domes, spheres and bubbles, architecture loses its great power to enact new listening modes, to challenge and suggest new acoustic typologies that are embedded within the city. From the auditory perspective, the dome is the ultimate demarcation of acoustic space; it represents a particularly forceful approach to creating a differentiation between the exterior and interior, and thus at the same time emphasizes and disregards the site context. The dome of *Palmtree Island (Oasis)* might equally present itself as internally empty, or containing within it any number of other environments such that its obvious auditory connotations remain. What is within the dome cannot be heard from the exterior, and in effect, whatever sound worlds are within are simply a proxy for an otherness to the sounds of the city. In this sense, the *Monumento Continuo* and *Palmtree Island (Oasis)* share the same acoustic function: through their implied form and materiality, both reflect back into the environment any sounds that approach, while simultaneously providing a sanctuary and hidden acoustic world to the outside. For *Palmtree Island (Oasis)*, this interior sound world can be seen but not heard, while for the *Monumento Continuo* we can only speculate and imagine the qualities of this otherness.

To read the architectural drawing, or the architectural diagram, as a rich source for the acoustic imagination, as a plateau that can be traversed through a critical listening, has been explored in these last two chapters as a means by which to go beyond the representation of architecture as fixed to the medium by which it is presented. The nature of the architectural drawing, of the render, the collage and the diagram has traditionally been concerned with the representation of ideas of the architectonic, of habitation, and even of the political and social implications of an articulation of space. But these elements of every drawing, of every architectural model of representation can also be amended through considering an auditory world that might also exist. An auditory realm that is strongly suggested by the very characteristics of form, materiality, program, structure and texture that any given representation possesses. Given the advent of technology and software that today play an ever-increasing role in providing acoustic analysis or auralizations of the architectural model, we can be lost in the notion that the acoustic simulation of the proposed building, of the notional articulation of space, might provide all that is required when considering the auditory experience of architecture. If critical listening is a tool for the auditory imagination, for considering what architectures of sound might mean, it is also one that seeks not to simply lay down any single or definitive solution or analytical framework to questions about acoustics. What critical listening ultimately seeks to provide then is a window into the acoustic world of architecture. It is a framework that imagines, through the language and consequences of acoustics and the philosophy of listening, that there are indeed unheard ramifications to any environment, to any proposal that places a form and a structure within a site.

Sound is all around us, it is an essential part of our daily lives and both repels and dispels our engagement with our surroundings. Thus, when space becomes articulated through a building, through a structure that finds a visual presence in the landscape, in the city or the built environment, its internal forces that act to stabilize and keep whole the sum of its parts similarly act to produce distinct acoustic typologies, however subtle or noticed these might be. In all of the iconic works of architecture explored here, the often-radical nature of the ideas presented through the representations have equally radical implications for what sounds might be expected, the behaviors, and what the acoustic signature or sound profile would be. That there are obvious social and political consequences from many of the explored icons of architecture, from the *Monumento Continuo* and *No-Stop City* to the *Überbauung Wien* and *Palmtree Island (Oasis)*, is immediately evident when considering their particular visual and material combinations. But this must also be summed with the auditory consequences, or imagined potentials, to give an even richer account of the representations. This is perhaps where the notion of a critical listening brings insights: that the idea of the architectural representation need not stop at the medium of the drawing, at the resolved idea expressed through the architectonic. It indeed goes much further when we seek to hear anew such representations as a way in which to complete the picture of the architectural idea, to bring forth the multisensory into the fold.

7
Acoustic Futures

Sound house
Sound plan
Order

Acoustic Futures

What then of the future sound of cities? So far, this question has been examined in relation to many of those iconic images, diagrams and collages that have perpetuated numerous mid- to late twentieth-century architectural practices. That the future of urban growth and the very real need to address the function of cities as complex systems of economic, cultural and social interactions has been explored and questioned through the numerous projects cited in previous chapters may lead us to believe the notion that an acoustic signature of the city will be ever-present, whether this be designed or simply randomly consequential. But of the city itself, as a concept, and particularly as a sounding environment, we can further examine how contemporary forces of technological advancement, new modes of listening and changes in expectations regarding the urban condition are shaping (very much in real time) the continual evolution of the city as a living organism: that which R. Murray Schafer duly notes as the idea of a city as an acoustic ecology.

If the city then is an acoustic ecology, it is also a series of embodied sound-spaces, and ultimately a reflection of an order. This particular order directly breeds sites in which visual space and sound-space are constantly being composed, adapted, evolved and recomposed through discrete changes in the acoustic horizon and acoustic arena. It is within these various localities, these myriad sites, that we find a type of sound laboratory emerging. It is a sound lab in the sense that spatial experiments are being conducted in which the outcomes are seemingly unknown or, at least for the most part, unheard at the time of design. Indeed, traditional approaches to architectural

Figure 82. Woodblock print (detail) from Francis Bacon's *New Atlantis* (1626). "**k:** Fruit much larger than its nature, **l:** Aids to improve hearing, **m:** Sound houses for studying sound, **n:** Sound conveyed in tubes over distances."

design in the urban environment have not directly considered the acoustic properties of the built environment at the time of design outside of the idea of the architectural facade as a type of skin or barrier to the exterior. When these auditory properties are addressed, they are often examined post-design because of other policy restrictions or other noise control ordinances.

Indeed, when Francis Bacon first wrote in 1627 of the function of the mythical island of Bensalem's sound houses, he similarly described the potential of such types of laboratories. For Bacon, such sites for the creation of sound-space could only be part of a utopian society whose technological advances in auditory design find a parallel in how our own mid-twentieth-century development of magnetic tape and the electronic music studio offered composers a new listening and production paradigm. But are such laboratories, such sound houses, to be found only in the contemporary electronic music studio? It could be forcibly argued that they have taken flight, escaped the confines of the studio and emerged to become absorbed into the very infrastructure of the modern city itself: the city as an architecture of sounds. Bacon writes:

> We also have sound-houses, where we practise and demonstrate all sounds and their generation. We have harmony which you have not, of quarter-sounds and lesser slides of sounds. Divers instruments of music likewise to you unknown, some sweeter than you have; with bells and rings that are dainty and sweet. We represent small sounds as great and deep, likewise great sounds extenuate and sharp; we make divers trembling and warbling of sounds, which in their original are entire. We represent and articulate all articulate sounds and letters, and the voices and notes of beasts and birds. We have certain helps which, set to the ear, do further the hearing greatly; we have also divers strange and artificial echoes, reflecting the voice many times, and, as it were, tossing it; and some that give back the voice louder than it came, some shriller and some deeper; yea, some rendering the voice, differing in the letters or articulate sound from that they receive. We have all means to convey sounds in trunks and pipes, in strange lines and distances. (Bacon 2007, p. 43)

The contemporary city itself is similarly awash in all manner of the above sounds, some emerging and being carried along musical lines, from sites of music production—the street, the park, the club, the café—while others emerge from social and human–machine interactions, mass mechanization, pocketed natural environments and the pervading technological hegemony of digital networks. Perhaps the "sound-houses" of Bensalem have simply transformed to become the modern city, its streets and its rich auditory space and its numerous acoustic signatures. But for Barry Blesser and Linda-Ruth Salter, the striking aural utopia of Bacon's Bensalem represents a telling insight into our evolving relationship with technologies for auditory design and the seeming widespread democratization of auditory technologies. Indeed, even at the time of Bacon's *New Atlantis*, his contemporary visionary Athanasius Kircher's (1602–1680) experiments and postulations on the nature of sound as the earthly counterpoint to heavenly light similarly saw built projects that utilized technological advancements to create amplifying devices integrated into architectural form (Figure 83).

Figure 83. Athanasius Kircher's illustration of a device for amplifying and conveying sound

But for Schafer and Truax it is the model of Bacon's sound houses as experimental sound laboratories that, in light of the nature and approach of soundscape composition, rightly foresaw the need for a site for auditory modeling or simulation of future environments. With the advent though of mobile technologies, smart phones and a greater openness concerning the use of sound for demarcating time as an auditory warning, and as a measure of human interaction, the sound houses of Bensalem are no longer delineated through specialized, closed, sedentary architectural structures. Indeed, Blesser and Salter nominate the rise of architectural acoustics in the nineteenth century and its twenty-first-century creative foil, aural architecture, as a distinctive manifestation of evolving attitudes within architectural design towards anticipating the role of technology in delivering novel multisensory experiences within the built environment. As such, we might easily consider that the city itself has become both a test bed and a lab for the production and experience of new sound worlds. Perhaps to examine Bacon's notion of sound houses through the lens of critical listening may bring us to the notion then of the modern city as a sound-space laboratory.

Indeed, for Michael Pacione, it is the notion of a city as much more than its territorial or spatial expanse that assists in defining it as something that can exist beyond its physical boundaries:

The city is also a social entity and a locus for social reproduction, comprising the myriad interlaced behaviour and activity patterns of its inhabitants and communities, each of which exhibit idiosyncratic preferences and lifestyle characteristics. The fundamental dialectical relationship between the social and the spatial is a hallmark of the city and of city life. Within this reciprocal relationship social forces operate to influence the physical environment of the city while concomitantly the spatial characteristics of the city act to condition the social behaviour of citizens. (Pacione 2002, p. 1)

From these social interactions and the nature of the form, program and materiality of the city come particular auditory experiences and expectations too. These are what Pacione notes as the reciprocal relationship between city inhabitants and their immediate auditory surroundings: that we both influence and are influenced by our perception of the spatial and auditory environment. As Robert Beck argues, "the physical and interpersonal properties of the environment are distributed in space, and personal environmental space is shaped by the configurations of these properties." (Beck 1967, p. 18)

This is the basis of the discipline of ecological psychology and of the study of behavior setting. Indeed, as its founder J. J. Gibson noted, "specific to the organism in its environment: information enables me to encounter my surroundings, to regulate my encounters, and to be aware of my activities in the living world." (Reed 1996, p. 7) Thus as Gibson's colleague Roger Barker noted, the basic notion of ecological psychology is an examination of the ecology of the environment, an investigation into the "life space" of an inhabitant as a means to more fully understand the impact of spatial infrastructures and other influences on behaviors. To consider the ecological environment is to consider "the nature of the units of the phenomenon studied. The essential nature of the units with which ecology deals is the same whether they are physical, social, biological, or behavioral units." (Barker 1968, p. 11)

In Barker's description of these structures he also suggests types of circuits that arise (Figure 84) that are necessarily a function of iterative units. According to Barker,

the subject matter of ecological psychology cannot be represented by an arc joining, via receptor, central and effector systems, ecological objects and events on the afferent and efferent sides of persons; it must be represented by circuits that incorporate the behavior of persons with objects and events of the ecological environment to form independent circuits. (Barker 1968, pp. 138–39)

Sound plan

This awareness indeed of the sounding environment and the potential influence of architecture and urban planning as ecological units that curate and produce new sound worlds has spurred what Ingrid Leman-Stefanovic and Stephen B. Scharper note as efforts "supported and encouraged by citizen organizations that are dedicated to limiting or eliminating the excessive 'noise pollution' generated by vehicles, outdoor appliances, and stereos." (Oddie 2012, p. 168) In fact, such a change in the auditory environment of modern cities can be found in the conclusions of a 2007 study by Anita Gidlöf-Gunnarsson and Evy Öhrström in which the authors noted that "it has been estimated that about 80 million (approximately 20 %) of the European Union's population suffer from noise levels considered unacceptable (above 65 dB in so-called 'black area') and an additional 170 million are living in 'grey areas' exposed to noise levels between 55 and 65 dB." (Gidlöf-Gunnarsson & Öhrström 2007, p. 115) The consequences of such acoustic conditions have been well documented through numerous studies into the link between stress effects manifested in physiological systems and psychosocial behavioral patterns (Skånberg & Öhrström 2002; Clark & Stansfeld 2007; World Health Organization 1999), indicating that the acoustic quality of urban space will remain an important contemporary health issue with increased population densities. Though such studies refer only to pure SPL (sound pressure) levels of sound sources rather than user expectations of particular sounds, sound source preferences, the semiotics of sounds, or threshold levels of acceptance within particular urban areas, there is still strong evidence that the acoustic environment of the contemporary city, and in particular its future sustainability, will need constant redress for its effective management.

That noise is a particularly contested area for urban design given its wide-ranging definition among different sociocultural groups has duly led Björn Hellström to describe it as more of a subjective qualitative measure of a sound for a particular auditor, while Charles Gurney hears noise as a "sound that is out of place." (Gurney 1999) The emphasis of specialist acoustic knowledge that is the hallmark of both aural architecture and acoustic ecology may end up becoming their greatest hindrance if designers are to take on and apply aural design into urban spaces. Given both disciplines have arisen from thinkers and practitioners whose modus operandi involves a lifelong role in sound and acoustics means that to design an urban auditory experience necessarily implies possessing the ability to understand what is currently heard within a site according to its users, and furthermore, what a new design may desirably present to

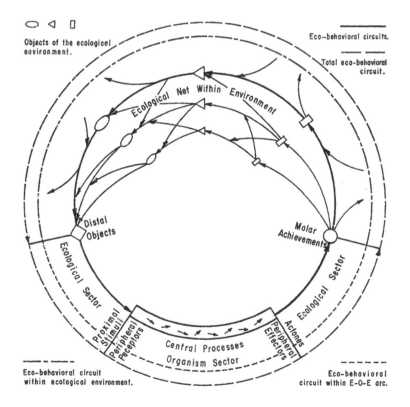

Figure 84. "Eco-behavioral circuits. The solid, directed lines represent the circuits; the broken lines are labelling guides."

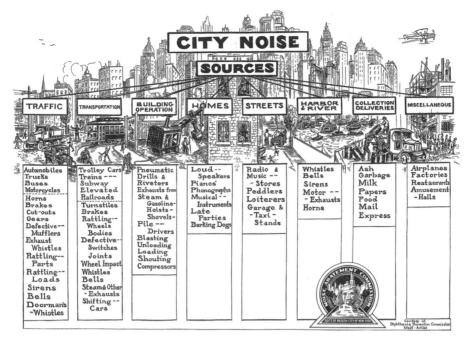

Figure 85. Edward Brown et al., *City Noise: The Report of the Commission Appointed by Dr. Shirley W. Wynne, Commissioner of Health, to Study Noise in New York City and to Develop Means of Abating It*, 1930. Frontispiece.

the ecology of such a site—a key distinction and goal of what I have outlined so far as critical listening. Indeed, the lack of such a usable framework of critical listening for understanding the link between sound and architecture may quite easily lead to the playback of soundscape compositions over loudspeakers, which would of course seem to defeat the contention that the auditory environment is indelibly linked to tangible space. Also deferred would be the innovative idea that sound might feasibly embody an architectural program or a project brief and thus present a creative opportunity rather than a regulatory constraint.

However, where specific acoustic goals have to be resolutely upheld, such as within concert halls or recording studio environments, the gap in auditory knowledge between the roles of acoustician and architect has been effectively maintained. Here, the complete separation between architectural design and the tweaking of a design through acoustic analysis by a team of room acousticians has meant that the optimization of the aural qualities of a space has sat in a convenient and respectable relationship to its process of design. But for Rafael Pizarro, Ted Sheridan and Karen Van Lengen, this separation of disciplinary knowledge has left architecture in a state of acute deafness. In spite of this assumption, it would seem that for the meta-theory of critical listening to become more readily applicable within architectural design and urban planning, those disciplinary boundaries and knowledge bases must somehow be made more porous and breakable. Indeed, the acoustician Jian Kang suggests an alternate longer-term solution for achieving a greater porosity between disciplinary knowledge areas through his call for new digital design tools for auralizing urban design models. (Kang 2010, p. 412)

Acoustic Futures

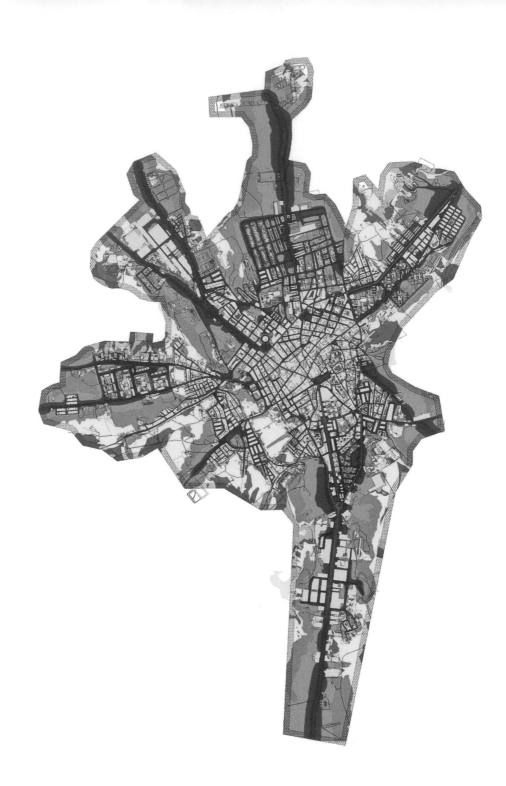

Figure 86. Noise map of the Spanish city Linares. Zones with greatest SPL values are shown in red.

But the notion of "design" here used by Kang is one only used to describe the elements of any given soundscape, which through zoning or other urban framework restrictions can be attenuated, muted or accentuated according to the given program. Perhaps one of the restrictions on novelty that has arisen within the recent work of acousticians working within the urban realm to "design" new soundscapes is their reliance on a standard usurpation of noise engineering strategies. Here, rather than engaging in the act of new spatial designs, architectural models that produce new types of acoustic signatures, or a broader addressing of the facets of critical listening such as form and materiality, staid and somewhat conservative approaches see the problem being tackled purely from a "top-down" policy stance rather than a "bottom-up" design stance.

Kang's proposal then for a software solution that communicates the auditory qualities of an urban environment closely approaches Blesser and Salter's contention that aural architecture is a design arena that will be enacted only through digital tools. Even though architecture seems to be glaringly absent, what such a proposal does envisage is that listening to an urban sound design and the acoustic relationship that it establishes between its users may become a ubiquitous approach for future urban planning frameworks. Currently, such information about design impact regarding acoustic qualities is still constructed objectively, and communicated through the standard scientific models of plotted data, tabulations and complex noise mappings.

The move away from purely visual representations of acoustic data into the more tangible area of experiencing the intended auditory qualities of an urban design directly through listening will certainly be a requirement for any truly innovative approach to the design of the future city. Indeed, the most basic premises of the disciplines of soundscape studies and aural architecture stem from their potential to enable architectural praxis to communicate via the auditory channel, for which the design process then must be one concerned with optimizing, adjusting or morphing architectonic qualities to communicate particular visual and acoustic affects. But for this strategy to have any real impact, architecture and architectural design itself must be present and not just seen as a given or a proxy. To readily accommodate the acoustic impact of design decisions, particularly within a parametric paradigm, requires an immediacy between hearing the connection that form, materiality, structure and texture have on the impact of the design's ability to communicate an intended acoustic signature: what Rivka Oxman nominates as a "performative design framework." (Oxman 2009) In such a framework, architecture would gain the potential to become more than what is immediately seen, and moreover, the case of whether sounds inhabit the space or space is produced by the sounds is a question only relevant to how one hears the design.

Order

That both aural architecture and soundscape studies have nominated themselves as somewhat equipped to tackle, or at least present, alternative frameworks for conceptualizing sound as a design parameter still leaves the processes of architectural design in need of new ears. This is particularly true in regard to the acoustic future of the built environment. To consider the meta-theory of critical listening then in regard to contemporary architecture and the future city is to thus propose a new conceptual framework in which the order of architecture is conceived as an articulation of space,

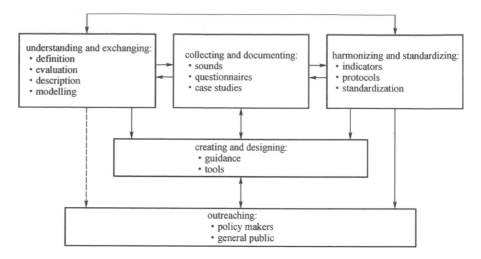

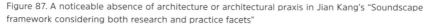

Figure 87. A noticeable absence of architecture or architectural praxis in Jian Kang's "Soundscape framework considering both research and practice facets"

for which the order of sounds is inherently enfolded within it. Critical listening is then a conduit and mediation tool between understanding the realm of the articulation of space, that which Timothy Morton suggests is the "circumambient, or surrounding world," (Morton 2007, p. 33) and the order in the sounds themselves: that is, their qualities and behaviors. The fundamental concept of these two orders is what I have derived from that which theoretical physicist David Bohm noted as the "implicate" and "explicate" orders.

For Bohm, and in a much more general manner, the notion of the "implicate order," which is also referred to as the "enfolded" order, is the idea that there is a deeper and much more fundamental order of reality present. In addition, Bohm also argues that there exists an explicate or "unfolded" order which describes those phenomena and other abstractions that are most readily perceived by humans:

> In the enfolded [implicate] order, space and time are no longer the dominant factors determining the relationships of dependence or independence of different elements. Rather, an entirely different sort of basic connection of elements is possible, from which our ordinary notions of space and time, along with those of separately existent material particles, are abstracted as forms derived from the deeper order. These ordinary notions in fact appear in what is called the "explicate" or "unfolded" order, which is a special and distinguished form contained within the general totality of all the implicate orders. (Bohm 1980, p. xv)

This characterization though is one that is equally fit and useful for describing the relation between the realm of architecture and the realm of acoustics and sound. As Ervin Laszlo contends, "because all things are given together in [Bohm's] implicate order, there are no longer any chance events in nature; everything that happens in the explicate order is the expression of order in the order of the implicate realm." (Laszlo 1995, p. 38) In regard to the meta-theory of critical listening, here too we might appropriately consider that architecture itself represents a structure or order, which in the built environment equates to the notion of Bohm's implicate order. In the city, for example, the order of architecture is the articulation of tangible space in which form and materiality provide a structure that enfolds all other phenomena: in particular, sound events. These sound events, which can be described according to their texture, the underlying program from which they arise and their structure, are unfolded in time (the very definition of sound as a time-based process). Current approaches to the research and investigation of sounds within the urban environment by acousticians using the pretext of soundscape studies have thus sought out ways to find a common "standard" or metric for scientifically describing qualities of sounds encountered by city inhabitants regarding their expectations. (Brown et al. 2011; Guastavino 2006) But what seems lacking in these approaches, particularly in regard to the notion of critical listening explored so far, is the lack of an examination of the connection between the unfolding order of sounds and the enfolded structure of architecture that is the built environment.

Sounds and the sound world of the city is necessarily a function of the greater implicate order that is architecture. Sounds are unfolded within the built environment and concurrently the built environment enfolds sound sources. Without the very idea of a medium, a landscape or architecture (however subtle, random or considered), this unfolding of an acoustic identity is muted, negated and annihilated. But similarly, architecture and the built environment is actually transversely constructed according to the acoustic unfolding: that is, due to the structure of the sounds themselves. This is evidenced in the very and most basic manner in which program serves not only as a force that shapes approaches to architectural design, but as a function within the assemblage of critical listening. From any given site program arise activities and thus sounds and an acoustic signature or sound profile. Given the program is one that shapes the approach to architectural design and the articulation of space, the sound world too is a dimension that complements and similarly assists in producing the experience of architecture. As Pallasmaa noted, "an architectural work is not experienced as a collection of isolated visual pictures, but in its fully embodied material and spiritual presence," (Pallasmaa 2005, p. 44) in which the acoustic dimension is inevitably a factor that brings a heightening of the multisensory. Thus, without human presence, or the development of functional spaces that pursue particular social programs, the specializations of human progress or the inevitable uptake in every human epoch of new technologies, architecture as an enfolded or implicate order would become unnecessary. Thus the connection between the implicate order and the explicate order in regards to acoustic events and acoustic signatures runs deeply through all manifestations of the articulation of form and the very fundament of architectural design. Hence as Laszlo argued, "everything that happens in the explicate order is the expression of order in the order of the implicate realm." This in turn means that the realm of the acoustic environment of the city and of architecture is equally an expression of the physical articulation of space in which the order unfolds: an order within, yet of another order.

The acoustic (explicate) and architectural (implicate) orders are thus inseparable yet appear, and have been so far commonly considered, as engaged in different problems, in different approaches to design and in a different aesthetics. Such a construct then suggests that the knowledge realms of acoustics and architecture are ostensively separable, or perhaps more succinctly, completely fragmented from the idea of completeness or wholeness. That there has been a wealth of recent research in the field of applied acoustics and noise engineering regarding the development of urban planning models (Mags et al. 2006) attests to how the urban environment is traditionally divided into policy areas. The compartmentalization of phenomena denies the true relation between auditory phenomena and the designed environment in which they unfold. This type of thinking is also found in contemporary approaches to generating soundscape evaluation strategies (Zhang & Kang 2007; Brown et al. 2011; Jeon et al. 2011) where metrics and norms are sought. Both of these approaches to understanding the sound realm of the city attest to the hegemonic notion of the "top-down" approach as absolute. But rather than providing real solutions to the problem of noise and the expectations of city dwelling, what is achieved is a fragmentation of the urban environment into disconnected problems. This occurs because of the sole focus on the explicate order of sounds and acoustic zones rather than a more complete examination of the relation between the explicate order and the order in which it is enfolded: that of the implicate order of architecture.

The meta-theory of critical listening is thus a means by which to disrupt the notion of a fragmentation of the implicate order that is architecture and the common approach so far developed between acoustics and architectural design: that of the separation of knowledge and of design praxis. The assemblage of critical listening posits the facets of texture, structure, form, program and materiality. As I outlined in Chapter 3, these are parts of a whole which form relations between each other and, when understood and examined together, provide a greater knowledge of the condition that is the explicate and implicate order. By this I mean the relation between characteristics of sound and all physical qualities of the articulation of space. Indeed, traditional investigations into acoustic phenomena, or the proposals and methods of Schafer and soundscape studies, have solely focused on the explicate order. Here, they have sought to bring attention to the unfolding of sound sources and their properties, qualities and semiotics. But where once the notion of soundscape had been used by the acoustic ecology movement and other electroacoustic composers as a framework for aesthetic means, and to draw attention to the sounds of the environment around us, in its new scientific clothes, it is currently being touted as a viable concept for controlling and "designing" new soundscapes. This emphasis though on planning models and scientific approaches to sound design has most likely discouraged architects, urban designers and landscape architects (those clearly who have the most to gain) from creatively applying innovative sound design within the built environment. What has been continually communicated within the last five years then is the absolute necessity now for the acoustic health and sustainability of future cities to be finally addressed via a new approach to urban sound design and thus architecture. But for this to be most readily achieved, we require a radical rethinking of the current disjunction and fragmentation between architecture and sound so that designers and planners can begin to address the multisensory qualities of architectural experience as a parameter that can be distinctly embodied by urban forms.

Thus critical listening seeks to provide a means towards generating a deeper investigation into the whole as two interconnected orders. This move against fragmentation is posited within the facets and their individual realms. Critical listening then is a meta-theory in the sense that the notion of texture and structure, which might be parameters enough to only consider the explicate order (as is common within the discipline of acoustic ecology), should also be considered against the facets of form and materiality (important elements of Blesser and Salter's aural architecture) as well as the notion of program (an indigenous concept vital in architectural design). An acoustic future of the city then must be a consideration of both a "top-down" and "bottom-up" framework. The facets of form and materiality necessarily have implications beyond the visual sense, as do the elements of texture and structure. We can easily imagine that a changed program may render not only the form and materiality of an architectural design as unsuitable, but equally the new texture and structure of the sound profile as problematic to the goals of a design. To fragment explicate and implicate orders as consisting of solely independent and absolute qualities causes less than optimized conditions to perpetuate. If the role of architecture, particularly in the city and urban realm, is to be one of unifying the forces and needs of social, cultural and even economic factors into a spatial coherence, then the wholeness of critical listening seeks to provide a multisensory approach to achieve these ends.

From this approach, the dynamics of sound sources as an unfolding in the explicate order can be assessed and considered within the deeper implicate order of architecture. This means then that the acoustic horizon, the sound profile of a site and the ensuing acoustic signature of architectural environments are a process of the mesh between the global physical articulations of space and the local phenomena of auditory objects. In fact, we can further consider that the relation between the acoustic horizon and the acoustic arena is a direct expression between implicate and explicate order. The idea of the acoustic arena as existing on an infinite plane can also be understood as a manifestation of the grid within the explicate order. The unfolding of the sound events within the explicate order is also a demarcation of the grid within this order. As the acoustic arena is privileged from the point of reference of the listener, the dimension of this arena and the area of the grid in which it operates within the infinite plane is an expression of the explicate order. Conversely, the acoustic horizon is an expression of the implicate order. Here, because of the articulation of architectural form throughout the infinite plane, often particular distant sound sources are heard, which themselves are a function of the implicate order. We can thus deduce from this characterization that at times the implicate order of architecture exists such that it distinctly defines the visual horizon. In an isolated room, the explicate order and unfolding of sounds within the acoustic arena, and indeed the acoustic horizon share the boundary of the visual horizon. Here then, the two orders may appear sealed as one. In other situations in which the acoustic arena and acoustic horizon mark out their area on the grid differently, we can ascertain that the implicate order must extend beyond the current visual horizon.

The city today and its acoustic future then can be read, or more pertinently, heard, as a potential laboratory in the same manner that Bacon's "sound-houses" of Bensalem functioned to find how a new range or library of experimental sounds can find their way into the very fabric of the everyday. The very notion of the city as a sound house was of course a defining quality of the aesthetic that John Cage pursued. Though Cage's aesthetics were more broadly concerned with the negation of the idea of "musical" sound, his approach to understanding sound was one that did not attempt to divide the realm between sound as being more aesthetically meaningful within the rarefied musical context. If anything, sounds for Cage are utilitarian, social phenomena that express the notion of a deeper order within society, regardless of whether they are sourced from a musical context or the city. Hence, like Bohm, Cage would have equally agreed with the notion that "man's natural environment has correspondingly been seen as an aggregate of separately existent parts, to be exploited by different groups of people." (Bohm 2005, pp. 1–2) Sounds too, for Cage, had suffered the same fate in which distinctions between value judgments and contexts had hindered the breadth and depth of music as a social process born from human creativity. Bacon's notion of the sound house and its proprietary as a laboratory then might provide a means by which to test and usurp the facets of critical listening as a way in which to innovate design in the urban realm, to branch out from the fragmentation of acoustic measurement as a means to an end.

Ultimately, critical listening is a framework in which to consider the urban realm and architecture as manifestations of a series of ongoing experiments in which the acoustic signatures of the city are constantly becoming transformed and refined. These signatures are then ones that are gradually moving towards coherence. But until now, it would seem that these experiments have been somewhat random and unconsidered, or at least fragmented and not unified. To address the whole and the notion of the explicate and implicate orders as a particular condition may produce many more striking results such that the future sound of cities may yet provide a balanced and adjudged synthesis between the implicate order of architecture and the explicate life of sounds that propagate within architecture.

8
"Like Quail Clucking ..."

"Like Quail Clucking…"

> One day, while trying to drive in the chaotic traffic of Tehran, with each move I tried to make provoking taps on the horns of cars beside, behind, and advancing towards me, I remarked to a hitch-hiker I had picked up, that after five blocks of this I felt like a road lizard on bad amphetamines. Oh, they are not, like us Westerners, using the horn as a warning or a threat, he said. They are like quail clucking as they feed on a ripe wheat field. They are, he meant, creating a sound environment with which they symbiotically merge with one another. (Lingis 1994, p. 107)

To return to where this book started, that is, with the notion of an architecture of the ear, is to perhaps contend that the ear's geometry, structure and spatiality is much like the implicate order of the architecture of our built environment. The ear's form and materiality function to curate particular types of listening experiences that become interpreted in the brain as sensation and thus produce a notion of space as well as an awareness of its program, texture and structure. From listening and the ear also come the ideas of acoustic scale and the limits of the acoustic horizon and the ephemeral bounds of the acoustic arena. Thus the sounds produced by bodies (of humans, of fauna and flora), technologies or architectonic features of an environment are those particular expressions of the unfolding or explicate order. But it is notable that these expressions are necessarily forged through, and simultaneously part of, that totality of all phenomena, which itself is an enfolded structure.

To hear, as Alphonso Lingis's hitchhiking companion implies, that the antiphonal calling of quail functions as an acoustic community built through a layering of individual voices is to similarly suggest that an analogous symbiotic merging is also found in our contemporary built environment. Each sound source of such a community is a distinct entity, yet when heard as a whole, we are able to grasp its condition as one intrinsically dynamic in its scale, rhythm and reach. This condition is thus the relation between sounds as they are produced and unfolded, and the effects of architectural and landscape forms to influence and curate particular acoustic behaviors in these sonic phenomena. These behaviors in turn greatly impact our daily lives, interpersonal interactions, expectations, movements, health and well-being.

To identify this symbiotic merging is thus also a chance to reflect on the connection between the architecture of the ear and the architecture of the implicate order that surrounds us. As Michel Serres noted in his idea of the box within us and its replication within our environment: "every possible kind of audible finds sites of hearing and regulation. It is as though the body were constructed like a box, a series of boxes, through which these cycles pass." (Serres 2008, p. 111) To read the ear as just such a box then is to identify how its architecture is a crucial characteristic in the forming of sensation and the manner in which listening produces particular patterns in behavior and enforces the notion of an auditory center, the "I," as the interface between the internal and external worlds. But as a box, the ear is perhaps also a physical expression of the implicate order, which duly returns us again to Geoffrey Scott's "architecture of humanism," where the ear and the building are a merged conglomeration:

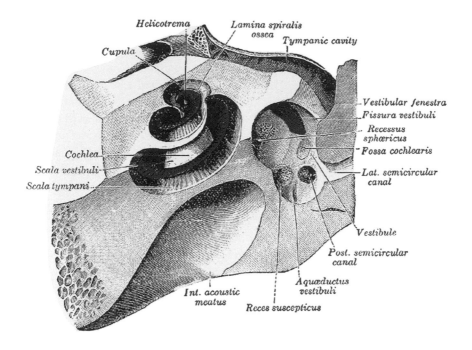

Figure 88. "The cochlea and vestibule, viewed from above. All the hard parts which form the roof of the internal ear have been removed with the saw."

> We have looked at the building and identified ourselves with its apparent state. We have transcribed ourselves into terms of architecture … The whole of architecture is, in fact, unconsciously invested by us with human movement and human moods. Here, then, is a principle complementary to the one just stated, we transcribe architecture into terms of ourselves. This is the humanism of architecture. (Scott 1914, pp. 121–213)

The meta-theory of critical listening posits that the co-creation and experience of sound-space is also a creation of an architecture of sounds that is indelibly tied to the assemblage of form, materiality, structure, program and texture. These facets of the whole then account for the total sum of articulations of visual and auditory space, that is, of both implicate and explicate orders. The architecture of the ear then enfolds acoustic stimuli that approach, interact and interface with it. Indeed because of the geometry of the cochlea waves are propagated through its entirety, from its base (close to the middle ear) to its apex (the top or center of the spiral). This structure dictates a relationship between a geometric or architectural form and a sound source and functions in an identical way to how our surrounding auditory world—as the juxtaposition between the digital, the mechanical and the natural—is crafted, cajoled, interfaced and directed by the architecture of our surroundings.

To consider the architecture of the ear as a structure that subtly shifts, amplifies and highlights particular ways of hearing (Jülicher et al. 2002, p. 16) similarly suggests that the architecture of our environment is too an auditory system ripe with influence and numerous consequences for our activities and our sedentary occupation within it. It is a logical consequence then that we can say that through architecture we hear in a particular fashion. The architecture of the built environment then can be understood as an auditory opportunity, a means by which to enable new types of hearing, such that we ultimately hear through architecture's ears. That which occurs at the facade of the building (or the pinna) and those further encounters at the perforations at doors or windows (the tympanic membrane) provide a means by which to conceptualize, like Scott did, an order that enfolds those passing, ephemeral acoustic events. The building and the landscape too similarly produce sounds (heard and unheard yet always unfolding), just like those arising from the tympanic membrane, not to mention the production of sounds through the myriad programs within various interior spaces we encounter.

Lingis's conception then of the manner in which a city like Tehran articulates an auditory experience through a symbiosis of competing yet complementary sound actions also suggests that the modulus of the active and aware listener is a mediator between the explicate and implicate orders. The fact that the ear itself is a producer of sounds, or *otoacoustic emissions*, points towards both its I/O and threshold condition. We might say then that critical listening is the awareness of this interface between the implicate architecture of the ear itself and the surrounding built environment as an iteration of this form. It is both an input and an output in which the implicate order enfolds sound behaviors through filtering and amplification, while the explicate order of unfolding sounds occurs via the instrument of the body. The approach of critical listening is thus the recognition of this condition, or this threshold structure, in which the unfolding of sounds is acutely of the order both of an implicate architecture and of an explicate phenomenon or sensation.

The architecture of sounds that is the traffic of Tehran then can be read as a space of distinct sound actions. These actions might be coordinated or seemingly random events on the grid but inevitably arise from a program and thus produce space as a function of the unfolding order. This unfolding of sounds is collected and interfaced by the implicate order that is the architecture of the ear. The ear then delivers and coordinates an interpretation of sensation that describes the facets of texture and structure. The sounds themselves though appear and disappear according to the form and materiality of the surfaces of an environment and the conditions of the medium of the atmosphere (wind, air temperature, air pressure). The shifting dimensions of the acoustic horizon and acoustic arena thus become markers of the relation between explicate and implicate orders. They are sensations of acoustic scale delivered through the ear and interpreted by the brain. But at the same time that they are products of an unfolding, they are too a manifestation of an implicate order, an apparent enfolding of physical space.

To say that critical listening is a type of spatial auditory thinking requires a template or structure in which not only to organize concepts, but equally to locate the listener. That the listener is there to begin with might not appear obvious, but nonetheless they are located in an environment as somebody who is an active agent, and therefore, a potential critical listener. The notion then of wholeness that Böhm spoke of means that an ensuing connectedness is ever present throughout all manifestations of apparent materiality and form given an active and critically minded listener. This is perhaps simply the acceptance of the auditory as a potential structural partner to the

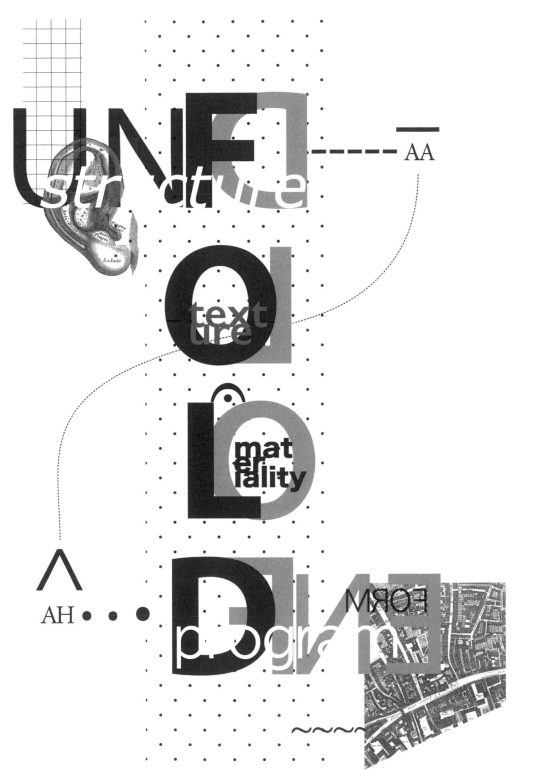

Figure 89. Diagram 3: The concepts of critical listening

"Like Quail Clucking..."

visual articulation of space, or, apropos, a chance to examine a sensuous semiotics of site. The facets of materiality and form are thus necessarily of the same structural importance as the descriptions of sounds as embodied in a particular texture and structure, which are correspondingly a function of an engaged program.

But as a theory of the auditory dimension and its potential to inform architecture, critical listening has specifically been called out in this book as a way to acoustically engage architectural design, and as a means to interrogate architectural thinking. The built works that have been examined in this book have thus been nominated as exemplar projects because they have incorporated notions about sound and acoustics as primary ideals that have catalyzed the concept of architecture as a multisensory encounter. The diverse range of work from practitioners such as NOX, Bernhard Leitner, Hodgetts + Fung Design and Architecture and Paul de Kort has resisted traditional approaches to design in which the acoustic signatures or auditory encounters of the resolved projects are merely a consequence or necessity of a less than whole, visually focused methodology. This move away from fragmentation, where both the enfolded and unfolding structures of sound and architecture are considered as intimately bound and capable of influencing each other, results in a coherence that unites structural, auditory and spatial articulations to produce multisensory experiences within built forms.

Critical listening has been applied here not only as a means of reading and theorizing such extant built works, but equally as a way in which to hear the potential of those iconic architectural representations that have made a significant mark on architectural representation within the twentieth century. From Archigram, Archizoom and Haus-Rucker-Co, the potential of critical listening has been as an aid to imagine those acoustic futures that are embedded within the language and spatial articulation inherent in such iconic projects. What should become apparent from these examinations then is that the auditory qualities of architecture are an embedded quality: they exist whether they are planned, designed or randomly acquired by the designer.

The logical outcome of the facet of program is a sound signature for which its particular sounds embody various acoustic types or characteristics that are described through the facets of texture and structure. These unfolding phenomena are then subsequently guided, corralled and influenced through a design's materiality and form. But it is the inseparability of this assemblage in producing an auditory experience of architecture that provides the constructs of the acoustic horizon and acoustic arena with a particular currency and influence. It is through this influence that an engulfing net is cast that covers not only our immediate environs or the single site we find ourselves in, but the greater built environment as the spatial fabric of our daily lives moves ever outwards across the infinite grid.

We might imagine then an architectural future in which the design of a wholeness lies in the indivisibility between the unfolded and enfolded orders: that is, between sounds and architecture as equal articulators of a lived experience. This future would be one in which the design of the built environment is the design of a multisensory experience in which our interactions are ones that assist in producing architectures—those both seen and heard; when design not only becomes a consideration of the myriad needs of social, economic, environmental or programmatic notions, but also acoustic qualities, the issues of noise abatement, health problems and site specificity become a seamless and integrated aspect of architecture as spatial articulator and producer of place.

Whether such a stance might be conceivable only in a utopia akin to Bacon's Bensalem denies the ease with which critical listening seeks it applicability into current design praxis. To consider any architectural design as a potential architecture of sounds is to simply apply a strategy of active and informed listening. Through this approach, the auditory image acts as a veil to the more commonly appropriated visual images that express and convey the essence of an architectural idea. That designs are visually analyzed, read and considered for their structural, spatial and cultural impacts already means that a level of disciplinary knowledge and interpretation is always necessary in understanding their strengths, innovations and ideology. To hear then another "hidden" layer of acoustic information within the architectural representation only deepens the notion of architecture as a function of the human condition, as a purveyor of human sensations. It similarly alludes to the richness and broad nature of architectural design and how the auditory channel must be conceived as a naturally occurring subset of the taxonomy that is architectural knowledge. If the theory of critical listening then has but a single aim, it is to simply open up and draw attention to the auditory realm as an already vibrant, coexistent and forceful event-maker in our lives. Its presence then has the potential to shape our future relationships and behaviors, our spatial interactions and our place-making, and thus draw us ever closer to the essence of architecture as the ongoing processing of an ideal in which space is conceived, built, sensed and ultimately lived.

Postlude

Wang opened his apartment door. The air was close inside, but before he could begin to even catch his breath, having decided to walk the last three floors in order to avoid encountering his desperate neighbor Jin Jin, his sofa called to him with longing intent — "feeling tired?" it whispered as small wavelets rippled across its cushions. Stepping inside, the door slid automatically shut behind him without even a slight suggestion of effort, no "click" or comforting faux-mechanistic sound signal announcing that the outside world was now to be dissolved and forgotten. Any trace of the exterior of the apartment-cum-cocoon was now quickly erased, tellingly marked only through the soft yet somehow salacious bellow of the air pressure adjustment between his apartment and the antechamber on the other side of the door. Living on the ninetieth floor had its peculiarities, but these were outweighed by what was found beyond the walls: an endless blue sky that met the eyes and the ears directly, and depending on the time of year, with an utmost force of light and sound. This other room, as Wang had often mused, must be the true interface to nature that the First-order followers had preached of. But he had no time for philosophy or any deep religious convictions; soundrags and the acoustic protest movement were both time-consuming, and indeed under the present circumstances risky enough.

Gazing outwards from the womb-like confines of his couch, the floor-to-ceiling mirrored windows functioned not only as the walls but as the eyes of the apartment. He could see that clouds had begun to gather around the Pinnacle, Tower T6 and what looked like Peak Tower T29. Though he couldn't really make out its distinct trapezoidal shape, that eternal neon pink signature glow and continuous air traffic — like fireflies busy swarming in pale light — was enough to give away its identity. It was growing dark now and as the fading rays of the sun began to refract off his neighboring sister apartment tower Shin-Roppongi 2, Wang fidgeted at the base of the couch for his phone. Having received an ancient Bash script from Janovich, he ran the code to enable a hack of the apartment control system. Slowly, tentatively and of course illegally, the wall-window began to laboriously open to reveal the sky and the walls of towers beyond. Wind began to flow in through the now-ajar opening. The air was frigid and the sound of the wind conveyed merriment, almost as if it found pleasure in its sweeping flow into the negative space of the apartment. Like filtered pink noise as it gradually moved across the spectrum, taking the nooks and hollows of the furniture, floor and kitchen, it swam through the apartment hungrily seeking out other frequencies to overwhelm, mesh, combine and synthesize with.

With the wind came the clouds too. Against a striated blue-pink sky they hung effortlessly on the walls of the other towers, consuming their mirrored surfaces until the propagation of dull pearl lights within each core became the only means by which to recognize their postmodernist forms. Wang imagined the clouds as cellular-organized white noise: a beautiful and simplistic acoustic organism that would initially congregate around the fiftieth floor; then, as it spread and grew in volume, would self-filter to transform into pink noise at the eightieth floor and beyond. In fact, the clouds, through the proxy of the wind, seemed to be the only acoustic reminder of life from the streets below. Brief amplified swirls and explosions of drone traffic and occasional electroacoustic warning alarms were the only suggestion that far below existed another world, a silent society, an acoustic community of near-mutes. But for Wang, it was the sky and its organs that were the deliverers of an auditory reminder of that other community, that other body: the sky, the air, the atmosphere and the weather—an openness and eternal freedom from any restraint or second-guessing. Though the ecology of the megacity was one in which the paradigm of human activities as producers of sounds was constantly being repressed, negated and disassembled, up here, above the low-lying smog of acoustic regulation, nature and the notion of the environment as an engulfing in auditory experience reigned in an endless freedom only matched by the vastness of the sky itself.

It was dark in the apartment now. The couch had sensed Wang's body temperature and had also adjusted its own warmth to counter the coolness of the air and invading clouds that had rapidly consumed the entire apartment. The interior atmosphere of the living room had been cannibalized, transformed, and this new enfolded interior volume began to lap like a wave at the bottom of the couch. Hanging from the ceiling, puffs of opaque white blobitecture cowered above a mist, itself thick, curvaceous and self-intersecting, yet completely nebulous. Droplets had already begun to appear on the walls as the mist began to waft over an ocean that gently began to ripple across the floor having found its way through the now-porous facade, its current and eddies forming ephemeral geometric patterns bathed in a choppy cream-colored foam.

Wang's heavy eyelids belied the creeping white noise that he had begun to notice, or at least come to accept as present in the apartment. It seemed to be located somewhere deep in his memory, at the left back quarter of his head, a call back to some other time in which he had lived. But in spite of its apparent familiarity, its creeping persistence had slowly begun to shift the dimensions and qualities of the room. After escaping the confines of his memory, it had immediately sought out the living room corner and seemed to be flowing both in and out from a data port in the wall. This caused everything, the facade, the walls, the windows and what was left of the floor, to start to modulate. A beautiful dance of wavelets and traces of complex manifolds began appearing all around him, both manipulating local surfaces and producing new surface-spaces in the voids between all visible objects. This courtship was met with the ensuing absorption of all the objects that surrounded him into the unrelenting shifting clouds and ocean that had now become the space of his apartment. The white noise increased sharply in volume until it became an obvious signal of something coming. How Wang had figured such a semiotics to be the case he couldn't be sure, perhaps he was simply remembering just another fantastic street sermon he had heard from the First-order followers. As he saw a dark figure come into view where his window once stood, the white noise ceased with a brilliant and percussive sharp downward ramp that left the room pregnant with a silent *fermata*.

It seemed logical and practically inevitable to Wang that the man standing in front of him was his missing colleague Tilsky. But what was more unusual about the encounter was that Tilsky was no longer Tilsky, but somebody called Torikai. How that was communicated to Wang was also a mystery, he just knew it wholeheartedly, so it appeared unnecessary to discuss the matter directly. Moreover, Torikai seemed wholly fixated on

Postlude

187

a small and intricately decorated black laminate box in front of him. "As an *otoniwashi* these secrets must be held safe and passed on only through the lineage." As Wang was trying to understand the meaning of this cryptic sentence, quite unexpectedly, something sprang forth from the box. To say "something" would be to imply that this "thing" had form and dimensions. Wang didn't initially perceive the image of the thing as a three-dimensional object located in space at all, but more as a fourth-dimensional enfolding of the apartment around a point that somehow hung interstitially above the box. Shortly after this foundational sensation evaporated, a very concise series of symbols manifested themselves, tickling his eyelids and dancing a spiral trajectory around the box before haphazardly dissipating into the mist-cloud-ocean that had stubbornly persisted throughout this whole episode. "Ah, *nani beati*, my happy little dwarfs," exclaimed Torikai with increasing excitement. In that moment, Wang turned his head as he had sensed something behind him, not a thing as such, but a presence that was embodied in an absolutely beatific sound. Looking around he saw nothing in particular within the mist but heard a curious bleating that circled around waist height. The sounds increased in number and moved slowly around the space, happily conversing with each other across a small amplitude-modulating bandwidth and appearing to bump into one another in a particularly cheerful fashion that marked each communal encounter with a *coloratura glissandi* pitch smear to mark the chatter point and information exchange.

Wang was still trying to account for exactly how many "happy dwarfs" had invaded the apartment when he saw Torikai ostensively planting both the species *tintinnabula* and *harpae regalis* on a wall that Wang could not remember ever having in his apartment. It was not really a wall that could be described in the ordinary sense of a partition between two spaces; it was more like a grid or a plane of no absolute thickness, but equally solid enough that it demarcated space-time: it was both in space and outside the space of their immediate environs. Across the grid Wang again found some graffiti of ephemeral notation briefly tracing out a trajectory before disappearing into the grid itself. "My wind bells and majestic harps, they thrive in any low-fidelity environment," proclaimed Torikai proudly. A soft and ethereal high-pitched ringing, rich in a complex frequency spectrum, emerged from the points that Torikai had located for his creations on the grid. Then came the sounds of a string instrument, but without the obvious percussive "pluck" of a finger working a tensile metallic string, only the resonant and reverberant unfolding of the ensuing envelope and its interaction with the architecture of a room, not this room per se, but a cathedral it seemed. The two lines complemented each other in their opposing fixed positions on the grid, marking off a small acoustic arena in which *beatae nano* seemed all too happy to explore the area between and underneath.

"How about a few *vitium ridentes* and *vitis pulchrae* for the roof?" gestured the *otoniwashi*. Wang had only then begun to understand what value Torikai's service had been. As a "sound gardener" it was now clear how these magnificent and soniferous fantasies would function—as a pleasure garden of acousticelights! Wang thought immediately of the potential for curating extraordinary acoustic encounters that would challenge the current muted state of megacity auditory regulations. But a small sharp explosion that seemed to be located somewhere at his feet muted his hollow chuckle. Quickly jumping out of the way, Wang heard the sound rise rapidly as it made its way directly to the roof and beyond in the matter of a few seconds. Soon the entire ocean was sending out various-sized sound rockets, each taking off at the same pitch but through their modulating rhythmic structure and the Doppler effect finding all manner of melodic interactions as they passed high above Wang and up through to the top of the building and into the embrace of the sky. These "laughing foibles" were offset by deep sub-frequency "crawlers" that seemed to inhabit a space deeper than the entire distance to the street. "The *vit pulchrae* are best used sparingly," advised the master. Accordingly, Wang felt his body starting to pulsate in communion with the deep sub-frequencies of the species. Each cycle appeared to both sweep away the ocean-mist to reveal the floor beneath while at the same time causing him to be lifted along on their enormous, far-reaching fundamentals.

The extraordinary sound scene had grown in its proportion and brilliance, both filling what Wang knew to be the physical boundaries of his apartment while at the same time producing a new type of interactive living sound-space that somehow extended beyond the building. "But no *ototeien* could be complete without at least a few flowering annuals, like *bulbus natans* or *oculi sui afflicti*," Torikai suggested. Directly above Wang's head droplets appeared, small black opaque spheres that began to resonate and then transform rapidly into chains of symbols, which spun on tilted axes before dissipating into the singularities from which they had originally emerged. Wang heard the "floating bulbs" first. "They feed off VF you know," exclaimed Torikai. "Enough stimulus from the band range of the human voice and they start to flower." Immediately Wang noticed the "bulbs" starting to sprout, followed by their counterparts the "cheering eyes." Their pitch kernels had an extremely simplistic sine wave oscillation mechanism, but this became increasingly richer and varied as Torikai whispered the short mantra *utsukushi chisana mono* towards them in a calm and soothing tone. Feeding off the human voice spectra, they started to become richer and more full sounding, their textures transforming from monochromatic sketches to deeply polychromatic portraits. They lost all roughness and became smeared and rounded in their envelopes, each articulating within a small but varied pitch range that was marked by a wonderfully percussive ramping envelope.

The combination of the elements, which were perfectly planted by the master, produced a glorious and organic polyphony of transcendent calls. It may have been regarded as a *Motet* in earlier times as it was a series of interleaving lines that with such rich trajectories, textures, bandwidths and frequencies synthesized to produce a new type of auditory experience. This sound garden though was one in which not only did Wang perceive sound to be contained and functioning within the site of his apartment, but somehow too, a new space arose from the sounds and their interactions with objects, people, surfaces and the forms of the building and city beyond.

Looking down, Wang noticed that he was now holding the small ornate black box and the mysterious sound garden master Tilsky, or his alter ego Torikai, was gone. Wang looked skywards, as it now appeared that his apartment had completely vanished and all that remained was the cloud-mist-ocean. The perfect ensemble of sounds and their ethereal polyphony continued on just as a light source emerging from the box started to greatly increase in its illumination. Soon everything was immersed in a perfect light ray that vibrated sympathetically too as a sound wave whose intensity constantly shifted upwards in pitch and volume until space and time seemed to collapse under the weight of an untold singularity: "The lineage continues," Wang heard himself say.

Bibliography

Mags Adams, Trevor Cox, Gemma Moore, Ben Croxford, Mohamed Refaee, and Steve Sharples. Sustainable Soundscapes: Noise Policy and the Urban Experience. Urban Studies, 43(13): 2385–2398, 2006.

Theodore Adorno. Sound Figures, trans. R Livingston. Stanford University Press, Stanford, CA, 1999.

Zeynep Çelik Alexander. The Core that Wasn't. Harvard Design Magazine, 35: 85–89, 2012.

Stan Allen. The New Cosmopolitans: Realigning the Global and the Local. Harvard Design Magazine, 35: 74–83, 2012.

Kirsti Andersen. Brook Taylor's Work on Linear Perspective: A Study of Taylor's Role in the History of Perspective Geometry. Including Facsimiles of Taylor's Two Books on Perspective. Springer Science & Business Media, New York, 1992.

Archizoom Associati. Città, catena di montaggio del sociale: Ideologia e teoria della metropoli (City, Assembly Line of Social Issues: Ideology and Theory of the Metropolis). Casabella, 350(51): 22–34, 1970.

Sophie Arkette. Sounds Like City. Theory, Culture & Society, 21: 159–168, 2004.

Rudolf Arnheim. The Dynamics of Architectural Form: Based on the 1975 Mary Duke Biddle Lectures at the Cooper Union. University of California Press, Los Angeles, 1977.

J. F. Augoyard and H. Torgue. A l'écoute de l'environnement: Répertoire des effets sonores. Éditions Parenthèses, Marseille, 1995.

Pier Vittorio Aureli. The Project of Autonomy: Politics and Architecture within and against Capitalism. Princeton Architectural Press, Princeton, 2008.

Pier Vittorio Aureli. The Possibility of an Absolute Architecture. MIT Press, Boston, 2011.

Pier Vittorio Aureli. Manfredo Tafuri, Archizoom, Superstudio, and the Critique of Architectural Ideology. In Architecture and Capitalism: 1845 to the Present, pages 132–149. Routledge, London, 2013.

Gaston Bachelard. The Poetics of Space. Beacon Press, Boston, 1969.

Francis Bacon. The New Atlantis. Filiquarian Publishing LLC, Minneapolis, 2007.

Jin Baek and Yoon-Jeong Shin. Accidental yet transformative: site-specificity of the turbine hall of Tate Modern. Architectural Research Quarterly, 19(1): 49–60, 2015.

J. G. Ballard. The Sound-Sweep. The Four-Dimensional Nightmare. Penguin Books, Middlesex, 1965.

Roger Barker. Ecological Psychology: Concepts and Methods for Studying the Environment of Human Behavior. Stanford University Press, Stanford, 1968.

Thomas Barr. Manual of Diseases of the Ear. James Maclehose, Glasgow, 1909.

Robert Beck. Spatial Meaning, and the Properties of the Environment. In David Lowenthal, editor, Environmental Perception and Behavior, pages 18–41. University of Chicago, Chicago, 1967.

Tulga Beyerle and Karin Hirschberger. A Century of Austrian Design: 1900–2005. Walter de Gruyter, Berlin, 2006.

Lawrence Bird and Guillaume LaBelle. Re-animating Greg Lynn's Embryological House: A Case Study in Digital Design Preservation. Leonardo, 43(3): 243–249, 2010.

Barry Blesser and Linda-Ruth Salter. Spaces Speak, Are You Listening? Experiencing Aural Architecture. MIT Press, Boston, 2007.

David Blumberg. Suspended moment: The fermata in Luigi Nono's string quartet Fragmente—Stille, An Diotima. In Irmengard Rauch and Gerald F. Carr, editors, Semiotics Around the World: Synthesis in Diversity: Proceedings of the Fifth Congress of the International Association for Semiotic Studies, Berkeley, 1994, volume 1, pages 595–598, Walter de Gruyter, Berlin, 1997.

David Bohm. Wholeness and the Implicate Order. Routledge, London, 1980.

Albert Borgmann. Technology and the Character of Contemporary Life. University of Chicago Press, Chicago, 1984.

Fritz Bornemann. Auditorium of the German Pavilion at EXPO 70. Bauwelt, 40: 1492–1494, 1970.

Étienne-Louis Boullée, Architecture, Essay on Art, trans. Shelia de Vallée (Paris: Bibliothèque Nationale Paris), page 91 1976.

Andrea Branzi. No-Stop City: Archizoom Associati. Hyx, Orléans, 2006.

Geoffrey Broadbent. Recent developments in architectural semiotics. Semiotica, 101(1–2): 73–101, 1994.

A. L. Brown, J. Kang, and T. Gjestland. Towards standardization in soundscape preference assessment. Applied Acoustics, 72: 387–392, 2011.

Earle Brown. Transformations and Developments of a Radical Aesthetic. In Christoph Cox and Daniel Warner, editors, Audio Culture: readings in modern music, pages 189–195. Continuum, New York, 2004.

Michel Brunet, Franck Guy, David Pilbeam, Hassane Taisso Mackaye, Andossa Likius, Djimdoumalbaye Ahounta, Alain Beauvilain, Cécile Blondel, Hervé Bocherens, Jean-Renaud Boisserie, Louis De Bonis, Yves Coppens, Jean Dejax, Christiane Denys, Philippe Duringer, Véra Eisenmann, Gongdibé Fanone, Pierre Fronty, Denis Geraads, Thomas

Lehmann, Fabrice Lihoreau, Antoine Louchart, Adoum Mahamat, Gildas Merceron, Guy Mouchelin, Olga Otero, Pablo Pelaez Campomanes, Marcia Ponce De Leon, Jean-Claude Rage, Michel Sapanet, Mathieu Schuster, Jean Sudre, Pascal Tassy, Xavier Valentin, Patrick Vignaud, Laurent Viriot, Antoine Zazzo, and Christoph Zollikofer. A new hominid from the Upper Miocene of Chad, Central Africa. Nature, 418: 145–151, 2002.

Craig Buckley. From Absolute to Everything: Taking Possession in "Alles ist Architektur." Grey Room, 28: 108–122, 2007.

Mark Burry. Scripting Cultures, Architectural Design and Programming. John Wiley & Sons, New York, 2011.

David Byrne. Playing the Building, 2016. http://www.davidbyrne.com/ archive/art/art_projects/playing_the_building/ [Accessed: 27 April, 2016.].

John Cage. Variations IV. Peters Edition, New York, 1963.

John Cage. A Year from Monday: Lectures and Writings. Calder and Boyars, New York, 1968.

Alessandra Capanna. Music and Architecture: A Cross between Inspiration and Method. Nexus Network Journal, 11(2): 257–271, Birkhäuser-Verlag, 2009.

Pablo Martínez Capdevila. The Interior City. Infinity and Concavity in the No-Stop City (1970–1971). Inicio, 4: 130–132, 2013.

Edmund Snow Carpenter. Eskimo. University of Toronto Press, Toronto, 1959.

Paul Carter. Auditing Acoustic Ecology. Soundscape. The Journal of Acoustic Ecology, 4(2): 12–13, 2003.

Roberto Casati and Achille C. Varzi. Holes and Other Superficialities. MIT Press, Boston, 1995.

William J. Cavanaugh, Gregory C. Tocci, and Joseph A. Wilkes. Architectural Acoustics: Principles and Practice. John Wiley & Sons, London, 2010.

C. Clark and S. A. Stansfeld. The Effect of Transportation Noise on Health and Cognitive Development: A Review of Recent Evidence. International Journal of Comparative Psychology, 20(2): 145–158, 2007.

B. de Coensel, A. Bockstael, L. Dekoninck, D. Botteldooren, B. Schulte-Fortkamp, J. Kang, and M. E. Nilsson. The soundscape approach for early stage urban planning: A case study. In Internoise 2010, Noise and sustainability, Lisbon, Portugal, 13–16 June 2010.

Peter Cook. Six Conversations. Academy Editions, London, 1993.

Peter Cook. Archigram. Princeton Architectural Press, Princeton, 1999.

Le Corbusier. Spirit of Truth. In Richard Abel, editor, French Film Theory and Criticism 1917–1939, pages 111–113. Princeton University Press, Princeton, 1998.

Le Corbusier. The Modulor: A Harmonious Measure to the Human Scale, Universally Applicable to Architecture and Mechanics. Birkhäuser, Basel, 2004.

Leonardo da Vinci. The Note Books of Leonardo da Vinci, ed. by E. MacCurdy. George Braziller, New York, 1955.

Peter J. Davies. Beethoven in Person: His Deafness, Illnesses, and Death. Greenwood Press, Westport, 2001.

Miguel de Beistegui. Immanence—Deleuze and Philosophy. Edinburgh University Press, Edinburgh, 2010.

Penelope Dean. No Strings Attached. Harvard Design Magazine, 35: 22–35, 2012.

Manuel Delanda. A New Philosophy of Society: Assemblage Theory and Social Complexity. Continuum, London, 2006.

Manuel Delanda. Philosophy and Simulation: The Emergence of Synthetic Reason. Continuum, New York, 2011.

Manuel Delanda. Emergence, Causality and Realism. Architectural Theory Review, 17(1): 3–16, 2012.

Gilles Deleuze and Félix Guattari. A Thousand Plateaus, trans. Brian Massumi. Continuum, London, 2004.

Gilles Deleuze and Claire Parnet. Dialogues II. Columbia University Press, New York, 2007.

Richard Deming. Living a Part: Synecdoche, New York, Metaphor, and the Problem of Skepticism. In David LaRocca, editor, The Philosophy of Charlie Kaufman, pages 193–207. University Press Kentucky, Lexington, 2011.

René Descartes. L'Homme. Charles Angot, Paris, 1664.

René Descartes. Principles of Philosophy, trans. V. R. Miller and R. P. Miller. Kluwer Academic Publishers, Dordrecht, 1983.

Eva Díaz. Dome Culture in the Twenty-first Century. Grey Room, 42: 80–105, 2011.

Johanna Drucker. The Visible Word: Experimental Typography and Modern Art, 1909–1923. University of Chicago Press, Chicago, 1997.

David Dunn. Purposeful Listening in Complex States of Times, 1997/1998. http://www.davidddunn.com/david/scores/Plicsot. pdf [Accessed: 30 April, 2016.].

S. Egusa, Z. Wang, N. Chocat, Z. M. Ruff, A. M. Stolyarov, D. Shemuly, F. Sorin, P. T. Rakich, J. D. Joannopoulos, and Y. Fink. Multimaterial piezoelectric fibres. Nature Materials, 9: 643–648, 2010.

Peter Eisenman. Duck Soup. Log, 7(Winter/Spring): 139–413, 2006.

Sam Elkington. Disturbance and Complexity in Urban Places: The Everyday Aesthetics of Leisure. In Sean Gammon and Sam Elkington, editors, Landscapes of Leisure: Space, Place and Identities, pages 24–40. Palgrave Macmillan, London, 2015.

Nishina Emi, Kawai Norie, Honda Manabu, and Oohashi Tsutomu. Design concept of sound environment based on the hypersonic effect: Research and application of sound ecology. In Kozo Hiramatsu, Tadahiko Imada, and Keiko Torigoe, editors, The West Meets East in Acoustic Ecology, pages 372–380. Hirosaki University, Hirosaki, Japan, 2006.

Robert Erickson. Sound Structure in Music. University of California Press, Los Angeles, 1975.

Robin Evans. In Front of Lines that Leave Nothing Behind. AA Files, 6 (May): 88–96, 1984.

Andrew Feenberg. Heidegger and Marcuse: The Catastrophe and Redemption of History. Routledge, New York, 2004.

Lucy Flint. Piet Mondrian, Ocean 5, 2007. http://www.guggenheim. org/new-york/collections/collection-online/artwork/3009 [Accessed: 1 May, 2016.].

Robert Fludd. Utriusque cosmi maioris scilicet et minoris metaphysica. Typis Hieronymi Galleri, Openheim, 1617.

James D. Foley. Computer Graphics: Principles and Practice. Addison-Wesley Professional, Reading, MA, 1996.

Allen Forte. The Structure of Atonal Music. Yale University Press, New Haven, 1973.

Michael Fowler. Sound Worlds of Japanese Gardens: An Interdisciplinary Approach to Spatial Thinking. Transcript-Verlag, Bielefeld, 2014.

Michael Fowler. Sound as a considered design parameter in the Japanese garden. Studies in the History of Gardens and Designed Landscapes, 35(4): 312–327, 2015.

George Michelsen Foy. Zero Decibels: The Quest for Absolute Silence. Simon and Schuster, New York, 2010.

Ursula Franklin. Silence and the Notion of the Commons. Soundscape. The Journal of Acoustic Ecology, 1(2): 14–17, 2000.

Deborah Gans. The Le Corbusier Guide. Princeton Architectural Press, Princeton, NJ, 2006.

A. Gidlöf-Gunnarsson and E. Öhrström. Noise and well-being in urban residential environments: The potential role of perceived availability to nearby green areas. Landscape and Urban Planning, 83 (2–3): 115–126, 2007.

Johann Wolfgang von Goethe and Wallace Wood. Conversations with Eckermann: Being Appreciations on Many Subjects. Washington M. Walter Dunne, New York, 1901.

Thomas Gold. Hearing. II. The Physical Basis of the Action of the Cochlea. Proceedings of the Royal Society B, 135(881): 492–498, 1948.

Henry Gray. Anatomy of the Human Body. Lea & Febiger, Philadelphia, 1918.

Walter Gropius. Idee und Aufbau des Staatlichen Bauhauses Weimar. Bauhausverlag GmbH, Munich, 1923.

John Grzinich. New Maps of Time, 2016. http://www.maaheli.ee/main/new-maps-of-time/ [Accessed: 27 April, 2016.].

C. Guastavino. The Ideal Urban Soundscape: Investigating the Sound Quality of French Cities. Acta Acustica, 92: 945–951, 2006.

Charles Gurney. Rattle and Hum: Gendered Accounts of Noise as a Pollutant: An Aural Sociology of Work and Home. In Health and Safety Authority Conference, York, 6–9 April 1999. HSA Conference.

Galia Hanoch-Roe. Musical Space and Architectural Time: Open Scoring versus Linear Processes. International Review of the Aesthetics and Sociology of Music, 34(2): 145–160, 2003.

Colin Hansen. Understanding Active Noise Cancellation. Spon Press, London, 2001.

Maria Anna Harley. Music of Sound and Light: Xenakis's Polytopes. Leonardo, 31(1): 55–65, 1998.

Karsten Harries. The Ethical Function of Architecture. MIT Press, Boston, 1998.

Lawrence Harvey. The Occupation of Space: Sound Sites, exhibition catalogue. Span Galleries, Melbourne, 1999.

Lawrence Harvey. Improving models for urban soundscape systems. Sound Effects, 3(3): 113–137, 2013.

Stephen W. Hawking. Black hole explosions? Nature, 248: 30–31, 1974.

K. Michael Hays. Architecture's Desire: Reading the Late Avant-Garde. MIT Press, Cambridge, 2010.

Martin Heidegger. Being and Time, trans. J. Macquarrie and E. Robinson. Harper & Row, New York, 1962.

Martin Heidegger. The Question Concerning Technology. In William Lovitt, editor, The Question Concerning Technology and Other Essays, pages 3–35. MIT Press, Cambridge, 1968.

Björn Hellström. Noise Design. Bo Ejeby Förlag, Göteborg, 2003.

Steven Holl, Juhani Pallasmaa, and Alberto Pérez-Gómez. Questions of Perception—Phenomenology of Architecture. William Stout Publishers, San Francisco, 2006.

Hans Hollein. Alles ist Architektur. Bau, 1(2): 1–32, 1968.

Hans Hollein and Walter Pichler. Forms and Designs, 1963, trans. Kurt Rheinfurt, 1963. http://www.hollein.com/ger/Schriften/Texte/Architecture [Accessed: 4 May, 2016.].

Santiago Huerta. Structural Design in the Work of Gaudí. Architectural Science Review, 49(4): 324–339, 2006.

Geoffrey Hunter. Metalogic: An Introduction to the Metatheory of Standard First Order Logic. University of California Press, Los Angeles, 1973.

Tim Ingold. Against Space: Place, Movement, Knowledge. In Peter Wyn Kirby, editor, Boundless Worlds: An Anthropological Approach to Movement, pages 29–44. Berghahn Books, New York, 2009.

J. Y. Jeon, P. J. Lee, J. Y. Hong, and D. Cabrera. Non-auditory factors affecting urban soundscape evaluation. Journal of the Acoustical Society of America, 130: 3761–3770, 2011.

J. Y. Jeon, J. Y. Hong, and P. J. Lee. Soundwalk approach to identify urban soundscapes individually. Journal of the Acoustical Society of America, 134: 803–812, 2013.

F. Jülicher, S. Camalet, J. Prost, and T. A. J. Duke. Active Amplification by Critical Oscillations. In A. W. Gummer, editor, Biophysics of the Cochlea: From Molecules to Models: Proceedings of the International Symposium Held at Titisee, Germany, 27 July – 1 August 2002, pages 16–27. World Scientific Publishing Co., Singapore, 2003.

Tahl Kaminer. Architecture, Crisis and Resuscitation: The reproduction of post-Fordism in late-twentieth-century architecture. Routledge, London, 2011.

Sharon Kanach. Music and Architecture by Iannis Xenakis. Pendragon Press, New York, 2008.

Jian Kang. From understanding to designing soundscapes. Frontiers of Architecture and Civil Engineering in China, 4(4): 403–417, 2010.

Toomas Karmo. Disturbances. Analysis, 37(4): 147–148, 1977.

D. T. Kemp. Stimulated acoustic emissions from within the human auditory system. The Journal of the Acoustical Society of America, 64 (5): 1386–1391, 1978.

Frederick Kiesler. Pseudo-Functionalism in Modern Architecture. Partisan Review, 16: 733–742, 1949.

Michael Kimaid. Modernity, Metatheory, and the Temporal-Spatial Divide: From Mythos to Techne. Routledge, London, 2015.

Jeffrey Kipnis. Hybridizations. Architecture + Urbanism, 296(5): 62–65, 1995.

Athanasius Kircher. Phonurgia nova sive conjugium mechanico-physicum artis & naturae paranymta phonosophia concinnatum. Rudolph Dreherr, Kempten, 1673.

Richard Kostelanetz. Conversing with Cage. Psychology Press, New York, 2003.

Bernie Krause. Anatomy of a Soundscape: Evolving Perspectives. Journal of the Audio Engineering Society, 56(1–2): 73–80, 2008.

Hanno-Walter Kruft. A History of Architectural Theory: From Vitruvius to the Present. Princeton Architectural Press, New York, 1994.

Raymond Kurzweil. The Singularity is Near: When Humans Transcend Biology. Viking Press, New York, 2006.

Poul la Cour. Tidens naturlære. Gyldendalske Boghandels Forlag, Kjøbenhavn, 1903.

Brandon LaBelle. Acoustic Territories: Sound Culture and Everyday Life. The Continuum International Publishing Group Inc, New York, 2010.

Steven LaGrow and Marvin Weessies. Orientation & Mobility—Techniques for Independence. Dunmore Press, Palmerston, NZ, 1994.

Oren Lahav, Amir Itah, Alex Blumkin, Carmit Gordon, Shahar Rinott, Alona Zayats, and Jeff Steinhauer. Realization of a Sonic Black Hole Analog in a Bose-Einstein Condensate. Physical Review Letters, 105 (24): 1–18, 2010.

Peter Lang and William Menking. Superstudio: Life Without Objects. Skira, Milan, 2003.

Ervin Laszlo. The Interconnected Universe: Conceptual Foundations of Transdisciplinary Unified Theory. World Scientific, Singapore, 1995.

Liane Lefaivre. Everything is architecture. Harvard Design Magazine, 18: 1–5, 2003.

Bernhard Leitner. Wasserspiegel, 1999. http://www.bernhardleitner.at/works [Accessed: 30 April, 2016.].

Daniel Libeskind. Countersign (Architectural Monographs No 16). Wiley-Academy, New York, 1991.

J. C. R. Licklider. Phenomena of Localization. In A. Bruce Graham, editor, Sensorineural Hearing Processes and Disorders, pages 123–127. Little Brown and Co., Boston, 1967.

Alphonso Lingis. The murmur of the world. In Walter Brogan and James Risser, editors, American Continental Philosophy, pages 95–113. Indiana University Press, Bloomington, 1994.

Kevin Lynch, Tridib Banerjee, and Michael Southworth. City Sense and City Design: Writings and Projects of Kevin Lynch. MIT Press, Boston, 1995.

Greg Lynn. Folds, Bodies & Blobs: Collected Essays. La Lettre volée, Brussels, 2004.

Angus J. Macdonald. Structure and Architecture. Routledge, London, 2007.

Brian Massumi. Parables for the Virtual: Movement, Affect, Sensation. Duke University Press, Durham, 2002.

Susan McClary. Feminine Endings: Music, Gender, and Sexuality. University of Minnesota Press, 1991.

Pierre von Meiss. Elements of Architecture: From Form to Place. Routledge, London, 2010.

Mohammed A. Mian. Project Economics and Decision Analysis: Probabilistic Models. PennWell Books, Tulsa, Oklahoma, 2002.

Andrea Mina. Why are Cuttlefish Tickled Pink? In Ross McLeod, editor, The Sensuous Intellect, pages 156–167. RMIT University Press, Melbourne, 2006.

Timothy Morton. Ecology without Nature. Harvard University Press, Cambridge, 2007.

Jamie Murray. Deleuze & Guattari: Emergent Law. Routledge, London, 2013.

Shane Murray. Architectural Design and Discourse. Architectural Design Research, 1(1): 83–102, 2005.

Adolfo Natalini. How Great Architecture Still was in 1966 …: Superstudio and Radical Architecture, Ten Years On. In Martin van Schaik and Otakar Máčel, editors, Exit Utopia: Architectural Provocations, 1956–76, 185–190. Prestel, Munich, 2005.

Dika Newlin. The Later Works of Ernest Bloch. Musical Quarterly, 33: 443–59, 1947.

Günter Nitschke. Japanese Gardens: Right Angle and Natural Form. Taschen, Cologne, 1999.

Marcos Novak. Computation and Composition. In Architecture as a translation of music, pages 66–69. Princeton Architectural Press, New York, 1994.

Flann O'Brien. The Third Policeman. Pan Books Ltd, London, 1967.

Richard Oddie. Other Voices: Acoustic Ecology and Urban Soundscapes. In Ingrid Leman-Stefanovic and Stephen B. Scharper, editors, The Natural City: Re-envisioning the Built Environment, pages 161–173. University of Toronto Press, Toronto, 2012.

OMA. Yokohama Masterplan, 1992. http://www.oma.eu/projects/1992/yokohama-masterplan/ [Accessed: 30 April, 2016.].

Walter J. Ong. Orality and Literacy: The Technologizing of the Word. Routledge, New York, 1982.

Tsutomu Oohashi, Emi Nishina, Manabu Honda, Yoshiharu Yonekura, Yoshitaka Fuwamoto, Norie Kawai, Tadao Maekawa, Satoshi Nakamura, Hidenao Fukuyama, and Hiroshi Shibasaki. Inaudible High-Frequency Sounds Affect Brain Activity: Hypersonic Effect. The Journal of Neurophysiology, 83(6): 3548–3558, 2000.

Michael Ostwald. Architectural theory formation through appropriation. Architectural Theory Review, 4(2): 52–70, 1999.

R. Oxman. Performative Design: A Performance-Based Model of Digital Architectural Design. Environment and Planning B: Urban Analytics and City Science, 36(6): 1026–1037, 2009.

Michael Pacione. The City: The City in Global Context. Psychology Press, New York, 2002.

Hyungmin Pai. The Portfolio and the Diagram: Architecture, Discourse, and Modernity in America. MIT Press, Boston, 2002.

Juhani Pallasmaa. The Eyes of the Skin: Architecture and the Senses. John Wiley & Sons, Chichester, 2005.

Wendy S. Parker. Does matter really matter? Computer simulations, experiments, and materiality. Synthese, 169: 483, 2009.

Keith Ansell Pearson. Viroid Life: Perspectives on Nietzsche and the Transhuman Condition. Routledge, London, 2012.

Asher Peres. Karl Popper and the Copenhagen interpretation. Studies in History and Philosophy of Science Part B: Studies in History and Philosophy of Modern Physics, 33(1): 22–34, 2002.

Mark Pimlott. Without and Within: Essays on Territory and the Interior. Episode Publishers, Rotterdam, 2007.

Rafael Pizarro. Teaching to understand the urban sensorium in the digital age: lessons from the studio. Design Studies, 30: 272–286, 2009.

R. Plomp. Rate of Decay of Auditory Sensation. The Journal of the Acoustical Society of America, 36(2): 277–282, 1964.

Dominique A. Potvin, Kirsten M. Parris, and Raoul A. Mulder. Geographically pervasive effects of urban noise on frequency and syllable rate of songs and calls in silvereyes (Zosterops lateralis). Proceedings of the Royal Society of London B: Biological Sciences, 278(1717): 2464–2469, 2010.

William T. Preyer. Die Erklärung des Gedankenlesens nebst Beschreibung eines neuen Verfahrens zum Nachweise unwillkürlicher Bewegungen. Grieben, Leipzig, 1886.

David Prior and Francis Crow. Warwick Bar Masterplan, (2005–6). http://www.liminal.org.uk/portfolio/warwick-bar-masterplan/ [Accessed: 30 April, 2016.].

Uta Priss. Formal concept analysis in information science. Annual Review of Information Science and Technology, 40: 521–543, 2006.

Wolf D. Prix. 10th Architecture Biennale Venice 2006 Austrian Pavilion Press Release. http://overview.labiennale.at/2006/downloads/ BIE_Shape_Space_Net_Eng.pdf [Accessed: 4 May, 2016.], 2006.

Ronald M. Radano. Interpreting Muzak: Speculations on Musical Experience in Everyday Life. American Music, 7(4): 448–460, 1989.

Franco Raggi. Radical Visions. Domus, 945: 89–102, 2011.

R. H. Randall. An Introduction to Acoustics. Dover Publications, New York, 1951.

Edward S. Reed. Encountering the World: Toward an Ecological Psychology. Oxford University Press, New York, 1996.

Resolution: 4 Architecture. Modern Modular, 2016. http://www.re4a.com/the-modern-modular/ [Accessed: 29 April, 2016.].

R. S. Rhodes and J. B. McClure. The audiophone. In K. A. Coleridge, editor, The Pamphlet Collection of Sir Robert Stout, volume 38, pages 3–45. Victoria University of Wellington Library, Wellington, 1987.

Terence Riley. The Changing of the Avant-garde: Visionary Architectural Drawings from the Howard Gilman Collection. Museum of Modern Art, New York, 2002.

Helen Rosenau. Boullée & Visionary Architecture. Academy Editions, New York, 1976.

Lewis Rowell. Thinking About Music: An Introduction to the Philosophy of Music. University of Massachusetts Press, Boston, 1984.

Simon Sadler. Archigram: Architecture without Architecture. MIT Press, Boston, 2005.

Joel Sanders and Karen Van Lengen. Mix House, 2006. http://www.joelsandersarchitect.com/ [Accessed: 26 April, 2016.].

R. Murray Schafer. The Soundscape: Our Sonic Environment and the Tuning of the World. Destiny Books,
Rochester, VT, 1977a.

R. Murray Schafer. Five Village Soundscapes. A. R. C
Publications, Vancouver, 1977b.

R. Murray Schafer, Barry Truax, and Hildegard Westerkamp. The Vancouver Soundscape 1973. Cambridge
Street Records, Burnaby, 1973.

Joseph Schillinger. Schillinger System of Musical
Composition. C. Fischer, Inc., New York, 1946.

Willem Schinkel and Liesbeth Noordegraaf-Eelens. Peter
Sloterdijk's Spherological Acrobatics: An Exercise
in Introduction. In Willem Schinkel and Liesbeth
Noordegraaf-Eelens, editors, In Medias Res: Peter
Sloterdijk's Spherological Poetics of Being, pages
7–28. University of Amsterdam, Amsterdam, 2011.

Patrik Schumacher. The Autopoiesis of Architecture
Volume II: A New Agenda for Architecture.
Wiley & Sons, London, 2012.

Geoffrey Scott. The Architecture of Humanism: A Study in
the History of Taste. Houghton Mifflin, Boston, 1914.

Michel Serres. The Five Senses: A Philosophy of Mingled
Bodies, trans. Margaret Sankey and Peter Cowley.
Continuum, London, 2008.

Ted Sheriden and Karen Van Lengen. Hearing Architecture. Journal of Architectural Education, 57(2):
37–44, 2003.

Marjorie Siegel. More than Words: The Generative Power
of Transmediation for Learning. Canadian Journal of
Education/Revue Canadienne de l'éducation, 20(4):
455–475, 1995.

Tanja Sihvonen. Players Unleashed!: Modding the Sims
and the Culture of Gaming. Amsterdam University
Press, Amsterdam, 2011.

Herbert A. Simon. Theories of Decision-Making in
Economics and Behavioral Science. American
Economic Review, 49(3): 253–283, 1959.

A. Skånberg and E. Öhrström. Adverse health effects in
relation to urban residential soundscapes. Journal
of Sound and Vibration, 250(1): 151–155, 2002.

Peter Sloterdijk. Bubbles: Spheres I. Semiotext,
Los Angeles, 2011.

Chris Smith. An architecture below Perception.
In Miriam Mlecek Claudia Perren, editor, Perception
in Architecture: Here and Now, pages 30–37.
Cambridge Scholars Publishing, Newcastle, 2015.

Robert Somol and Sarah Whiting. Okay, Here's the Plan.
Log, 5: 5–7, 2005.

Robert Somol and Sarah Whiting. Notes around the
Doppler Effect and other Moods of Modernism.
In A. Krista Sykes, editor, Constructing a New Agenda,
Architectural Theory 1993–2009, pages 188–203.
Princeton Architectural Press, Princeton, 2010.

Douglas Spencer. The Alien Comes Home. In Laurence
Davis and Peter Stillman, editors, The New Utopian
Politics of Ursula K. Le Guin's The Dispossessed,
pages 95–110. Lexington Books, Oxford, 2005.

Heiner Stahl. Sounding out Erfurt: Does the Song Remain
the Same? In Gwyneth Cliver and Carrie Smith-Prei,
editors, Bloom and Bust: Urban Landscapes in the
East since German Reunification, pages 169–194.
Berghahn Books, New York, 2014.

Laurent Stalder. Turning Architecture Inside Out:
Revolving Doors and Other Threshold Devices.
Journal of Design History, 22(1): 69–77, 2009.

Standards Australia. Design for access and mobility, Part
4 tactile indicators, 2002. http://www.saiglobal.com/
PDFTemp/Previews/OSH/as/as1000/1400/N14284.
pdf [Accessed: 3 May, 2016.].

Sven Sterken. Towards a Space-Time Art: Iannis Xenakis's
Polytopes. Perspectives of New Music, 39(2):
262–273, 2001.

Karlheinz Stockhausen. Aus den sieben Tagen. Universal
Edition, Vienna, 1968.

William Henry Stone. Elementary Lessons on Sound.
Macmillan & Co., London, 1879.

Yoshio Sugimoto. An Introduction to Japanese Society.
Cambridge University Press, Cambridge, 1997.

Louis H. Sullivan. The tall office building artistically
considered. Lippincott's Magazine, March: (339)
403–409, 1896.

Superstudio. Utopia, Antiutopia, Topia. In, 7: 93–96, 1972.

Daisetz Suzuki. Essays in Zen Buddhism: Second Series.
Rider, London, 1974.

R. A. Tange. The history of otosclerosis treatment:
A survey of more than a century's search for the
best treatment of the disease. Kugler Publications,
Amsterdam, 2014.

Brook Taylor. New principles of linear perspective, or the
art of designing on a plane the representations of
all sorts of objects, in a more general and simple
method than has been done before. John Ward,
London, 1749.

Lisa Taylor and David Claringbold. Acoustics of the
Sydney Opera House Concert Hall. In Proceedings
of the International Congress on Acoustics 2010,
Sydney, 23–27 August 2010.

Georges Teyssot. Aldo van Eyck's Threshold: The Story
of an Idea. Log, 11(Winter): 33–48, 2008.

Georges Teyssot. An enfolded membrane. In Pablo
Lorenzo-Eiroa and Aaron Sprecher, editors,
Architecture in Formation: On the Nature of
Information in Digital Architecture, pages 35–46.
Routledge, London, 2013.

Jeremy Till. The vanity of form. The Journal of
Architecture, 4(1): 47–54, 1999.

Marvin Trachtenberg. Architecture and Music Reunited: A New Reading of Dufay's "Nuper Rosarum Flores" and the Cathedral of Florence. Renaissance Quarterly, 54(3): 740–745, 2001.

John D. Trimmer trans. The Present Situation in Quantum Mechanics: A translation of Schrödinger's "cat paradox" paper. In J. A. Wheeler and W. H. Zurek, editors, Quantum Theory and Measurement, pages 152–167. Princeton University Press, Princeton, 1983.

Barry Truax. Handbook for Acoustic Ecology, 1999a. http://www.sfu.ca/sonicstudio/handbook/ [Accessed: 29 April, 2016.].

Barry Truax. Composition and Diffusion: Space in Sound in Space. Organised Sound, 3(2): 141–146, 1999b.

Barry Truax. Acoustic Communication. Ablex Publishing, Westpoint, 2001.

Bernard Tschumi. Architecture and Disjunction. MIT Press, Boston, 1996.

Bernard Tschumi. Architecture as event. http://www.tschumi.com/history/ [Accessed: 29 April, 2016.].

Kuniichi Uno. The Enemy of Architecture. In Gary Genosko, editor, Deleuze and Guattari, Critical Assessments of Leading Philosophers, pages 1015–1020. Routledge, London, 2001.

Edwin van der Heide and Lars Spuybroek. Son-O-House, 2004. http://www.evdh.net/sonohouse/ [Accessed: 30 April, 2016.].

Aldo van Eyck. Place and occasion. In Alison Smithson, editor, Team 10 Primer, page 101. MIT Press, Cambridge, 1968.

Robert Venturi, Denise Scott Brown, and Steven Izenour. Learning from Las Vegas: The Forgotten Symbolism of Architectural Form. MIT Press, Cambridge, 1977.

Paul Virilio and Claude Parent. Architecture Principe, 1966 et 1996, trans. George Collins. L'Imprimuer, Besançon, 1996.

Konrad Wachsmann. The Turning Point of Building. Reinhold Publishing Corporation, New York, 1961.

Charles W. Warren. Brunelleschi's Dome and Dufay's Motet. Musical Quarterly, 59(1): 92–105, 1973.

J. K. Waters. Blobitecture: Waveform Architecture and Digital Design. Rockport Publishers Inc., Gloucester, 2003.

Mike Webb. Boys at Heart. In Peter Cook, editor, Archigram, pages 2–3. Princeton Architectural Press, Princeton, 1999.

Bernhard Wedler. Baut ruhige Wohnungen. Bundesministerium für Wohnungsbau, Bad Godesberg, 1957.

Steven Weinberg. Dreams of a Final Theory: The Scientist's Search for the Ultimate Laws of Nature. Knopf Doubleday Publishing Group, New York, 2011.

Pieter Van Wesemael. Architecture of Instruction and Delight: A Sociohistorical Analysis of World Exhibitions as a Didactic Phenomenon (1798–1851–1970). Uitgeverij 010 Publishers, Rotterdam, 2001.

Hildegard Westerkamp. Soundwalking as Ecological Practice. In Tadahiko Imada Keiko Torigoe and Kozo Hiramatsu, editors, The West Meets the East in Acoustic Ecology, pages 84–89. Hirosaki University, Hirosaki, 2006.

Rudolf Wille. Restructuring lattice theory: an approach based on hierarchies of concepts. In I. Rival, editor, Ordered Sets, pages 445–470. Reidel, Dordrecht, 1982.

R. G. Winther. Eco-devo as a Trading Zone. In Alan C. Love, editor, Conceptual Change in Biology: Scientific and Philosophical Perspectives on Evolution and Development, pages 459–482. Springer, 2014.

Sander Woertman. The Distant Winking of a Star, or the Horror of the Real. In Martin van Schaik and Otakar Máčel, editors, Exit Utopia: Architectural Provocations, 1956-76, pages 146–155. Prestel, Munich, 2005.

K. E. Wolf. A first course in formal concept analysis: How to understand line diagrams. SoftStat'93 Advances in Statistical Software, 4: 429–438, 1993.

Robert Woodbury. Elements of Parametric Design. Routledge, Abingdon, 2010.

Robert F. Woodbury and Andrew L. Burrow. Whither design space? Artificial Intelligence for Engineering Design, Analysis and Manufacturing, 20(2): 63–82, 2005.

World Health Organisation. Guidelines for Community Noise. WHO, D. H. Schwela, B. Berglund, and T. Lindvall, eds. Geneva, 1999.

Henry Wotton. The Elements of Architecture. Da Capo Press, New York, 1970.

James E. Young. Daniel Libeskind's Jewish Museum in Berlin: The Uncanny Arts of Memorial Architecture. In Barbie Zelizer, editor, Visual Culture and the Holocaust, pages 179–197. The Athlone Press, London, 2001.

Miriama Young. Singing the Body Electric: The Human Voice and Sound Technology. Ashgate Publishing, Ltd, Farnham, 2015.

L. Yu and J. Kang. Modeling subjective evaluation of soundscape quality in urban open spaces: An artificial neural network approach. Journal of the Acoustical Society of America, 126(3): 1163–1174, 2009.

M. Zhang and J. Kang. Towards the Evaluation, Description and Creation of Soundscape in Urban Open Spaces. Environment and Planning B: Urban Analytics and City Science, 34(1): 68–86, 2007.

Picture Credits

Figures p. 15, 18, 20, 188/189: Copyright 2015, Michael Fowler.

Figure 1: la Cour 1903, p. 100.

Figure 2: Gray 1918, Fig. 904.

Figure 3: Bilder copyright 2017 Google, DigitalGlobe, GeoBasis-DE/BKG, GeoContent.

Figure 4: Wedler 1957.

Figure 5: Copyright 2010, Michael Fowler.

Figure 6: Copyright City of Markham/Varley Art Gallery of Markham.

Figure 7: Gray 1918, Fig. 910.

Figure 8: Barr 1909, p. 91. Image courtesy of the Bernard Becker Medical Library Washington University School of Medicine in St. Louis.

Figure 9: Rhodes & McClure 1987, Volume 38. Creative Commons Attribution-Share Alike 3.0, New Zealand Licence. Image courtesy of the University of Wellington Library, http://nzetc.victoria.ac.nz

Figure 10: Reprinted with permission from R. Plomp. "Rate of decay of auditory sensation." *Journal of the Acoustical Society of America*, 36(2): 277–282, 1964. Copyright 1964, Acoustic Society of America.

Figure 11: Gray 1918, Fig. 921.

Figure 12: Copyright 2008, Michael Fowler.

Figure 13: Photo by Sam Horine, Courtesy Creative Time.

Figure 14: Descartes 1664.

Figure 15: Preyer 1886.

Figure 16: Copyright FLC/2017, ProLitteris, Zurich.

Figure 17: UAV 713.9013 (Fig. 8), olvwork383957. Harvard University Archives, reprinted with permission.

Figure 18: Redrawn from diagram by Estebandgj, 2014, Creative Commons Attribution-Share Alike 4.0 International license.

Figure 19: public domain

Figure 20: Image couresy of the National Library of Ireland.

Figure 21: Copyright 2017, ProLitteris, Zurich.

Figure 22: "View of the reverberation chamber at IETR laboratory, Rennes" by Manuamador, 2010. Used under Creative Commons Attribution-Share Alike 3.0 Unported license/desaturated from the original.

Figure 23: Still Photograph from "SYNECDOCHE, NEW YORK" used with permission from Sidney Kimmel Entertainment. Copyright Kimmel Distribution, LLC. All Rights Reserved.

Figure 24: Copyright: Archive of the Stockhausen Foundation for Music, Kürten (www.karlheinzstockhausen.org).

Figure 25: Copyright: Archive of the Stockhausen Foundation for Music, Kürten (www.karlheinzstockhausen.org).

Figure 26: Thompson 1917, p. 1062. Redrawn from the original.

Figure 27: Image courtesy of the Fachgebiet Audiokommikation, Technische Universität Berlin.

Figure 28. Image used with permission and courtesy of RESOLUTION: 4 ARCHITECTURE, 150 West 28th Street, Suite 1920 New York, NY 10001.

Figure 29: Copyright 2015, Michael Fowler.

Figure 30: Copyright 2015, Michael Fowler.

Figure 31: Brook Taylor 1749, p. 231.

Figure 32: Copyright 2015, Michael Fowler.

Figure 33: Copyright 2015, Michael Fowler.

Figure 34: Copyright Atelier Leitner, used with permission.

Figure 35: Copyright Atelier Leitner, used with permission.

Figure 36: Paul de Kort Visual Artist in collaboration with H + N + S Landscape Architects, Year of execution 2013.

Figure 37: Stone 1879, p. 26.

Figure 38: Copyright 2015, Michael Fowler.

Figure 39: Copyright Hodgetts + Fung Architecture, used with permission.

Figure 40: Copyright 2015, Michael Fowler.

Figure 41: Score excerpt courtsey of David Dunn.

Figure 42: Image courtesy of Lars Spuijbroek.

Figure 43: Copyright 2015, Michael Fowler.

Figure 44: Iannis Xenakis, *Study for Polytope de Montréal*, c. 1967, ink on paper, 9 1/2 x 12 1/2 in. Iannis Xenakis Archives, Clichès Bibliothèque nationale de France, Paris.

Figure 45: Copyright Office for Metropolitan Architecture (OMA), Heer Bokelweg 149, 3032 AD Rotterdam, The Netherlands, www.oma.com.

Figure 46: "Picture of Beetham Tower Manchester" by Gadamy69, 2010. Licensed under the Creative Commons Attribution-Share Alike 3.0 Unported license.

Figure 47: Copyright 2015, Michael Fowler.

Figure 48: Courtesy Private Archive Hollein.

Figure 49: "Expo 1958 Philips Pavilion" by Wouter Hagens, 1958. Licensed under the Creative Commons Attribution-Share Alike 3.0 Unported, 2.5 Generic, 2.0 Generic and 1.0 Generic license.

Figure 50: Copyright 2015, Michael Fowler.

Figure 51: Schafer 1977b. Image courtesy of Barry Truax used with permission.

Figure 52: Schafer et al. 1973. Image courtesy of Barry Truax used with permission.

Figure 53: de Coensel et al. 2010. Re-printed with permission.

Figure 54: "Bauhaus teaching diagram" by SuperManu, 2007. Redrawn after original found in Walter Gropius. *Idee und Aufbau des Staatlichen Bauhauses Weimar*. Bauhausverlag GmbH, München, 1923. Licensed under the Creative Commons Attribution-Share Alike 3.0 Unported, 2.5 Generic, 2.0 Generic and 1.0 Generic license.

Figure 55: Copyright 2015, Michael Fowler.

Figure 56: Copyright 2015, Michael Fowler.

Figure 57: Image courtesy of Daniel Libeskind used with permission.

Figure 58: public domain

Figure 59: Earle Brown, *December 1952*, Copyright Music Sales Group, New York, 1961. Printed with permission.

Figure 60: Copyright Herron Estate, © 2017, ProLitteris, Zurich

Figure 61: Fludd 1617.

Figure 62: Copyright 2015, Michael Fowler.

Figure 63: public domain

Figure 64: Copyright 2015, Michael Fowler.

Figure 65: Copyright Peter Cook.

Figure 66: Copyright Peter Cook.

Figure 67: Copyright 2015, Michael Fowler.

Figure 68: Copyright 2015, Michael Fowler.

Figure 69: Descartes 1983.

Figure 70: Image courtesy Andrea Branzi used with permission.

Figure 71: Image courtesy Andrea Branzi used with permission.

Figure 72: Copyright 2015, Michael Fowler.

Figure 73: Superstudio (Frassinelli, Magris Alessandro e Roberto, Toraldo di Francia, Natalini): *The Continuous Monument: On the River, project*. Perspective, 1969. New York, Museum of Modern Art (MoMA). Cut-and-pasted printed paper, color pencil, and oil stick on board, 17 1/4 x 15 3/4' (43.8 x 40 cm). Gift of The Howard Gilman Foundation. Acc. n.: 1309.2000 © 2017. Digital image, The Museum of Modern Art, New York/Scala, Florence.

Figure 74: *Affiche avec les dessins axonométriques des Istogrammi*, 1972. Poster printed on paper, 49.7 x 70 cm, inv. A-010 026 004. Photographer: François Lauginie. Courtesy of the collection of the Frac Centre-Val de Loire.

Figure 75: Copyright 2015, Michael Fowler.

Figure 76: Copyright 2015, Michael Fowler.

Figure 77: Copyright Hans Hollein, Collection Centre Pompidou.

Figure 78: Copyright BBC Motion Gallery, 2017. Printed with permission.

Figure 79: Copyright 2015, Michael Fowler.

Figure 80: Model and rendering created by Alberto Herrera (www.albertoherrera3dart.com) based on the film. Image courtesy of Alberto Herrera used with permission.

Figure 81: Haus-Rucker-Co (Austria, established 1967–1992): *Palmtree Island (Oasis) Project*, New York, New York. Perspective, 1971. New York, Museum of Modern Art (MoMA). Cut-and-pasted printed paper with gouache and graphite and cut-and-pasted painted paper on silver gelatin photograph on board, 19 3/4 x 29 5/8 (50.2 x 75.2 cm). Wendy Evans Joseph Purchase Fund. Acc. n.: 482.2004. © 2017. Digital image, The Museum of Modern Art, New York/Scala, Florence.

Figure 82: public domain

Figure 83: Kircher 1673, p. 162.

Figure 84: From Ecological Psychology: concepts and methods for studying the environment of human behaviour. Roger Barker Copyright 1968 by the Board of Trustees of the Leland Stanford Jr. University. All rights reserved. Used with the permission of Stanford Unievrsity Press, www.sup.org.

Figure 85: Copyright, Noise Abatement Commission, Department of Health, City of New York, 1930.

Figure 86: "Mapa de ruido de Linares (Jaén, España)" by Avandtel, 2006. Rotated and cropped from original. Licensed under the Creative Commons Attribution-Share Alike 3.0 Unported license.

Figure 87: Jian Kang. From understanding to designing soundscapes. Frontiers of Architecture and Civil Engineering in China, 4(4): 403–417, 2010. Copyright 2010. Figure 1, "Soundscape framework considering both research and practice facets." With permission of Springer.

Figure 88: Gray 1918, Fig. 923.

Figure 89: Copyright 2015, Michael Fowler.

Graphic design: Jenna Gesse

Layout and typesetting: Kathleen Bernsdorf

Production: Kathleen Bernsdorf

Copy Editor: Raymond Peat

Editors for the Publisher: Petra Schmid, Sarah Schwarz

This publication is made possible with the support of the Alexander von Humboldt Foundation.

Paper: Magno Natural, 120 g/m²

Printing: BELTZ Grafische Betriebe, Bad Langensalza

Library of Congress Cataloging-in-Publication data

A CIP catalog record for this book has been applied for at the Library of Congress.

Bibliographic information published by the German National Library

The German National Library lists this publication in the Deutsche Nationalbibliografie;

detailed bibliographic data are available on the Internet at http://dnb.dnb.de.

This publication is also available as an e-book (ISBN PDF 978-3-0356-1329-2)

© 2017 Birkhäuser Verlag GmbH, Basel

P.O. Box 44, 4009 Basel, Switzerland

Part of Walter de Gruyter GmbH, Berlin/Boston

Printed on acid-free paper produced from chlorine-free pulp. TCF ∞

Printed in Germany

ISBN 978-3-0356-1322-3

9 8 7 6 5 4 3 2 1   www.birkhauser.com